THE CHRONICLER'S USE
OF THE DEUTERONOMISTIC HISTORY

HARVARD SEMITIC MUSEUM

HARVARD SEMITIC MONOGRAPHS

edited by
Frank Moore Cross

Number 33

THE CHRONICLER'S USE
OF THE DEUTERONOMISTIC HISTORY

by
Steven L. McKenzie

Steven L. McKenzie

THE CHRONICLER'S USE OF THE DEUTERONOMISTIC HISTORY

Scholars Press
Atlanta, Georgia

THE CHRONICLER'S USE
OF THE DEUTERONOMISTIC HISTORY

Steven L. McKenzie

© 1984
The President and Fellows of Harvard College

Scholars Press Edition, 1985

Publication of this volume was made possible
by a partial grant from Rhodes College.

Library of Congress Cataloging in Publication Data

McKenzie, Steven L., 1953–
   The chronicler's use of the Deuteronomistic History.

   (Harvard Semitic monographs ; 33)
   Bibliography: p.
   1. Bible. O.T. Chronicles—Criticism, interpretation,
etc. 2. D document (Biblical criticism) I. Title.
II. Series: Harvard Semitic monographs ; no. 33.
BS1345.2.M34 1985   222'.606   85–11743
ISBN 0–89130–828–8 (alk. paper)

Printed in the United States of America
on acid-free paper

TABLE OF CONTENTS

ACKNOWLEDGEMENTS

The admission that if one sees further than his predecessors it is only because he stands on the shoulders of giants has never been truer that in the case of the present volume. The research presented here relies heavily on foundations laid by scholars of past generations as well as significant advances by contemporary scholars. I am indebted to an extensive history of research on Chronicles and the Deuteronomistic History.

There are certain individuals, however, to whom I owe a particular expression of gratitude. Professor Frank Moore Cross of Harvard University suggested this topic and patiently directed my research at the dissertation stage. He spent hours carefully reading rough drafts of chapters, discussing them with me, and making numerous valuable suggestions. He constantly prodded me toward more thoroughness and precision. It was also he who suggested that I publish this work in the HSM series.

Professor Michael Coogan of Harvard also read the chapters in rough draft and made many useful suggestions. His cheerful assurance that I was making progress and really would finish was invaluable.

I wish to thank Rhodes College for contributing a partial grant towards the publication of this volume. Dr. Charles Lemond of Rhodes helped to make the task of revision much less painful by setting up my dissertation on that marvelous labor saving device, the computer.

My parents first brought about my interest in Biblical Studies through their devotion to the Bible. They have encouraged me in every possible way in my academic pursuits.

Most of all, I want to express my gratitude to my wife, Vilma, and my two daughters, Christina and Bonnie. Vilma spent many late hours typing my dissertation. Christina and Bonnie tried hard to understand why their father spent so much time away from them working on his "chapters." They have unselfishly borne the sometimes inhumane existence of a family of a graduate student in the humanities during the past five years, at the same time supplying the most important ingredient in the entire enterprise: perspective.

Steven L. McKenzie
Christmas, 1983

ABBREVIATIONS

This work follows the abbreviations listed in *CBQ* 38 (1976): 438–53. Additions or variations to that list follow:

A	Codex Alexandrinus
ALQ	Cross, *The Ancient Library of Qumran*
B	Codex Vaticanus
BANE	*The Bible and the Ancient Near East*
C	Chronicles
Chr	the Chronicler (= Chr 1)
CMHE	Cross, *Canaanite Myth and Hebrew Epic*
DDS	Weinfeld, *Deuteronomy and the Deuteronomic School*
DH	the Deuteronomistic History
Dt	the old Deuteronomic law code
Dtr (1 and 2)	the Deuteronomist, Dtr 1 = the seventh century compilor of DH, Dtr 2 = the exilic editor of DH
G	the majority Greek text
JSOT	*Journal for the Study of the Old Testament*
K	Kings
KTU	Die keilalphabetischen Texte aus Ugarit
L	the Lucianic recension or the majority of Lucianic MSS (b,o,c$_2$,e$_2$ in S and K; b,e$_2$ in C)
M	the Masoretic Text
NAB	*New American Bible*
OTL	Old Testament Library
rell	*reliqui*, the rest of the Greek MSS
S	Samuel
ÜS	Noth, *Überlieferungsgeschichtliche Studien*

Chapter 1

THE CONTEMPORARY DEBATE
OVER THE WRITING AND PURPOSE
OF THE DEUTERONOMISTIC HISTORY

The appearance of M. Noth's *Überlieferungsgeschichtliche Studien* initiated a new phase in the study of the historical material of the Old Testament./1/ In it, Noth argued that the material now standing in the books of Joshua through Kings was actually the result of a single composer. The Deuteronomist (Dtr), as Noth called him, had collected traditions about Israel's history, and on the basis of those traditions had written his own history of Israel. Noth dated this work of Dtr to the middle of the sixth century B.C./2/ Dtr's activity consisted of three major tasks, according to Noth. First, he collected traditions about Israel's history. Secondly, he chose from his collection certain traditions which he wished to record because of their appropriateness for his interests. Thirdly, Dtr linked the different traditions together and harmonized their differences./3/

Dtr structured his history by means of a series of speeches in a common "Deuteronomistic" style and language inserted into the mouths of major characters in Israel's history at significant junctures of that history (Josh 1:11–15; 23; 1 S 12:1–25; 1 K 8:12–51). Elsewhere Dtr's remarks are found in narrative form (Josh 12; Judg 2:11–22; 2 K 17:7–18, 20–23). The speeches effectively arranged the material in Dtr's history into periods. Josh 23 comes at the end of the Conquest period, 1 S 12 at the end of the period of the judges, and 1 K 8 closes the first part of the monarchy./4/ Dtr further structured his history by prefixing to it an old form of the book of Deuteronomy (Deut 4:44–30:20 minus later additions), which he had already encased within his own framework (Deut 1–3 plus part of 4 and 31:1–13 plus *34. By means of this framework, Dtr cast all of Dt into the form of a speech of Moses./5/

According to Noth, Dtr's objective in his history was completely negative. Dtr traced the thread of apostasy and decline
through Israel's history in order to demonstrate to his exilic contemporaries that Yahweh's judgment in the destruction of Israel
and Judah was totally justified./6/ This negative orientation
toward the history of his people is particularly visible in his presentation of Josiah. Despite all of the good done by Josiah, Judah
still fell because of the centuries of evil in its people and its
kings. Dtr's criticism of the monarchy was especially harsh. The
theme of evil in the monarchy is evident in Dtr's treatment of
Saul's rise to kingship, where he supplemented older traditions
in order to render the overall view of the monarchy negative. It
was, after all, the monarchy which was primarily responsible for
the falls of Israel and Judah.

Noth went even further in his view of Dtr's negative outlook.
Not only did Dtr paint a picture of continuous decline, but he
offered no prospect for future hope, not even the simple return of
the exiles. Deportation was the final end as described by Dtr in
Deut 4:25–28; Josh 23:15b–16; 1 S 12:25. The prayer of Solomon in
1 K 8:44–53 requested only that Yahweh might hear the prayers of
the exiles offered in the direction of Jerusalem. There was no hope
beyond that simple request. Furthermore, in 2 K 25:27–30 Dtr
merely reported the fact of Jehoiachin's release from prison out of
his respect for historical facts. The account offered no real hope for
the exiles./7/

Noth's essay brought about a shift in focus in scholarly treatments of Deuteronomy and the former prophets. Most scholars
began to treat these books as essentially a single historical work.
Thus, Noth's most important observation in *ÜS* has been widely
accepted. Other facets of Noth's original conclusions have also
achieved some degree of scholarly consensus. For example, his
argument about the structure of DH has been only slightly
revised by the addition of 2 S 7 and 1 K 13 to the series of
speeches and narratives in Deuteronomistic style which provide
the structure for DH./8/ However, there have been numerous
attempts to refine Noth's theory. It is not possible to summarize
here the vast amount of material on DH since the appearance of
ÜS, but major revisions have centered in two related areas: (1)
authorship and date of DH, and (2) the purpose of DH.

With regard to the authorship of DH there has been a growing
trend among scholars to reject Noth's theory that a single exilic

composer is essentially responsible for DH./9/ A few prefer to see DH as the product of a Deuteronomistic school. E. W. Nicholson and M. Weinfeld are both proponents of this position./10/ Others have found evidence for two or more redactional levels in different parts of DH, though there is disagreement as to the dates of the respective redactions. Aside from those who wrote before the appearance of *ÜS* (see note 22), the two most important advocates of a dual redaction of DH are F. M. Cross (see below) and R. Smend./11/ Smend claims to find evidence in Josh 1:7-9; 13:1b-6; 23; Judg 2:17, 20-21, 23; 1:1-2:9 that a secondary redactor interested in Law (DtrN) has reworked the original history (DtrG). He gives no date either for DtrG or DtrN. His conclusions have been expanded by W. Dietrich who argues for an intermediate stage of redaction by prophetic writers (DtrP)./12/ The same basic approach has also been applied by others, especially in 2 K 22./13/ There are major problems with the methodology employed in this approach. First, Smend's initial work, upon which the subsequent studies were based, concentrated on passages whose condition is very disturbed and uncertain in terms of literary criticism. Consequently his own conclusions must be regarded with a good deal of scepticism. More serious is the problem with the criteria used to isolate material from different redactions. This approach distinguishes different redactional levels in DH merely on the basis of the emphasis a certain passage places on a theme such as law, prophecy, or covenant. Such themes are best attributed to a single author./14/ They do not contrast but rather compliment each other as important elements throughout the history and culture of Israel and the Ancient Near East.

With regard to the purpose of DH, two major articles have appeared. G. von Rad argued that over against the theme of judgment ("Law") there is a contrasting theme of grace ("Gospel") running throughout DH./15/ Dtr's history was actually the history of Yahweh's word at work. His prophets had foretold destruction because of the people's disobedience. The destruction finally came, but Dtr had to explain why Yahweh had postponed it for so many evil generations. This he did by his understanding of Yahweh's grace, especially as it was concretely manifested in the reiteration of the guarantee of an eternal Davidic dynasty found in the Nathan oracle of 2 S 7. It was because of Yahweh's gracious promise to David that Judah endured as long as it did. But this element of tradition based on the Nathan oracle of 2 S 7 had

another role to play in DH. Passages such as 1 K 2:4; 8:20, 25; 9:5
which reiterate Yahweh's promise to David represent a cycle of
Messianic conceptions which, in the time of the exile, furnished
the basis for the hope that the Davidic dynasty (and with it the
kingdom of Israel) would be reestablished. Of the theological components of judgment and grace, the latter was the weaker, as indicated by the fact that the accounts of the end of Judah and the
later monarchy say nothing about the Nathan oracle. Dtr was
faced with a difficult theological dilemma. He could neither abro-
gate the severity of the judgment which had occured nor concede
that the promise about David's *nîr* had failed./16/ His only alternative was to leave his account of history open to the possibility of
restoration. This he did in the final pericope of his work (2 K
25:27–30). Although it was not explicit, von Rad argued that there
was theological meaning in the notice about Jehoiachin's release
from prison. It was at least a demonstration that the Davidic line
had not come to an end and pointed to the place where Yahweh
could begin again with his people.

Another discussion of Dtr's purpose has been contributed by
H. W. Wolff./17/ For Wolff, it is inconceivable that an Israelite
in the exile would undertake to write a history of his people with
the sole intention of showing that their final destruction came as
their just desserts from a righteous God. He further criticizes
Noth for his explanation of 2 K 25:27–30. The assertion that Dtr
includes the notice about Jehoiachin's release merely out of his
respect for historical events contradicts Noth's own demonstration of Dtr's choosing and ordering his sources. Therefore, one
may well question Noth's thesis about Dtr's purpose on the basis
of this final passage.

At the same time Wolff criticizes von Rad's attempt to find
hope in the promise of an eternal dynasty. Wolff argues that the
promise to David is subordinated, at least for Dtr, to obedience
to the Mosaic covenant. Thus, since the kings of both Israel and
Judah abandoned the law of Moses, the promises made in the
Nathan oracle and reiterated elsewhere were no longer valid.
Against von Rad's interpretation of 2 K 25:27–30 is the fact that
this notice contains no mention of the Nathan oracle, which one
would expect, if von Rad were correct, on the basis of Dtr's
promise–fulfillment schema demonstrated elsewhere by von Rad
himself.

Wolff points out that the very length of DH compels one to

raise the question of Dtr's purpose in the work. If he wished to revive the hope of his people by means of the Nathan oracle, why did he include material from Moses to Samuel? On the other hand, if he wished only to demonstrate Yahweh's execution of the Mosaic curses in Israel's final end, he need not have described the ebb and flow of centuries of history.

Wolff, then, begins by discussing the material about the premonarchical period. Here, particularly in the "judges" material, Dtr narrates his history in a frequently recurring pattern: the people sin and Yahweh sends a deliverer. A similar pattern occurs at the beginning of the monarchy. The people sin by asking for a king, and Yahweh shows his judgment for their rebellion in the form of a thunderstorm (1 S 12:17–18). The people then cry out asking Samuel to pray for them (12:19), and Yahweh initiates a new phase of Israel's history in granting a king. The first part of the pattern is found also in the exile and the events preceding it. The people have sinned, and judgment has come upon them in the form of the destruction of their state and in their exile. Dtr writes for the purpose of showing his contemporaries that they must cry out now to Yahweh in confession of their sins, in prayers for deliverance, and in a new willingness to obey the law of Moses. This is the next step of the pattern of Yahweh's dealings with Israel and the beginning of a process that may lead to Yahweh's gracious deliverance.

Dtr expresses in another way what Israel must do in order to invoke Yahweh's grace. They must return to Yahweh. Wolff points out the frequent use of the verb *šûb* in key Deuteronomistic passages (Deut 4:29–31; 30:1–10;/18/ 1 S 7:3; 2 K 17:13; 23:25; and especially 1 K 8:46–53). In all of these passages, particularly Solomon's speech, the return of the people to Yahweh is seen as the key to Yahweh's delivering grace toward his people. The message for the exiles is clear. If they will return to Yahweh, he may also repent of the destruction he has brought on them and initiate a new phase in their history and relationship with God. Israel's only hope, therefore, lies not in the Davidic monarchy, but in the return of the people to Yahweh.

These insights of von Rad and Wolff represent very important contributions to the understanding of DH. Each of them points to a serious gap in Noth's thesis. Each, especially Wolff, observes the tension in DH between the Mosaic and the Davidic covenants. Together, they render untenable the thoroughly negative view of

Dtr's purpose as presented by Noth. However, von Rad and Wolff both fall short with regard to the same major interest of Dtr, the promise of an eternal dynasty to David. Von Rad notices this theme, but he fails to see all of its implications for the understanding of DH. Wolff's attempt to explain the promise as conditional in the mind of Dtr fails to take seriously enough the allusions to the promise in material dealing with the later kings of Judah (1 K 15:3–5a; 2 K 8:18–19).

F. M. Cross recognizes that the two problem areas of authorship and date on the one hand and purpose on the other are intimately related, at least in K. Cross argues that the theme of the Davidic promise is the key to understanding the purpose and composition of DH./19/ He finds two contrasting themes in K. One is the sin of Jeroboam I. Ahijah's prophecy regarding Jeroboam's kingdom in 1 K 11:29–39 indicates that Jeroboam would have a "sure house" if he obeyed the law of Moses. When Jeroboam and his successors continually failed to fulfill this condition, the covenant curses were prophesied and then enacted upon them (1 K 14:7–11; 15:29; 16:1–4; 21:17–29; 22:37–38; 2 K 9:1–10:11)./20/

This theme stands in contrast to the second theme of the promise of an eternal Davidic dynasty which stems from the royal Judean theology. The key passage here is 2 S 7./21/ While Jeroboam is viewed as the prototype of unfaithfulness, David is clearly the ideal king. This is evident from the fact that the promise to David is repeatedly mentioned or alluded to in DH (1 K 11:12–13, 34–36, 15:3–5a; 2 K 8:18–19). Also, the good kings of Judah are sometimes compared with David (e.g., Asa in 1 K 15:11 and especially Josiah in 2 K 22:2). What is particularly striking is the climax of this theme in the portrait of Josiah as the true successor of David. The reform of Josiah has already been previewed in 1 K 13:2–5 where Josiah is mentioned by name and cast as the opposite of Jeroboam, the precise role of David in the schema of DH. The account of Josiah's reforms is longer than that of the good deeds of any other approved king of Judah. In fact, Josiah is the only king in the entire history of Israel—David and Solomon included—who is viewed as righteous without reserve (2 K 23:25). Josiah is viewed as the new David, and it is hoped that his reforms will lead to a restoration of the Davidic empire.

The persistence of this theme of hope in the Davidic monarchy, and more concretely in Josiah, is strong evidence for a primary, Josianic edition of DH. Cross refers to this edition as Dtr 1. He argues that the edition was written as a program for the reform of Josiah. Here his view accords well with the stress which Noth himself places on the importance of Josiah's reign in influencing Dtr./22/ The Josianic edition of DH, according to Cross, called the remainder of the Northern kingdom to return to Judah, to Yahweh's only legitimate shrine in Jerusalem, and to his only legitimate monarch, a Davidide./23/ Even stronger, the work of Dtr 1 called Judah to return wholeheartedly to Yahweh in the reforms of his Davidic king, Josiah, so that Yahweh would restore all of Israel to its former greatness under David.

Cross continues by arguing for a second, exilic edition of DH which he calls Dtr 2. He begins by noting the validity of some of the arguments by earlier literary critics for two levels of redaction in K, one pre-exilic and the other exilic./24/ He strengthens these arguments by pointing to the two major themes of Dtr 1 and by his observation that before the material about Manasseh no hint of doom appears. The work of Dtr 2 consisted mainly of two functions: (1) bringing DH up to date by recounting Josiah's death, giving information about the last few monarchs of Judah, and narrating the fall of Jerusalem and the subsequent exile; (2) explaining the destruction so soon after Josiah as the result of Manasseh's wickedness. Particularly revealing for Dtr 2's work is the passage in 2 K 21:2–15. Cross shows that the attribution of Judah's fall to Manasseh's unforgivable sins in this passage is secondarily attached and not integral to the history. The same is true of other passages which blame Judah's demise on Manasseh. In revising the work before him Dtr 2 gives no hint of hope in the Davidic monarchy. In fact, Cross holds that he has overwritten and contradicted that earlier hope discovered by von Rad. The muted hope of repentance isolated by Wolff is best explained, according to Cross, by Dtr 2's faithful preservation of Dtr 1 and his modest retouching of the earlier work. The fact that there is no lengthy peroration on the fall of Judah as there had been on the fall of Israel is another indication of separate levels of editing in the two accounts. It is also an indication that Dtr 2 was, as Cross puts it, "less articulate" than Dtr 1.

After establishing that there were two editions of DH, Cross suggests that other passages in the work probably came from Dtr 2 on the basis of their view of the Davidic covenant as conditional or their threats of defeat and captivity which seem addressed to the exiles and call for repentance or promise restoration./25/ Cross lists the following passages as falling under one of these two criteria: Deut 4:27–31; 28:36–37, 63–68; 29:27; 30:1–10; Josh 23:11–13, 15–16; 1 S 12:25; 1 K 2:4; 6:11–13; 8:25b, 46–53; 9:4–9; 2 K 17:19; 20:17–18. Of course, he considers the end of DH, 2 K 23:26–25:30, as Dtr 2 material, and he views Deut 30:11–20 and 1 K 3:14 as suspect passages.

Cross offers, in my opinion, convincing evidence for the existence of two redactions of DH and for the purpose behind the work of Dtr 1. The purpose of Dtr 2 is more difficult to ascertain. If he does offer hope to the exiles, it is certainly not explicit. Even von Rad argued only that 2 K 25:27–30 suggested a point at which Yahweh could begin again with his people./26/ Wolff has discerned in the whole of DH the theme of the return of the people to Yahweh. As Levenson puts it, "the ground of hope is. . . the moral freedom of Israel and God's accessibility and that of his revelation."/27/ This theme of return is appropriate for the work of Dtr 1. It is, of course, quite possible that Dtr 2 has appropriated the theme of return in order to offer hope to his own generation. It is extraordinary that Dtr 2 includes no peroration on the fall of Judah, no statement that the covenant with the Davidic dynasty has been irreparably broken. Cross attributes this to an inarticulate Dtr 2. It may also indicate that Dtr 2 finds some hope in Yahweh's gracious promises if only the people will return. Therefore, I am not willing to deny all hope to Dtr 2, though if he did hold such a hope, it was largely a matter of his interpretation of Dtr 1.

Friedman has added two arguments to those adduced by Cross for two editions of DH./28/ First, he has gathered evidence pointing to a fundamental change in the narrator's perspective after Josiah's account. Here he depends partially on two patterns in DH noticed by von Rad. Von Rad pointed out that the kings of Israel and Judah were evaluated on the basis of their fulfillment or transgression of the regulation regarding the centralization of worship. Thus, all of the Israelite kings were condemned out of hand because of the existence of the shrines at Dan and Bethel. Similarly, all Judean kings except Hezekiah and Josiah fell short in allowing the *bāmôt* to stand. Von Rad also noted a second pattern, one of prophecy and fulfillment in DH. However, as Friedman notes, both of these patterns cease to occur after Josiah. Furthermore, he adds that a third pattern, the

comparison of the kings of Judah to David, which is standard for
kings from Ahaz to Josiah, again ceases to occur after Josiah.
These changes in pattern indicate, according to Friedman, a
change in editorial perspective after the time of Josiah.

The second supplementary argument adduced by Friedman
is that Josiah is clearly the focus of Dtr 1. The striking *vaticinium ex eventu* in 1 K 13:2 is one trace of such a focus. Other
traces occur in the linking of the Mosaic period to that of Josiah
in a variety of ways. The most obvious, of course, is the finding
of the Mosaic law during Josiah's reign. Friedman details other
links in terminology between Josiah and his reforms on the one
hand and the Deuteronomic description of Moses and the law on
the other. Friedman's point is that from the very beginning of
the work it points to and builds up to Josiah as its real hero and
Josiah's time as its real concern./29/

Next, Friedman turns his attention to a discussion of the passages which he attributes to Dtr 2. He argues not only on the
basis of thematic grounds, as did Cross, but also on the basis of
literary grounds that the following passages are additions of Dtr
2: Deut 4:24–31; 8:19–20; 28:36–37, 63–68; 29:21–27; 30:1–10,
15–20; 31:16–22, 28–30; 32:44 plus the insertion of the Song of
Moses; 1 K 9:6–9; 2 K 21:8–15; 23:26–25:26. In addition, other
passages are probably, though not certainly, Dtr 2 additions, or
show signs of light retouching by Dtr 2: Josh 23:15–16; 1 K 6:11–
13; 2 K 17:19, 35–40a; 22:16–20.

In arguing that there are deliberate links between Dt and
Josiah which Dtr 1 has made in order to prove the perfection of
Josiah, Friedman has had to deal extensively with the view
expressed earlier by J. Levenson that the entire book of the Torah
in Deuteronomy comes not from Dtr 1 but has been inserted by
Dtr 2./30/ Levenson's arguments for the insertion of the Dt corpus
by Dtr 2 occur on three levels. First, on the basis of literary considerations he argues for an exilic framework around Dt (Deut 4:1–40
and 29:21–28 + 30 + 31:16–22, 24–29). Secondly, by virtue of a
comparison between passages within the exilic framework and
passages ascribed by Cross to Dtr 2, Levenson concludes that the
exilic framework of Dt should be attributed to Dtr 2. However,
there is some doubt as to whether the passages cited by Levenson
are really Dtr 2 additions. Of the five verses used by Levenson as
examples of Dtr 2 material (1 K 8:23, 47, 51; 2 K 20:18; Josh 23:11),
none is regarded by Friedman as Dtr 2. Furthermore, there is

some circularity involved in Levenson's argumentation. Three of the five alleged Dtr 2 passages come from 1 K 8:23–53. But in another article Levenson determines that 1 K 8:23–53 is a Dtr 2 insertion on the basis of comparisons with the framework which he has isolated around Dt./31/ This points out a need to establish objectively, at least in a part of DH, what material definitely stems from Dtr 2.

In the third level of Levenson's argumentation he compares the theology of Dtr 1 with that of Dt and Dtr 2 on five points, covenant, kingship, centralization of worship, mixed marriage, and celebration of the Passover by country priests, in order to demonstrate that the framework around Dt accords theologically with Dtr 2 against Dtr 1. Friedman replies in detail to Levenson's view of these five themes in his own treatment of DH./32/ A discussion of these themes lies beyond the scope of the present work, and I am not primarily concerned with Deuteronomy where the debate between Friedman and Levenson has centered. However, the fact that they can come to very different conclusions about such theological issues points again to a need to establish objectively the location and extent of Dtr 2 passages in order to understand the theology of DH in its different editions.

Two recent contributions by Nelson and Peckham make the need for objective criteria even clearer./33/ Both use literary criticism as their primary tool for isolating Dtr 2 material. Peckham confines himself to Deut 5–11 where he attributes to Dtr 2 far more material than do Cross or Friedman. It is clear that in his view Dtr 2 is no longer responsible merely for light retouching of DH, but has significantly redacted the earlier edition. Nelson concentrates on material outside of Deuteronomy. His methodology is most similar to that of Friedman. He treats a series of passages which he ascribes to Dtr 2. Although his list is apparently not meant to be complete it overlaps to an extent with the passages attributed by Cross and Friedman to Dtr 2. Still there are major differences.

The survey of work on DH presented above can be summarized as follows. Noth's major tenet that Deuteronomy through Kings was a single historical work has been almost universally accepted. Cross has, in my view, corrected Noth's theory by demonstrating that there were two editions of DH, a Josianic and an exilic one. Difficulty has occurred in the various attempts to isolate the material introduced by the exilic editor. Neither literary criticism nor investigation along the lines of theology has succeeded in achieving a consensus on this question. There is agreement with Cross that the material which blames Manasseh for Judah's demise and, of course, the material about the period after Josiah is from Dtr 2. However, of Cross's other two criteria for finding Dtr 2 passages, one, the threat of captivity which seems explicitly directed at the exiles, is admittedly somewhat subjective. The other, that of the conditionality of the Davidic covenant, has been significantly and independently revised by Friedman and Nelson./34/ This does not mean that the above criteria are invalid. However, there is a clear need for some additional, objective criterion to assist in the investigation of Dtr 2 material along with literary criticism, theology, and content. One goal of the present work is to contribute precisely at this point, i.e., by investigating the possibility that such a criterion may exist in the way in which the Chronicler has used DH. The next step, therefore, and the subject of the next chapter is a survey of recent work in Chronicles.

NOTES

/1/   (Halle: Max Niemeyer, 1943). Hereafter *ÜS*.

/2/   Ibid., 10–12. Noth argued that except for the settlement/conquest material, the material about Saul and David, and also apparently, the Elijah–Elisha cycle, the traditions collected by Dtr show no signs of prior collection.

/3/   Ibid., 97–99. The best example of Dtr's linking of traditions is the account of the period between the settlement/conquest and the monarchy where Dtr has linked traditions about different heroes with a list of judges into a running narrative in a chronological framework (see *ÜS*, 47–61). Noth stressed that Dtr had a profound respect for the traditions he used. This respect is clear from the fact that only once, in the narrative of Saul's rise to kingship (1 S 7:2–12:25), did Dtr deliberately alter the tradition which he received. This narrative was of fundamental importance for Dtr's view of the monarchy, yet even in this crucial passage Dtr cited the pro-monarchical passages without deletion. His alteration consisted in the addition of anti-monarchical passages (*ÜS*, 54–60).

/4/   Ibid., 5–6, 10. The later division into "books" corresponded with Dtr's division into periods only at the border between Joshua and

Judges. Dtr also structured the material chronologically to a degree. See Noth's discussion of the chronological references in *ÜS*, 18–26.

/5/   Ibid., 16–17, 38–40. The remainder of the material in Deut 31–33 is regarded by Noth as various secondary additions, and Deut 34 in its present form was added by the editor of the Pentateuch.

/6/   Ibid., 91, 95.

/7/   Ibid., 108.

/8/   On 2 S 7 see D. J. McCarthy, "II Samuel 7 and the Structure of the Deuteronomistic History," *JBL* 84 (1965): 131–38 and F. M. Cross, *CMHE*, 241–64. On 1 K 13 see W. E. Lemke, "The Way of Obedience: I Kings 13 and the Structure of the Deuteronomistic History," *Magnalia Dei* (ed. F. M. Cross, W. E. Lemke, and P. D. Miller; Garden City: Doubleday, 1976) 301–26. See also McCarthy, "The Wrath of Yahweh and the Structural Unity of the Deuteronomistic History," *Essays in Old Testament Ethics* (ed. J. L. Crenshaw and J. T. Willis; New York: KTAV, 1974) 97–110. Finally, R. Pratt has recently offered convincing evidence that Hezekiah's prayers in 2 K 19:14–19; 20:3 are Deuteronomistic compositions of the same type as others of the speeches in DH, especially Solomon's prayer in 1 K 8. See "The Incomparability of Hezekiah in the Deuteronomistic History" (unpublished paper, OT 200, Harvard University, Fall, 1982).

/9/   A notable exception is the recent work of H.-D. Hoffmann, *Reform und Reformen* (ATANT 66; Zurich: Theologischer Verlag, 1980). Hoffmann attempts to reaffirm Noth's view that DH is the work of a single, exilic author. Indeed, Hoffmann goes beyond Noth's view in arguing that Dtr is an author not a compiler of traditions. Hence, DH is actually a literary composition about the "history" of Israel's cult which does not rely on any official documents or traditional sources.

/10/   Nicholson's view is "that the Deuteronomic–Deuteronomistic circle was a prophetic circle." See *Deuteronomy and Tradition* (Philadelphia: Fortress, 1967) 118. Cf. 107–18, 123. Weinfeld's view is suggested by the title of his book *Deuteronomy and the Deuteronomic School* (Oxford: Clarendon, 1972). See pp. 1–9.

/11/   "Das Gesetz und die Völker, Ein Beitrag zur deuteronomischen Redaktionsgeschichte," *Probleme biblischer Theologie* (ed. H. W. Wolff; Munich: Chr. Kaiser, 1971) 494–509.

/12/   *Prophetie und Geschichte* (FRLANT 108; Göttingen: Vandenhoeck & Ruprecht, 1972). The work of DtrP is an extremely important element in Dietrich's view of DH. He attributes most of the prophetic stories in DH, at least in their present form, to the redaction of DtrP (cf. p. 145). In addition, he attaches dates to his three redactional levels. He dates DtrG to ca. 580 B.C., DtrN to ca. 560 B.C., and DtrP to sometime in the interim (pp. 139–44).

/13/ See R. Nelson, *The Double Redaction of the Deuteronomistic History* (Sheffield: JSOT, 1981) 22, n. 45, for references.

/14/ Dietrich attempts to confirm through literary means the various redactional layers that he suspects in individual passages on the basis of the themes they stress. His literary arguments are rarely convincing. Sometimes passages that contain similar information are seen as doublets and assigned to different redactors (pp. 115, 124, 128). At other times a similarity in information, language, or themes is the reason cited for assigning various passages to the same author. Thus, there is tension in the methodology. Furthermore, the expressions and themes at issue are so common that it is difficult to believe that they signal redactional layers. For example, Dietrich regards the expression *kōh 'āmar Yahweh 'elōhê Yiśrā'ēl* as a sign of DtrP's hand. It is difficult to see how such a common formula can be used as a valid criterion for isolating redactional hands. Compare the critique of Dietrich's work given by Hoffmann in *Reform*, 19–21.

/15/ *Studies in Deuteronomy* (SBT 9; trans. David Stalker; Chicago: Henry Regnery Co., 1953) 74–91. Reprinted in a different translation in "The Deuteronomic Theology of History in I and II Kings," *The Problem of the Hexateuch and Other Essays* (trans. E. W. T. Dicken; New York: McGraw-Hill, 1966) 205–21. Von Rad's Lutheran presuppositions are obvious in the contrast he builds between these two themes.

/16/ On the meaning of *nîr* in this promise see Paul D. Hanson, "The Song of Heshbon and David's *Nîr*," *HTR* 61 (1968): 297–320.

/17/ "Das Kerygma des deuteronomischen Geschichtswerk," *ZAW* 73 (1961): 171–86; reprinted in an English translation by F. C. Prussner in *The Vitality of Old Testament Traditions* (ed. W. Brueggemann and H. W. Wolff; Atlanta: John Knox, 1975) 83–100.

/18/ Wolff holds that Deut 4:29–31 and 30:1–10 are later additions by a member of the Deuteronomistic school to the primary work of Dtr. See his discussion "Das Kerygma," 180–84.

/19/ *CMHE*, 274–89. His views were originally published in "The Structure of the Deuteronomic History," *Perspectives in Jewish Learning*, Annual of the College of Jewish Studies 3 (Chicago, 1968) 9–24.

/20/ For a discussion of these Northern prophetic oracles see H. N. Wallace, "The Oracles Against the Israelite Dynasties" (unpublished

paper, OT 200, Harvard University, Fall, 1979). Wallace argues, correctly in my opinion, contra Cross, that the promise to Jeroboam is one
of an eternal dynasty like David's if Jeroboam is faithful as was David.
This view makes the contrast between David and Jeroboam even
stronger.

/21/ See *CMHE*, 219–73.

/22/ *ÜS*, 92–94.

/23/ The editorial comment of Dtr 1 in 1 K 12:19 makes it clear that
his view is indeed that the Northern kingdom rebelled against Judah.
In his view, the Northern kingdom has seceded. It is they who are the
apostates, the bastard government. Thus, throughout the work of Dtr 1
there is a strong polemic against Jeroboam and the Northern monarchy.
That Judah was the true successor of the united kingdom was clear to
Dtr 1 from the outcome of history. This bias often influences our
understanding of the history as well, since we too know how the story
ends. However, 1 K 12:11b–20, especially in its use of the expression
"all Israel," indicates that the general view of the division, particularly
in the North, must have been precisely the opposite. The very fact that
the majority of tribes and people accepted Jeroboam would indicate
that it was essentially only the clan of David which had seceded. The
Northern kingdom bore the heritage of united Israel; it was the true
Israel. The difference is a subtle but important one, and the use of the
term "Israel" by Dtr 1 is very important for interpreting the promise of
a Davidic dynasty as Dtr 1 understood it.

/24/ Cf. R. H. Pfeiffer, *Introduction to the Old Testament* (New
York: Harper Brothers, 1941) 178–87; J. Gray, *I and II Kings* (London:
SCM, 1963) 13–15, 38; O. Eissfeldt, *The Old Testament. An
Introduction* (trans. P. R. Ackroyd; New York: Harper & Row, 1965)
242–48, 297–301. For others see Nelson, *Double Redaction*, 13–19.
Perhaps most important was A. Jepsen (*Die Quellen des Königsbuches*
[Halle: Max Niemeyer, 1956]) who located the first redactor, a priest, in
the early exile and credited him with the basic structure of the history.
A second, prophetic redactor later in the exile enlarged the work of R 1
essentially using it as one of his sources. Jepsen states that his R 2 is the
same as Noth's Dtr.

/25/ As D. Hillers has demonstrated, the threat of deportation was
quite common in the Ancient Near East in treaties as a curse for treaty
breaking. Thus, such threats in the OT do not necessarily stem from the
exile. See Hillers, *Treaty Curses and the Old Testament Prophets*
(Rome: Pontifical Biblical Institute, 1964).

/26/ R. Friedman posits that 2 K 25:27–30 is not the work of Dtr 2 at all but an even later addition. He may well be correct. See *The Exile and Biblical Narrative* (HSM 22; Chico, CA: Scholars Press, 1981) 36.

/27/ J. Levenson, "Who Inserted the Book of the Torah?" *HTR* 68 (1975): 232. In a footnote on the same page Levenson goes on to say that there may be a more concrete ground of hope for Dtr 2 in the patriarchal covenant, but he does not elaborate.

/28/ *The Exile*, 1–43. See also his article, "From Egypt to Egypt: Dtr 1 and Dtr 2," *Traditions in Transformation* (ed. B. Halpern and J. Levenson; Winona Lake, IN: Eisenbrauns, 1980) 167–92.

/29/ Additional support for the position that Josiah is the real hero of DH has been supplied by Hoffmann in *Reform*. Hoffmann does not cite Cross's work on DH. He either overlooks it or ignores it. Yet, he refers throughout his book to the account of Josiah's reform as the real goal of DH. He discusses a number of motifs and themes of DH, all of which end with Josiah and point to him as the objective of the work. 2 K 22–23 is, for Hoffmann, the *Zielkomposition* of DH. See especially pp. 39–46, 169–270 of *Reform*. Hoffmann even refers to the programmatic nature of DH (p. 56). In spite of all this evidence seen by Cross as pointing to a primary Josianic edition, Hoffmann argues for an exilic date for DH. The few arguments that he gives for an exilic date are weak (cf. pp. 241–51). Hoffmann regards DH as a cultic history (see n. 9 above), but he never explains satisfactorily why such a work in the exile would focus so strongly on Josiah. His failure to take into consideration Cross's arguments regarding the editions of DH and their respective purposes is a significant shortcoming of his work.

/30/ "Who Inserted," 203–33.

/31/ "From Temple to Synagogue: 1 Kings 8," *Traditions in Transformation*, 143–66.

/32/ *The Exile*, 26–29.

/33/ Nelson, *Double Redaction*, and Brian Peckham, "The Composition of Deuteronomy 5–11," *The Word of the Lord Shall Go Forth* (ed. C. L. Meyers and M. O'Connor; Winona Lake, IN: Eisenbrauns, 1983) 217–40.

/34/ Friedman, *The Exile*, 12–13; Nelson, *Double Redaction*, 99–105.

Chapter 2
RECENT WORK ON CHRONICLES

"During the past generation the attention of Old Testament scholars has been drawn more and more to the problems connected with the Chronicler's great work. . . ." So began W. F. Albright's well known article on C in 1921./1/ The same statement could be made about the contemporary generation of OT scholars. Indeed, several recent studies of C from different aspects have completely altered the way in which C must be viewed. These studies have focused on the issues of the authorship of C, its date and purpose, and the Deuteronomistic source utilized by C. Naturally, the conclusions reached on these issues have significant implications for all other areas of C studies. This chapter will survey the most important contributions in recent generations by students of C to the three areas mentioned above as a background for the investigation of Chr's use of DH.

I. *Authorship*

The real question at issue here is the extent of Chr's original work. Until recently it has been the nearly unanimous consensus of scholars that C, Ezra, and Nehemiah were originally a single work by a single author./2/ There are four principal arguments for this position:/3/ (1) the doublet in 2 C 36:22–23 and Ezra 1:1–3a; (2) linguistic and stylistic similarities; (3) theological and ideological similarities; and (4) the evidence of 1 Esdras. The first argument is patently weak./4/ The presence of this doublet at the end of C and the beginning of Ezra does not establish either common or separate authorship; it can be interpreted either way. The question has focused on the other three arguments. The weakening of the general agreement on the theory of common authorship is due largely to the work of Japhet and Williamson who have convincingly challenged the assertion that C and Ezra-Nehemiah show close affinities in the areas of language and theology./5/ While their arguments are not of equal value, they have persuasively established that there are significant differences in these areas between C and Ezra-Nehemiah./6/

The fourth argument involves the question of the nature of 1 Esdras. Is it a compilation or a fragment of a translation of Chr's work? The latter view is not new, though at least until recent years its supporters have been in the minority./7/ H. H. Howorth was apparently the first proponent of the view./8/ C. C. Torrey and S. Mowinckel have been the principal advocates of the fragment view in this century and receive the credit for being the first to defend this view on truly critical grounds./9/ Much of Torrey's reconstruction is weak,/10/ but the major strength of his work is to point out the difficulties of the compilation view and the analogous situation to 1 Esdras reflected in the Greek versions of Daniel and Jeremiah. Mowinckel's treatment is more sober than that of Torrey. He holds that 1 Esdras probably corresponds to the original form of Chr's work except for the tale in 1 Esdr 3:1–5:6 and a few later additions. He refutes individually the major proponents of the compilation theory. Mowinckel also points out the analogous situation in Daniel. In addition, he stresses the abrupt beginning and ending of 1 Esdras and the fact that Josephus' source was 1 Esdras as indications that 1 Esdras represents a fragmentary translation of Chr's original work. No theory of compilation has offered a convincing statement of the "book's" purpose to explain adequately the variations in 1 Esdras, especially its order, vis-à-vis Ezra-Nehemiah. Further support for the fragment view has recently been added by R. Klein./11/ He treats the Greek witnesses for C and Ezra-Nehemiah in the light of the evidence provided by the Qumran fragments for different textual families in the OT. He concludes that 1 Esdras represents the OG translation of Chr's work. Thus, its *Vorlage* was of the Egyptian text type which in turn reflects a shorter, frequently superior text to the Palestinian type found in C^M and 4QEzra and reflected in the later translation of Paralipomena and Esdras B.

The arguments presented by these scholars, especially Mowinckel and Klein, are strong and have convinced a growing number of students of 1 Esdras that it is indeed a fragment. However, Williamson has again taken up the defense of the compilation view./12/

In essence, Williamson believes that 1 Esdras is not the torso of a separate translation of Chr's work at all. He states that "it is surely *a priori* extremely unlikely that two such translations should have been independently produced within what would have to be considered a comparatively short space of time."/13/ Rather, he holds that 1 Esdras reflects a compilation of materials principally from C and Ezra-Nehemiah collected for the purpose of addressing a specific problem in the post-exilic period. His argument for this position is based largely on his interpretation of 1 Esdr 1:21–22. He argues that these two verses are integral to 1 Esdras and represent an addition that is "composed from a number of elements extracted from originally quite different contexts."/14/ The purpose of the addition is essentially the same as that of the plus in 2 Par 35:19a–d, namely, to explain Josiah's death and the exile in terms different from C's rigid theory of immediate retribution. This is done in 1 Esdr 1:21–22 by balancing the assertion that Josiah was upright (v 21) with the statement that the sins of others still led to Israel's condemnation (v 22). Verse 22 echoes the judgment on Manasseh's reign in 2 K 21:9//2 C 33:9. However, Manasseh is not explicitly mentioned in v 22 as he is in 2 Par 35:19a–d. The reason for this difference, according to Williamson, is that 2 Paralipomena was able to refer to Manasseh because Manasseh's reign had been described earlier in his account, while 1 Esdras' veiled reference to Manasseh must mean that its narrative began after Manasseh's reign. Thus, 1 Esdras never covered all of 1–2 C. Therefore, Williamson suggests that 1 Esdras was compiled sometime after the conclusion of C for the purpose of filling "a need for self-justification in face of the contrast between the glories of the monarchical days and the prevailing disappointing conditions."/15/

Williamson's position is replete with problems. In the first place, he does not take into consideration a whole range of recent work on the text of the OT, particularly Klein's treatment of the Greek text of C which entails an analysis of the evidence of 1 Esdras./16/ To see 1 Esdras in the context of the textual evidence furnished by other OT books is to place it in an entirely new light. One recognizes in the relationship of 1 Esdras to C and Ezra-Nehemiah a situation very similar to that of M and G in Jeremiah./17/ Two different text types are represented, the shorter of the two being the better. There are, as Klein observes, a priori no other reasonable explanations for 1 Esdras./18/ The shorter text of 1 Esdras is not due to the type of

abbreviation found in 2 Maccabees and sometimes in 2 C. Nor
do 1 Esdras' omissions vis-à-vis C and Ezra-Nehemiah reflect the
same type of selective omission visible in Josephus and C.
1 Esdras generally appears to follow its *Vorlage* clause by clause,
and there is no pattern to its omissions from the received text
of C and Ezra-Nehemiah. To conclude that the differences
between 1 Esdras and C^M are due to a translator's work is to
propose a unique case. In short, Williamson speaks of the a priori difficulty of seeing 1 Esdras as a separate translation, but in
light of the recent work done in textual criticism in the OT,
one's first reaction a priori is to view 1 Esdras as the representative of a different text type from that found in the *textus receptus* of the canonical books.

There are also problems with Williamson's understanding of
1 Esdr 1:21–22. My view of these two verses will be given in
greater detail in chapter 6. For now, however, it is enough to
observe that the meaning of these verses, especially v 22, is
obscure. As Torrey observed long ago, the text of these verses as it
stands is almost certainly corrupt./19/ Verse 21 and possibly the
first phrase of v 22 (up to *chronois*) speak of Josiah in a favorable
way. However, the remainder of v 22 refers to those who sinned
worse than the nations, thus apparently bringing about Israel's
downfall. Surely those who sinned to such an extent were not seen
as products of Josiah's reign. Yet the text as it stands clearly
ascribes the *hēmartēkotōn* and the *ēsebēkotōn* to a previous
account of Josiah's reign (*ta kat' auton de anagegraptai*). The only
possible antecedent of *auton* is *Ioseiou*. Williamson's own
translation makes it clear that Josiah's reign is on view./20/

> And the deeds of Josiah were upright in the sight of his
> Lord, for his heart was full of godliness. The events of
> his reign have been recorded in the past, concerning
> those who sinned and acted wickedly toward the Lord
> beyond any other other people or kingdom, . . .

It may be that Manasseh was originally referred to in v 22. The
reference to sinning more than the nations here is similar to the
statement made about Manasseh in 2 K 21:1//2 C 33:9. However, if Manasseh was explicitly mentioned it would undermine
Williamson's argument about an implicit reference to Manasseh
here./21/ The point is that there is absolutely nothing in 1 Esdr
1:21–22 that indicates that 1 Esdras began after Manasseh's reign

or that 1 Esdras is a compilation. If Williamson takes 1 Esdr 1:21–22 as it stands it refers to sinners in the reign of Josiah and says nothing about Manasseh. Should he agree that 1 Esdr 1:21–22 is now corrupt he can hardly determine from such a corrupt text whether it mentioned Manasseh, where 1 Esdras began, or whether it was a compilation.

Finally, Williamson's understanding of the purpose of the compilation that he sees in 1 Esdras is not convincing. According to Williamson 1 Esdras was occasioned not only by Josiah's death but also by the problem posed by the exile for which K and C offer different explanations./22/ C's explanation, says Williamson, according to its theme of immediate retribution, is that the exile was due solely to the sins of Zedekiah and his contemporaries. A part of the reason for the compilation of 1 Esdras, Williamson suggests, may have been to counteract this theory of immediate retribution which had created a need for self-justification in the struggling post-exilic community. But why would a compiler include C's explanation of the exile (1 Esdr 1:45–50//2 C 36:12–17) if his work was meant to clarify such ambiguities? Why not leave it out? Furthermore, Williamson essentially asks one to believe that with one verse, whose present meaning is obscure, the compiler of 1 Esdras attempts to counteract a major theological tenet in the work of 1–2 C. In addition, Williamson's explanation does not account for all the evidence. If 1 Esdras attempts to counteract C's theology, why does it include material from Ezra and Nehemiah? Finally, why would a compiler rearrange the order of pericopes? How would the revised order help to realize the compiler's purpose? In short, Williamson's theory of the purpose of 1 Esdras raises more problems than it solves. In fact, his entire understanding of 1 Esdras as a compilation simply cannot be accepted. On the other hand, the position that 1 Esdras represents a different and frequently superior text type not only explains the evidence satisfactorily but also accords well with recent advances made in the understanding of the development of the OT text.

Williamson continues his consideration of 1 Esdras by focusing on the question of the ending of 1 Esdras and the testimony of Josephus./23/ He agrees that the ending of 1 Esdras is broken off and that Josephus used 1 Esdras as his source in *Ant* XI. 1–158 followed by the Nehemiah memoirs (Neh 1:1–7:4) in *Ant* XI. 159–83. He argues that most of the rest of the Nehemiah material (chapters 8–13) was omitted by Josephus because it lay outside of his interests, or he had already dealt with it in following 1 Esdras./24/ He goes on to argue against Mowinckel's suggestion that, based on Josephus' evidence, 1 Esdras originally ended with the account of the celebration of *Sukkōt* found in Neh 8:13–18./25/ Williamson's position is that there is no real evidence from Josephus' account as to the original length of 1 Esdras. He states that Josephus as a Jew with priestly connections would have known the ordinances of *Sukkōt* well enough to compose his account in *Ant* XI. 154–158 without any *Vorlage*. Furthermore, the variations between Josephus' account and that of Neh 8:13–18 indicate that Josephus did indeed compose on his own here. Thus, Williamson concludes that Josephus' copy of 1 Esdras was probably in the same incomplete condition as is ours and that Josephus therefore furnishes no evidence regarding 1 Esdras' original ending.

Again Williamson's view must be rejected because he does not take the evidence of *Ant* XI. 154–158 with the seriousness that it merits. He asks one to believe a rather incredible set of coincidences. He agrees that Josephus used 1 Esdras as his source at least up to the point parallel with Neh 8:12. Both Josephus and Neh 8:13–18 then give an account of the celebration of *Sukkōt* and, as Williamson agrees, the ending of 1 Esdras is broken off after the point parallel with Neh 8:12. Furthermore, as Williamson again agrees, the Nehemiah memoirs are then presented separately by Josephus. In other words, Josephus clearly concludes the Ezra narrative with a parallel to Neh 8. What few differences do exist between Josephus' account of *Sukkōt* and that of Neh 8:13–18 are consistent with the results of Josephus' rewriting of his canonical sources elsewhere. Obviously, the easiest reconstruction of this evidence, particularly when it is seen that 1 Esdras represents a recension not a compilation, is that 1 Esdras also originally ended with the report of *Sukkōt* in Neh 8:13–18.

There is one more argument adduced by Williamson which merits a brief response. Williamson states it as follows./26/

> Comparison of the last three verses of Neh. 7 and the first phrase of 8:1 with Ezr. 2:68–70 and the first phrase of ch. 3 suggests that the time reference (*wyg' hḥdš hšby'y*) originally belonged with the preceding section, and not with the contents of ch. 8 as in the present

arrangement. It appears that 1 Esdras 9:37 translates the
heading, and thus could only have been effected after
Neh 8 had been combined with the preceding material.

My explanation of 1 Esd 9:37 agrees substantially with that
offered by Pohlmann./27/ Williamson criticizes Pohlmann's
view because it assumes that Neh 8 originally followed Ezra 10,
the very point that Pohlmann is trying to prove. However, I
have already rejected Williamson's theory that 1 Esdras is a
compilation on other grounds in favor of the view that it represents a distinct text type. Thus, the assumption is now justified,
and 1 Esdr 9:37 merely needs to be explained as it stands. With
Pohlmann I would observe that this verse suits its context perfectly after Ezra 10. It is striking that the three groups mentioned in 1 Esdr 9:37, the priests, Levites, and some from Israel,
are precisely the three groups, in the same order, that are
described in the previous verses as having married foreign
women. Secondly, it is clear that 1 Esdr 9:37 is quite different in
its details from both Ezra 2:70 and Neh 7:72. The singers, gate
keepers, and temple servants mentioned in the latter two verses
are not found in 1 Esdr 9:37. Also, 1 Esdr 9:37 says that the
priests, Levites, and Israelites lived in Jerusalem and in the country, while the other two verses do not make this statement. Furthermore, the phrase *tē noumēnia tou hebdomou mēnos* is
clearly not a translation of *wygʿ hḥdš hšbyʿy*. The phrases are
similar but not exact. The same thing could be said for the complete verse here. 1 Esdr 9:37 is similar to Neh 7:72 and Ezra 2:70
but not exactly the same. If the phrase *tē noumēnia tou hebdomou mēnos* is indeed secondary in 1 Esdr 9:37, it is possible that
its insertion has been influenced by the similar time phrase in
Ezra 2:70. A more likely source of the phrase is 1 Esdr 9:40
where nearly the exact expression is used. Finally, the similarity
of 1 Esdr 9:37 to Ezra 2:70 and the fact that the lists in Ezra 2
and Neh 7 are the same may have provided part of the motivation for shifting the account of the reading of the law and celebration of *Sukkōt* from its original position after Ezra 10 to its
present place in Neh 7:72–8:18.

To summarize, I have found in Williamson's arguments no
compelling reason for regarding 1 Esdras as a compilation. On
the contrary, the evidence in my view accords with the conclusion reached by Torrey, Mowinckel, and Klein.

This survey of the major issues involved in determining the

extent of Chr's work has shown the seemingly contradictory results produced by modern research on these issues. On the one hand, recent work on language and theology in C and Ezra-Nehemiah raises serious doubts that these books, at least as they stand, are the work of a single author. On the other hand, the evidence of 1 Esdras is a strong indication that C and Ezra (at least in part) originally were a single work. These results immediately suggest the possibility of redactional levels in C and Ezra-Nehemiah. This is precisely the proposal of F. M. Cross./28/ He brings together a variety of evidence including the practice of papponymy found in the fourth century Daliyeh papyri, the linguistic and theological differences between C and Ezra-Nehemiah, the understanding of 1 Esdras as a fragment of the OG translation, and Freedman's discussion of the purpose of Chr's work./29/ Cross uses all these pieces of evidence in building his reconstruction of the events surrounding the Judean restoration as well as different editions of C. As discussed above, 1 Esdras as we have it is defective. Cross agrees with Mowinckel that it concluded with the description of the reading of the law and the celebration of the high holy days now found in Neh 8:13–18. Further evidence for this conclusion, as Mowinckel again observed, is found in *Ant* XI. 1–158 where Josephus obviously follows the order of 1 Esdras and concludes his account with the celebration of Sukkot as does Neh 8. Thus, 1 Esdras reflects an earlier edition of this material before the Nehemiah memoirs were attached. The canonical books of C, Ezra, and Nehemiah are the final edition. Finally, on the basis of a discussion of Chr's purpose by D. N. Freedman,/30/ Cross posits an original edition of C which served as a program for the restoration of the kingdom under Zerubbabel. This original edition of the work concluded with the account of the founding of the second Temple in Ezra 3:13 (1 Esdr 5:65). In short, Cross reconstructs three editions of C. The first edition (Chr 1) was made up of 1 C 10-2 C 34 + the *Vorlage* of 1 Esdr 1:1–5:65 (= Ezra 3:13);/31/ the second (Chr 2) included 1 C 10-2 C 34 + the *Vorlage* of all of 1 Esdras; the third (Chr 3) consisted of the books of C, Ezra, and Nehemiah in their present form. The dates of the editions in Cross's reconstruction are as follows: Chr 1—shortly after the founding of the Temple in 520 B.C.; Chr 2— ca. 450 B.C. and Chr 3—ca. 400 B.C. because of the extent to which the genealogical entries in each reach./32/ Since Cross's view regarding the first edition of C rests primarily on his understanding of Chr's purpose, that will be the next topic of this survey.

II. *Purpose and Date*

Freedman's article suggesting a late sixth century date for Chr's work is refreshing./33/ He bases his conclusions on the purpose apparent in the major themes of C. He argues that Chr's purpose was "to establish and defend the legitimate claims of the house of David to pre-eminence in Israel and in particular its authoritative relationship to the temple and its cult."/34/ He goes on to propose that this purpose fits best in the setting of the return from exile and the rebuilding of the Temple under the Davidide, Zerubbabel. He dates the original work of Chr shortly after the completion of the Temple in 515 B.C. Freedman's sketch of the major themes and purpose of C is precisely correct, and the setting he suggests for the book is on the right track. Neither Freedman's methodology of determining the date of C from its themes nor his perception of Chr's concern for Temple and monarchy is new./35/ The stress of C on "city and ruler, temple and priest" as Freedman puts it/36/ is so obvious that it can hardly be denied. Indeed, every work on C of which I am aware acknowledges the importance for C of the Davidic monarchy and the Temple with its cult. Clearly the best setting for such strong concerns is the period of the return from exile and the attempt to reestablish both Davidic monarchy and Temple cult. Freedman has observed this fact without being distracted by other issues. Although his suggestion has not received the consideration it deserves,/37/ it raises serious questions for those who persist in dating C and Ezra-Nehemiah ca. 400 B.C. or later./38/ The stress on these themes simply cannot be explained adequately if C is given this late date. The notion that C's stress on the Davidic monarchy is due to a type of messianism in Chr 1 is out of the question because of the obviously programmatic nature of the material. Cross's revision of Freedman's suggestion refines the setting and purpose for Chr's work to account even better for the themes of Temple and monarchy./39/ He points to the narrative of the foundation of the Temple ending at 1 Esdr 5:65 (Ezra 3:13) as the appropriate ending for a propaganda work which seeks to reestablish the monarchy. Hence, a date shortly after 520 B.C. for the original edition of C is better than Freedman's initial proposal. The strength of Cross's proposal is that it provides a concrete historical setting as the motivation for the programmatic nature of C.

I have agreed, then, with Cross's reconstruction of editorial levels in C and Ezra-Nehemiah, including the date and propaganda work which he sees for Chr 1. His entire view of C, like his view of DH, is perhaps best seen in contrast to the conclusions of Noth./40/ Noth was correct in seeing C, like DH, as substantially the work of a single author/editor. In each case, however, the final form of the work blinded him from connecting the program espoused with the historical setting for which it was originally designed. This fault is particularly acute in Noth's treatment of C where he already recognizes the major themes of the book but is unable to find a truly appropriate setting for such themes during the period in which he dates C. Cross's reconstructions not only find proper settings for the major themes of DH and C, but his isolation of editorial levels in each work accords well with what is known from other OT material about the growth of biblical books.

III. *The Sources of C*

There are actually two questions involved with regard to Chr's sources. The first has to do with his use of canonical sources, especially S and K. The second concerns the existence of extra-biblical sources used by Chr. C, with its parallels in the books of S and K, offers a unique opportunity in OT studies to observe how a writer of an extended piece of biblical history has utilized his sources. Until recently, however, this area of research was generally dependent on an incorrect understanding of the nature of C's DH *Vorlage*. The nearly unanimous assumption among scholars who treated C was that the books of S and K upon which C was dependent were virtually identical with the *textus receptus*. Hence, any differences in C's parallels to S-K material were regarded as changes made by Chr himself./41/ The discovery of the 4QSam^a fragments has forced a change in this assumption. By a comparison of the textual witnesses, including 4QSam^a, W. Lemke has illustrated in detail the idea expressed earlier by Albright and Cross that S in a text type different from M underlies C./42/ A number of differences in C's text vis-à-vis

S^M which had formerly been regarded as Chr's changes have proved to be due to textual variation.

Just as important as his conclusion about the text type of C's S *Vorlage* was Lemke's statement of methodology. He showed that one can conclude that Chr is responsible for a variation from S only when no other witness to the text of S agrees with C and the variation attests a demonstrably consistent interest on the part of Chr. Essentially, Lemke has raised an important *caveat* against too quickly attributing to Chr differences from the text of S which may have already existed in C's *Vorlage*. This is not to say that Chr does not make tendentious changes in his *Vorlage*. He does, but Lemke has pointed out another reason for the variations between the canonical books of C and S.

Lemke's work has paved the way for further research in a variety of directions. Although his conclusion that Chr used a text of S different from the *textus receptus* has been widely accepted, its implications have not been reflected in many recent works on C./43/ Yet his work raises some important questions. Because of the important new information in 4QSam^a Lemke's work was limited to C's relationship to S. Do his conclusions hold true with regard to C's relationship to K? Lemke's conclusions were largely negative, pointing out the improper use that had been made of C. What can be said in a positive way about Chr's use of his S-K source and the insertion of his biases? By eliminating from consideration those differences in C vis-à-vis S-K that have arisen in textual transmission can one define Chr's interests more precisely? Are there reasons, besides textual corruption and tendentious change, for the differences between C and S-K?

The issue of whether Chr used sources unknown today actually overlaps with the final question raised above. While various sources have been proposed, the tendency has been to doubt the existence of the sources cited by Chr and to ascribe the information in Chr's account that is different from S-K to his own composition. Torrey, for example, emphatically denied that Chr had any extra-canonical sources./44/ Noth also regards Chr's references to other sources as a literary device, and he would clearly prefer to view any additional information in C as the product of the transmission and development of traditions. Nevertheless, he is compelled by the material to posit extra-biblical sources behind some of Chr's accounts./45/ Actually, there are several issues at stake in this matter. One concerns whether the sources cited by Chr are genuine or reflect a simple literary device on the part of Chr. Another question has to do with the nature of Chr's proposed source(s). How much of C's variant or additional information was from written sources and how much from simple oral tradition? Was there, as 2 C 24:27 suggests, a *midrash* of K available to Chr? Obviously, these are complex questions, and no attempt will be made here to deal thoroughly with them. The immediate concern is whether Chr used any extra-canonical sources at all. Where C contains different or additional information from S-K that does not derive from textual variation or from Chr's bias, it is certainly reasonable to propose that Chr has used a source unknown to us.

NOTES

/1/ "The Date and Personality of the Chronicler," *JBL* 40 (1921): 104–24.

/2/ See S. Japhet ("The Supposed Common Authorship of Chronicles and Ezra–Nehemiah Investigated Anew," *VT* 18 [1968]: 330–31) and H. G. M. Williamson (*Israel in the Books of Chronicles* [Cambridge: Cambridge University Press, 1977] 5, n. 3) for lists of scholars who have rejected the consensus.

/3/ Japhet, "Authorship," 331–32; Williamson, *Israel*, 5–6.

/4/ See Williamson, *Israel*, 7–11.

/5/ Along with the works of Japhet and Williamson cited above see Japhet's recently published dissertation, *The Ideology of the Book of Chronicles and its Place in Biblical Thought* (Jerusalem: Bialik Institute, 1977).

/6/ Cross has pointed out that some of Japhet's arguments are invalid because they are based on orthographic practices or the use of archaic or pseudo-archaic forms. See "A Reconstruction of the Judean Restoration," *Int* 29 (1975): 197, n. 58. Japhet's linguistic arguments have also been criticized by R. Polzin (*Late Biblical Hebrew: Toward an Historical Typology of Biblical Prose* [Missoula, MT: Scholars Press, 1976] especially p. 54, n. 56). Cf. M. Throntveit, "Linguistic Analysis and the Question of Authorship in Chronicles, Ezra and Nehemiah," *VT* 32 (1982): 201–16. For arguments from theology see R. Braun "Chronicles, Ezra, and Nehemiah: Theology and Literary History," *Studies in the*

Historical Books of the Old Testament (VTSup 30; ed. J. A. Emerton; Leiden: E. J. Brill, 1979) 52–64.

/7/ See C. C. Torrey, *Ezra Studies* (Chicago: University of Chicago, 1910) 12–18, and S. Mowinckel, *Studien zu dem Buche Ezra-Nehemia I: Die nachchronistische Redaktion des Buches. Die Listen* (SUNVAO II; Oslo: Universitetsforlaget, 1964) 16–17.

/8/ See his series of articles entitled, "The Real Character and the Importance of the Book of 1 Esdras," in *The Academy*, vols. 43–44 (1893). See also his series, "Some Unconventional Views on the Text of the Bible," in *Proceedings of the Society of Biblical Archaeology*, vols. 23–29 (1901–1907).

/9/ Torrey, *Ezra Studies*, 11–36, and "A Revised View of First Esdras," *Louis Ginzberg Jubilee Volume* (New York: The American Academy for Jewish Research, 1945) 395–410. Mowinckel, *Studien* I, 7–28. The more recent work by K.-F. Pohlmann (*Studien zum dritten Esra* [FRLANT 104; Göttingen: Vandenhoeck & Ruprecht, 1970]) gathers the major arguments.

/10/ His reconstruction of the original shape of both Ezra and 1 Esdras is not convincing. He argues that 1 Esdr 4:47–56 and 4:62–5:6 are part of Chr's original composition. He also includes the Nehemiah memoirs, albeit in a different order than M, within the original work. Furthermore, he argues that the Artaxerxes correspondence in 1 Esdr 2:15–25 has been transposed from its original position in Ezra 4:6–24. Finally, Torrey accepted Howorth's view that Esdras B represents Theodotion's translation, a view that has been refuted by several scholars; see Mowinckel, *Studien* I, 8–9.

/11/ "Studies in the Greek Texts of the Chronicler" (unpublished Ph.D. thesis, Harvard University, 1966).

/12/ *Israel*, 12–36. He is actually arguing against Pohlmann's work, *Studien zum dritten Esra*.

/13/ *Israel*, 15.

/14/ Ibid., 18

/15/ Ibid., 20–21.

/16/ Klein, "Studies in the Greek Texts."

/17/ See J. Gerald Janzen, *Studies in the Text of Jeremiah* (HSM 6; Cambridge, MA: Harvard, 1973).

/18/ Klein, "Studies in the Greek Texts," 16–19.

/19/ "Revised View." The corruption in v 22 is clear whether or not one agrees with Torrey's emendation.

/20/ *Israel*, 16.

/21/ This is an argument, incidentally, that makes little sense. If the compiler of 1 Esdras in Williamson's reconstruction expected his readers to know the story of Manasseh as recorded in K and C so well that he could make subtle allusions to it, as Williamson argues that he did in v 22, why could he not mention Manasseh by name?

/22/ *Israel*, 18–19.

/23/ Ibid., 21–29.

/24/ Williamson argues that *Ant* XI. 181 summarizes Neh 11, and XI. 182 summarizes Neh 13:4–14. He holds that Neh 13:15–21 was omitted for apologetic reasons because of its negative view of Jerusalem. Neh 8 is missing because it was already covered at the end of 1 Esdras according to Williamson.

/25/ Mowinckel, *Studien* I, 25–28.

/26/ *Israel*, 32.

/27/ *Studien zum dritten Esra*, 68–71.

/28/ "Reconstruction," 194–98. This article was originally published in *JBL* 94 (1975): 4–18.

/29/ On the Dâliyeh papyri see Cross, "Papyri of the Fourth Century B.C. From Dâliyeh: A Preliminary Report on Their Discovery and Significance," *New Directions in Biblical Archaeology* (ed. D. N. Freedman and J. C. Greenfield; New York: Doubleday, 1969) 41–62. On Freedman's article see below.

/30/ "The Chronicler's Purpose," *CBQ* 23 (1961): 432–42. See the discussion below under *Purpose and Date*.

/31/ Minus the story of the three youths in 3:1–5:6, which is a secondary insertion. See Cross, "Reconstruction," 196.

/32/ Cross has since nuanced his original reconstruction slightly. He originally viewed the addition of the genealogies in 2 C 1–9 as the work of the final editor. He now believes that much of this material was in the original edition. See his "Samaria and Jerusalem: The Early History of the Samaritans and Their Relations with the Jews (722–64 B.C.E.)," n. 45 (unpublished paper, Harvard University, 1983). The latter view is correct, not only because the material fits with Chr's inclusion of genealogies elsewhere but also because the inclusion of genealogies from the Northern tribes accords with Chr's pan-Israel interest. In addition, I would agree with D. L. Petersen (*Late Israelite Prophecy: Studies in Deutero-Prophetic Literature and in Chronicles* [SBLMS 23; Missoula: Scholars Press, 1977] 60) that the redactional work of Chr 2 and Chr 3 may have involved internal retouching within the first edition of C as well as additions to that edition. In the comparison of the texts of C and S-K in later chapters there are a few passages in C that appear to be secondary. However, I would stress that there is no evidence for systematic revision. All indications are that the internal redactional activity of Chr 2 and/or Chr 3 was very light.

/33/ "Chronicler's Purpose." So far as I am aware, this early a date had not been proposed before by a critical scholar. The dates generally given fall between 400–250 B.C.

/34/ Ibid., 441.

/35/ Compare, for example, Noth's discussion of precisely these themes in *ÜS*, 174–80. Because he is influenced by other considerations and regards C and Ezra-Nehemiah as the work of a single writer, Noth attempts to force the concern for these themes into a period which does not really fit (300–200 B.C.).

/36/ "Chronicler's Purpose," 437.

/37/ Aside from Cross's basic acceptance of the position, the only other voices in agreement have been J. D. Newsome ("Toward and Understanding of the Chronicler and his Purposes," *JBL* 94 [1975]: 201–17) and Petersen (*Late Israelite Prophecy*, 58–60).

/38/ Even the recent studies of Japhet and Williamson, which challenge traditional scholarly understandings of Chr's work, continue to date C ca. 400 without seriously considering the implications of the importance of the Davidic monarchy and the Temple for C. See Japhet, *Ideology*, especially pp. 187–212 and 375–412. Williamson's remarks about David on pp. 65–66 of his *Israel* show his understanding of the importance of the Davidic covenant for C. He dates C "at some point within the fourth century B.C." (86), but he does not discuss in detail how this date fits with the ideology of C as he sees it.

/39/ "Reconstruction," 197–99.

/40/ *ÜS*, 110–80.

/41/ Examples of this methodology are given throughout Lemke's thesis (next note) and need not be cited here.

/42/ "Synoptic Studies in the Chronicler's History" (unpublished Th.D. thesis, Harvard University, 1963). See his article "The Synoptic Problem in the Chronicler's History," *HTR* 58 (1965): 349–63. See also Albright, "The Judicial Reform of Jehoshaphat," *Alexander Marx Jubilee Volume* (New York: Jewish Theological Seminary, 1950) 62, and Cross, *ALQ*, 188–90; "The History of the Biblical Text in the Light of Discoveries in the Judean Desert," *HTR* 57 (1964): 292–97; and "The Contribution of the Qumran Discoveries to the Study of the Biblical Text," *IEJ* 16 (1966): 84–85.

/43/ Even recent commentaries which recognize that C's S *Vorlage* was not M continue to ascribe the majority of variations between S and C in parallel passages to C's *Tendenz*. See, for example, P. R. Ackroyd, *I II Chronicles, Ezra, Nehemiah* (Torch Bible; London: SCM, 1973), and J. M. Myers, *I and II Chronicles* (AB; New York: Doubleday, 1965). This is also one of the major problems of T. Willi's *Die Chronik als Auslegung* (Göttingen: Vandenhoeck & Ruprecht, 1972), who cites Lemke's thesis and article but fails to take seriously their implications. Some of the reasons cited by Willi for changes in C vis-à-vis S-K are valuable. However, quite often his suggestions would apply to copyists' work in C and need not be regarded as Chr's changes.

/44/ *Ezra Studies*, 227–31.

/45/ *ÜS*, 131–43. Besides arguing that certain individual reports, such as that about Hezekiah's tunnel in 2 C 32:30, were based on sources available to Chr. Noth also believed that a single source underlay C's various reports about the fortifications and defenses of the Judean kings. Similarly, the wars of Judean kings were based on a single source according to Noth.

Chapter 3

1 CHRONICLES

The goal of the next four chapters is to determine to what extent and in what ways Chr made use of DH as his source. The material in C//S-K is treated in four sections: 1 C//1 S 31–2 S 24 (David), 2 C 1–28// 1 K 1–2 K 17 (Solomon through Ahaz), 2 C 29:1–35:19//2 K 18:1–23:28 (Hezekiah to Josiah's death), and 2 C 35:20–36:23//2 K 23:29–25:30 (Judah following Josiah). This four-part division is not arbitrary. There is major change in the relationship of C to DH in each section.

In each section, the material in C and DH falls into three categories: (1) omissions from C of material extant in S-K, (2) additions in C not paralleled in S-K, (3) parallel passages. We are concerned in (1) and (2) principally with omissions and additions of entire pericopes. Minor pluses and minuses are dealt with in (3). (1) and (2) provide insight into the purposes and interests of Chr and the motives behind his use of sources. (3) shows the extent to which Chr relied on DH and the extent to which text types and textual corruption are responsible for the differences. In 2 C//K there is an additional category of material that is not strictly parallel in the two accounts but does deal with the same subject matter. Much of this material has probably been borrowed by Chr from a source other than K. In 1 C, the dependence on S is obvious. It has long been recognized that S is the major source for 1 C. The real question, therefore, has to do with the ways in which Chr used S for the story of David. As the previous chapter explained, the predominant view for many years has been that Chr wrote over his S source with frequent changes introducing his theological ideas. The major basis for this view was the understanding that Chr's source was S^M. However, since the S fragments from Qumran have made it clear that Chr's *Vorlage* was a different text type of S, the view that Chr extensively rewrote his S source must be reinvestigated.

The method of investigation employed here involves the

detailed comparison of parallel accounts in important textual
witnesses using the methods and tools of textual criticism. First,
parallel passages in S and C for which there is extant 4QSam^a
material will be compared. Although the percentage of 4QSam^a
material is small (ca. 10% of 2 S), its testimony is extremely
important. Of special significance are those readings of 4QSam^a
that agree with C against S^M. Such readings mean that Chr follows his *Vorlage* closely at that point. Secondly, I will compare
passages where S^M and C^M show significant disagreement, especially where Chr has been accused of tendentious change and
4QSam^a is not extant. Here a series of questions will be asked:
(1) Does the reading of C^M agree with that of any other important witness to S, particularly the OG or L, thus indicating that
Chr has used a text of S from a different textual tradition than
that of S^M? If this question is answered positively, then one must
conclude that the different reading in C is probably due to his
Vorlage, S in a different text type from M. (2) Do the readings
in the witnesses to S or C disagree among themselves indicating
that there is textual corruption within the S or C textual tradition that might account for the present difference between S^M
and C^M? (3) If textual evidence is wanting, do principles of textual criticism suggest that textual corruption may be responsible
for the difference between S^M and C^M? Do one or both appear
expansionistic? Is there evidence of haplography? If the answer
to either (2) or (3) is "yes" the passage in question must be disqualified as furnishing evidence for the way in which Chr used
S. (4) Finally, does the alleged change in C illustrate an interest
of Chr that appears consistently throughout C? If this final question cannot be answered positively one must be extremely cautious about attributing the different reading in C to tendentious
change or rewriting, especially if there is evidence that elsewhere Chr follows his *Vorlage* closely.

The similarity of this methodology to that adopted by Lemke
is obvious, although the objectives are different from his and cause
one to ask different questions of the material. In addition, I have
adopted as a working hypothesis Cross's theory of local text
types./1/ Thus, I am assuming that Chr used a Palestinian text of
S, the type to which 4QSam^a also belongs. The Egyptian text,
which developed from the Palestinian, is represented by the OG.
S^M is an example of the Babylonian type. Even if some aspects of
Cross's hypothesis prove to be incorrect, it is clear from the

number of passages where 4QSam^a and C^M agree against S^M that one is dealing with different textual traditions.

In regard to the history of recensions of the Greek Bible, Cross makes use, with some revision, of the important work done by D. Barthélemy./2/ For the present purposes the important point is that in 2 S 11:2–1 K 2:11 and 1 K 22:1–2 K 25:30 B and the majority of Greek manuscripts display *kaige* readings not OG./3/ Since Lucianic manuscripts are the only exception, they may attest OG or proto-Lucianic readings in these sections, and their importance is thus enhanced. A similar point may be made about the OL. It was translated from either an OG or proto-Lucianic manuscript of S. Therefore, it is an important witness and becomes even more important where B is *kaige*./4/

Another of my assumptions is Ulrich's conclusion that Josephus consistently and predominately used a Greek text of S in a slightly revised form of the OG that was closely affiliated with 4QSam^a./5/ That Josephus predominately followed S not C is clear from the survey in section I below of S material omitted by C. Josephus includes parallels to all of the passages under I except the poems in 1 S 2; 2 S 1; 22; and 23. Furthermore, the order of events and general information given in S is basically the same as that given in Josephus. The agreement of 4QSam^a, Josephus, and C^M against S^M in such passages as 1 C 21:16 has led scholars to reassert, with Mez and Thackeray, the value of Josephus as a witness to the text of S./6/ Nevertheless, Josephus must be used with caution, not only because of his loose style in reporting the accounts in his source, but also because it is almost always possible that he was using C. 1 C 21:16//2 S 24:16 is exceptional because it is clear from the context that Josephus was using a Greek translation of S not C at this point (see below on 1 C 21:16–17). But it is obvious from the passages in section B of this chapter that Josephus knew C in some form. Josephus contains parallels to 1 C 12:25–40; 13:1–4; 21:27b–22:1; 22:2–29:30, all of which are unparalleled in S. Hence, one cannot assume that whenever Josephus and C agree against S^M they both depend on a text type distinct from M. Neither does such a case automatically mean that Josephus has copied C, since they may represent a text type different from S^M. If there is no other textual evidence supporting the C = Josephus reading, one will usually have to suspend judgment about the origin of the reading. If there is evidence indicating that Josephus did not borrow from C, their common reading will be accepted as a real variant to S^M. The main value of Josephus, then, is corroborative.

In addition to his conclusions about Josephus, Ulrich also presents the evidence establishing the S tradition, not the C tradition, as the source for the agreement of 4QSam^a and C^M./7/ The strongest datum is the similarity of 4QSam^a and C^M with the OG, proto-Lucian, and the OL which places them both within the Palestinian textual tradition of S. In addition, I shall point out in the course of this chapter some specific passages where it is clear that 4QSam^a did not borrow from C.

I. *Material Omitted by Chr*

Some of Chr's interests can be deduced from the frequently large blocks of material in S for which there is no parallel in C. The list of blocks includes: 1 S 1–30; 2 S 1–4; 9; 11:2–12:25; 13:1–21:17; 22; 23:1–7.

A. *1 S 1–30*. Chr omits all of the stories about Samuel, the rise of kingship in Israel, and the kingship of Saul. His account begins with the death of Saul in order to show how Yahweh turned over (*wayyasseb*) the kingdom to David (1 C 10:14). It is clear from the allusion to Saul's enquiry of the witch of Endor in 1 C 10:14 and the reference to Samuel's prophecy about David in 1 C 11:3 that Chr is familiar with the traditions in 1 S 1–30. Thus, by omitting all that is pre-Davidic he focuses on David. He begins essentially with David, and even more significantly, with David as Yahweh's chosen king.

B. *2 S 1–4*. Most of this material describes the chaos between the reigns of Saul and David, particularly the contention of Ishbaal with David for the throne of Israel. Also included here is the conflict of Joab with Abner for the office of David's commander-in-chief. Therefore, David is not the central focus of these chapters. What is more, the events narrated in these chapters all occur before David takes Jerusalem, which is of prime importance to Chr as the central cultic site, as is obvious in 1 C 21. Finally, the omission of these chapters fits in well with Chr's pan-Israel interest (see section C below on 11:1–3).

C. *2 S 6:20b–23*. These verses describe Michal's reproach of David for dancing unclothed before the ark of Yahweh. In C's report (15:29//2 S 6:16) Michal's anger appears unwarranted. The rest of the story was probably omitted because it seemed to

Chr to detract from the role of David as the model king.

D. *2 S 9*. Although this chapter describes David's generous care of Mephibaal, it is not directly concerned with the paradigmatic presentation of David's reign and as such is omitted.

E. *2 S 11:2–12:25*. The absence of the entire narrative about David's adultery with Bathsheba and his subsequent murder of Uriah along with Nathan's oracle is striking. Obviously Chr has omitted the story because it does not fit his idealized view of David.

F. *2 S 13:1–21:17*. Also conspicuous by its absence is this extensive block of material which tells of the revolts of Absalom (chaps. 13–19) and Sheba (20). 2 S 21:1–17 explains how David's slaughter of seven members of Saul's family was an effort to atone for bloodguilt incurred by Saul in killing the Gibeonites. As a whole, these passages clearly place David in a negative light and detract from his status as the model king of Israel.

G. *2 S 22*. This chapter contains a psalm attributed to David "on the day when Yahweh delivered him from the hand of all his enemies and from Saul." It may have been omitted from C because of its association with the period before David's monarchy when he fled from Saul. At any rate, it has nothing to do directly with the reign of David and thus does not fall within Chr's main sphere of interest.

H. *2 S 23:1–7*. These verses are the poem known as the "Last Words of David." Again, the poem is not directly concerned with the paradigmatic Davidic monarchy and lies outside of Chr's main interests. It may also have seemed somewhat premature to Chr to include the "Last Words of David" at this point since he had a large body of other material about David yet to append (1 C 21–29).

The passages treated above have been intentionally omitted by Chr, and they all have in common that they view David in a negative light or are not directly concerned with the Davidic monarchy which Chr views as paradigmatic./8/

II. *Chr's Independent Material*

Chr's interests are also evident in the blocks of material peculiar to C.

A. *1 C 1–9*. It is uncertain exactly how much of this material comes from Chr 1. Some of it undoubtedly stems from Chr 3 who gave C its final form. As a whole, though, these chapters do accord with Chr 1's interests in genealogies and in pan-Israel (see Chap. 2 n. 32)./9/ Most of this material comes from sources outside of DH.

B. *1 C 10:13–14*. This brief summary passage serves to place the kingdom squarely in David's hands. The two verses also illustrate the schema of divine retribution which is extremely important for Chr.

C. *1 C 11:41b–47*. Chr's addendum here attests no particular bias other than his interest in lists. Its connection with the preceding verses is uncertain. It may simply be a loose list of names attached by Chr./10/ He has probably done the same thing with other lists that he presents.

D. *1 C 12*. Chr probably relies on sources outside of DH for these two lists of troops who came to David at Ziklag (vv 1–22) and Hebron (vv 23–40). Both lists, especially the second one which includes troops from all thirteen tribes, accord with Chr's pan-Israel theme. Chr does not exclude the Northern tribes from "Israel" but envisions a time when the Northern tribes will be reunited with Judah under one Davidic king.

Josephus contains a close parallel to vv 25–40 (*Ant* VII. 55–60). He probably borrows this list from C, since his account rarely furnishes so close a parallel as it does here. He borrows only the second list probably because of its association with Hebron where David was anointed. In fact, he inserts the list after David's anointing rather than after the names of David's mighty men where it appears in C (1 C 11:10–47).

E. *1 C 13:1–4*. These verses again betray a pan-Israel interest in the gathering by David of all Israel for the cultic celebration of bringing the ark up to Jerusalem. Chr's interest in the Levites and priests with their place in the cult is also apparent here. If this entire pericope is not an addition of Chr, he has certainly reworked it. Josephus (*Ant* VII. 78–79) shows familiarity with both the C and the S accounts. He mentions the priests and Levites, Kiriath-jearim, and David's gathering the leaders of the people for consultation, all of which are peculiar to C's account. At the same time, his reference to those who were in the prime of life (*en akmē tēs hēlikias*) seems to presuppose the *bāḥûr* found only in 2 S 6:1.

F. *1 C 14:17*. This brief addition again illustrates Chr's esteem for David as the ideal king whom Yahweh rewarded with an empire. The model of the Davidic monarchy is obvious, although Chr's view of David's reward is not unique. 2 S 8:14 makes a similar point.

G. *1 C 15:1–25a.* This material consists largely of lists of divisions of Levites established by David. Chr's interest in the Levites is clear. More significant, though, is the fact that David is credited with their organization. The extent to which David is credited with shaping the cult in C is astonishing in comparison to S where his function is almost entirely political./11/

H. *1 C 16:4–43.* This passage, which consists largely of quotations from Pss 105, 96 and 106, is prefaced with an account of David's organization of the Levites to make music in the cult. Again David is portrayed in the role of cult organizer.

I. *1 C 21:27–22:1.* It is surprising that Chr includes the narrative of David's census, since it is clearly viewed as a sin on David's part. The reason for its inclusion is apparent in this ending of the story, which describes the reason behind David's choice of Ornan's (*sic*) threshing floor as the precise spot for the altar of Yahweh within the Temple court. Chr stresses the centrality of the Jerusalem Temple in Israel's cult and David's establishment of that cult, even though doing so means tarnishing the image of David as model king.

J. *1 C 22:2–29:30.* This material is an extraordinary addition by Chr to his S source. It attributes the organization of the Jerusalem cult in nearly every detail to David. A number of Chr's interests are evident here. Of particular importance is David's division of the priests and Levites into various groups, each with a special duty in the cult (chaps. 23–26). Chr's pan-Israel interest is visible in 27:1–28:1 with the lists of the heads of the tribes of Israel and David's gathering them in Jerusalem to present Solomon as his successor. David is credited with formulating the plan for the Temple and securing many of the materials needed for its building (22:2–5; 28:11–19). David explains why he was unable to build the Temple himself—because he was a man of blood (22:8; 28:3). These two explanations are encased within two speeches of David which compare the themes "house of Yahweh" and "house of David" (22:6–16; 28:2–10). These themes are the same ones found in the Nathan oracle of 2 S 7//1 C 17 and reiterated in Solomon's temple dedication speech (1 K 8//2 C 6). Strangely enough, few scholars have noticed this similarity. However, the following list of expressions from 1 C 22:6–16;

28:2–10 clearly illustrates the degree to which these two speeches rely on the Nathan oracle and/or its reiteration in Solomon's dedication speech.

(1) 'm 1bb 1 1 C 22:7; 28:2; 1 K 8:17, 18//2 C 6:7, 8
kl 'šr blbbk 2 S 7:3// 1 C 17:2

(2) byt lšm Yhwh 1 C 22:7; 28:3; 1 K 8:17//2 C 6:7; 1 K 8:20//2 C 6:10; (cf. 1 K 5:19); 1 K 8:19//2 C 6:9 (cf. 1 K 8:19//2 C 6:9: l' tbnh hbyt)
byt lšmy 1 C 22:8,10; 28:3; 2 S 7:13; (1 K 8:18//2 C 6:8; 1 C 17:12: hw' ybnh ly byt; 1 C 28:6: hw' ybnh byty).

(3) whnhwty lw mkl 'wybyw msbyb 1 C 22:9
wYhwh hnyh lw msbyb 2 S 7:1
whnyhty lk mkl 'ybyk 2 S 7:11
(hnyh Yhwh 'lhy ly msbyb 1 K 5:18)

(4) whw' yhyh ly lbn w'ny lw l'b whkynwty ks' mlkwtw 'l yśr'l 'd 'wlm 1 C 22:10
ky bhrty bw ly lbn w'ny 'hyh lw l'b whkynwty 't mlkwtw 'd 'wlm 1 C 28:6–7a
wknnty 't ks' mmlktw 'd 'wlm 'ny 'hyh lw l'b whw' yhyh ly lbn 1 S 7:13–14a
wknnty 't ks'w 'd 'wlm 'ny 'hyh lw l'b whw' yhyh ly lbn 1 C 17:13–14a

(5) (w)yhy Yhwh 'mk 1 C 22:11, 16
Yhwh/h'lhym 'mk 2 S 7:3//1 C 17:3
w'hyh 'mk 2 S 7:9//1 C 17:8

In addition, there are two phrases in 1 C 22:13 which are common Deuteronomistic rhetoric:/12/ (1) l'śwt 't hhqym w't hmšptym 'šr ṣwh Yhwh 't Mšh (see especially Deut 4:1, 5, 14, 40; 5:1; 6:1; note also 1 K 9:4//2 C 7:17), and (2) hzq w'mṣ 'l tyr' w'l tht (see especially Josh 1:9; cf. Deut 31:7, 23; Josh 1:6, 7, 18). The latter expression is also found in 1 C 28:20.

It seems clear that Chr here followed the ancient historiographic technique of inserting speeches into the mouths of his characters as elsewhere in his work (cf. 2 C 13:4–12)./13/ However, it is also clear that in David's speeches in 1 C 22 and 28 Chr composes on the basis of Deuteronomistic material, particularly the Nathan oracle and Solomon's speech. In essence, these two Deuteronomistic passages are rephrased and placed in David's mouth. These two speeches, then, illustrate one usage which Chr makes of his Deuteronomistic source. He rewrites it, in this case to fit another context.

The material treated in sections I and II clearly reveals some of Chr's major interests. The focus of 1 C is obviously David. Chr portrays David's monarchy as the ideal era in Israel's history. David is, except for 1 C 21, the model king. Chr has structured the material in 1 C so that David's primary concern is the cult. 1 C 13 and 14 in effect reverse the order of the accounts found in 2 S 5–6 by narrating David's dealings with Hiram, the increase of his wives and children, and his wars with the Philistines after his initial attempt to bring up the ark to Jerusalem. The purpose of this structure seems to be to produce the impression that David's first act upon conquering Jerusalem is to bring up the ark./14/ David is essentially credited with the organization of the entire cult. Thus, Chr is also particularly interested in the Jerusalem cult and its organization. This portrayal of David as the model king and the importance of the king in the role of the guardian of the cult of Yahweh in Jerusalem and Israel fit well with the proposal that Chr wrote his work as a program for the restoration of the Davidic monarchy. "The Chronicler was not so much interested in writing a factual history—*wie es eigentlich gewesen*—as he wanted to write a history of theocracy as realized through the Davidic dynasty and the Jerusalem cult."/15/ In Chr's vision a new Davidide will reign over a united Israel, hence his pan-Israel interest. These interests are also visible in the synoptic material to which we now turn.

III. *Parallel Passages in S and C*

A. *Passages where 4QSam^a is extant./16/*

(1) 1 C 11:1–9//2 S 5:1–10
 (a) 1 S 5:1
 4QSam^a: [כ](ו)ל שב] מי יש[ראל] (not in Ulrich)
 M,G: כל שבטי ישראל ($\pi\alpha\sigma\alpha\iota$ $\alpha\iota$ $\phi\upsilon\lambda\alpha\iota$ $I\sigma\rho\alpha\eta\lambda$)
 1 C 11:1
 M,B: כל ישראל ($\pi\alpha s$ $I\sigma\rho\alpha\eta\lambda$)
 L: $\pi\alpha s$ $\alpha\nu\eta\rho$ $I\sigma\rho\alpha\eta\lambda$ (כל איש ישראל)

This example probably represents an intentional change on the part of Chr, introducing his pan-Israel interest. The "tribes of Israel" in S refers only to the Northern tribes, while in C "Israel" refers to the entire nation. The difference in interpretation is clearly seen in the light of 2 S 1–4 where "Israel" is obviously the Northern tribes who follow Ishbaal instead of David (2:8–11; 3:12,

17–19). As pointed out in section II above, there are various reasons for Chr's omitting 2 S 1–4. The omission is not due entirely to
his pan-Israel interest. But by omitting 2 S 1–4 Chr can introduce
his pan-Israel interest into 1 C 11:1–3 without extensive alteration
of his *Vorlage*. Thus, when "all Israel" gathered at Hebron to make
David king over "Israel" (1 C 11:1, 3) Chr speaks not of the Northern tribes alone, but of the entire nation./17/

(b) 2 S 5:1

4QSam[a]: לאמור

M: ויאמרו לאמר (8 MSS: ויאמרו לו לאמר)

B: και ειπαν αυτω

L: και λεγουσιν

1 C 11:1 M, G: לאמר (λεγοντες)

The C witnesses and 4QSam[a] preserve the old Palestinian
reading, לאמר. L probably preserves the old Egyptian reading,
ויאמרו. S[M] attests a conflate reading. B and the majority of Greek
manuscripts for S have been revised toward a form of the proto-
Rabbinic text (cf. the eight variant MSS)./18/

(c) 2 S 5:2

4QSam[a]: [ת]בהיו (not in Ulrich)

M: בהיות

1 C 11:2 M: גם בהיוב

גם in C is a dittography. It occurs twice before in both S[M]
and C[M].

(d) 2 S 5:3

4QSam[a], M,G: omit

1 C 11:3 M,G: כדבר יהוה ביד שמואל

Ant VII. 53: οτι τε βασιλευς υπο του θεου δια
Σαμουηλου του προφητου χειροτονηθειη

Spatial considerations make it impossible that 4QSam[a]
included this phrase./19/ Josephus seems to reflect the phrase.
He could have borrowed it from C, or each of them could have
found it in their similar *Vorlagen*. Chr is interested in prophecy
and its fulfillment in the history of Israel, but the same is true of
DH. Thus, the phrase is an expansion, but it is impossible to
determine whether it was introduced by Chr or was already
found in his *Vorlage*.

(e) 2 S 5:4–5

4QSam[a], OL, *Ant* VII. 53–55: omit/20/

M,G, Targum, Peshitta: Include

No parallel in 1 C 11.

The real question here is whether the material in vv 4–5 has been lost by haplography from the text underlying the witnesses without it or represents a secondary insertion as attested by the witnesses that have it. The first alternative is that the original reading was lost in the developing Palestinian tradition, hence it is lacking in C and 4QSam^a. The proto-Lucianic recension would have deleted the material from its OG *Vorlage* to bring it into conformity with a Hebrew text of the developing Palestinian tradition, hence it is lacking in the OL and Josephus. Finally, the material would have been restored in L to make it conform with the Rabbinic or proto-Rabbinic text. The second alternative is that the two verses represent a secondary insertion into the Rabbinic text of S, hence it was originally lacking in the witnesses to other text types. However, the material was inserted by an early reviser into the OG, and all subsequent G manuscripts included it. Neither of these alternatives is completely satisfactory. The first, besides appearing overly complex, furnishes no good mechanism for the supposed initial haplography. The second presupposes a revision of the OG toward the proto-Rabbinic text prior to the proto-Lucianic revision. Ulrich adopts the second alternative and argues for such a revision in 2 S 6./21/ Without further evidence, it is impossible to regard either of the alternatives as certain. In either case, there can be little doubt that Chr follows his *Vorlage* in this passage.

(f) 2 S 5:6

4QSam^a: ואנשיו (not in Ulrich)

M,B: ואנשיו (και οι ανδρες αυτου)

L: וכל אנשיו (και παντες οι ανδρες αυτου)

1 C 11:4

M,L: וכל ישראל (και πας Ισραηλ)

B: και ανδρες αυτου

The original reading is represented in S^M, 4QSam^a, and B(S). B(C) has borrowed its reading from B(S). L(S) expands with כל. C^M's reading reflects intentional change on the part of Chr. While the change in words is minor, the difference in meaning is striking. אנשיו in S refers to David's own army, excluding those from the North who had recently anointed David as their king. כל ישראל in C includes both Northern and Southern tribes. Chr's pan-Israel interest is evident.

(g) 2 S 5:6

4QSam^a: כי הסית[ו העורים והפסחים לאמר לא יבוא] דויד הנה

(Not in Ulrich)

M: כי אם הסירך העורים והפסחים לאמר לא יבוא דוד הנה

1 C 11:5 M,G: omit

While the readings of S^M and 4QSam^a differ slightly, they clearly agree against C in including this information. However, the meaning of this line is not completely clear in either witness, and it may be corrupt. Chr has probably omitted the line because of its obscure meaning. However, the omission is not due to any bias on the part of Chr.

(h) 2 S 5:8

4QSam^a: [ויאמר] ד[ויד] ביום ההוא כול [מ]כה [יבו]סי יגע בצנור

ואת הע[ו]רים ו[ה]ה[פסחי]ם שנאה נפש דויד [על] כן יאמרו עור ופסח

לוא [יבוא אל הבית]

M: ויאמר דוד ביום ההוא כל מכה יבסי ויגע בצנור ואת הפסחים

ואת העורים שנאו נפש דוד על כן יאמרו עור ופסח לא יבוא אל הבית

1 C 11:6 M: ויאמר דויד כל מכה יבוסי בראשונה יהיה לראש ולשׂר

ויעל בראשונה יואב בן צרויה ויהי לראש

As in the previous example, Chr has probably omitted the reference to the blind and lame because of its obscure nature. C's independent information about Joab going up first may come from a source other than S. Josephus also credits Joab with the capture of the city in an account similar to that of C (*Ant* VII 63–64), but he could be combining the accounts of S and C. It is difficult to see any consistent bias of Chr in this verse./22/

(i) 2 S 5:9

4QSam^a: לה [ויקר[א (Not in Ulrich)

M: ויקרא לה

G: και εκληθη αυτη

1 C 11:7

M: על כן קראו לו

G: על כן קרא לה (δια τουτο εκαλεσεν αυτην)

על כן in the C witnesses is probably an expansion. The other differences among the witnesses are insignificant. There is certainly no bias in C's reading.

(j) 2 S 5:9

4QSam^a, B: ויבנה עיר (και ωκοδομησεν αυτην πολιν)

M: ויבן דוד

L: και ωκοδομησεν την πολιν

1 C 11:8 M,G: ויבן העיר (και ωκοδομησεν την πολιν)

The reading of 4QSam^a and B is primitive. ויבנה is a long form of ויבן. C and L reflect incorrect word division. דוד is a corruption of עור./23/ Therefore, the Egyptian and Palestinian witnesses stand aligned against S^M.

(k) 2 S 5:9

4QSam^a: סביב מן](מ)[המלוא וביתה (not in Ulrich)

M: סביב מן המלוא וביתה

G: κακλω απο της ακρας και τον οικον αυτου

1 C 11:8

M,L: מסביב מן המלוא ועד הסביב ויואב יחיה את שאר העיר

B: κυκλω και επολεμησεν και ελαβεν την πολιν

Ant VII. 66: Δαυιδης δε την τε κατω πολιν περιλαβων και την ακραν ουναψας αυτη εποιησεν εν σωμα

There is obvious disarray among the witnesses to the text of C here. The origin of the reading in B (C) is uncertain./24/ It is possible that C^M's *Vorlage* differed from S^M in this verse. Josephus' reference to Joab as επιμελητην των τοιχων in this context seems to reflect a reading similar to C^M's ויואב יחיה את שאר העיר. In any case, C's reading is hardly due to any bias on Chr's part.

Of the eleven examples where 4QSam^a is extant for 2 S 5:1–10 it agrees three times with C^M against S^M (b, e, j), showing that Chr has followed his Palestinian *Vorlage* in these readings. In three cases (d, h, k) where 4QSam^a and S^M agree against C^M, Josephus' parallel to C and the lack of an obvious *Tendenz* in C leave open the possibility that these readings were found in C's *Vorlage*. In two cases (a, f) Chr's pan-Israel interest is responsible for the variations. In two other examples (g, h) Chr has omitted material that he found difficult to understand. Finally, in two cases (c, i) the variations are due to textual corruption. Therefore, 1 C 11:1–9//2 S 5:1–10 in its various witnesses indicates that Chr has adhered closely to his *Vorlage* with only two exceptions (a, f). In these two cases he made minor changes in his *Vorlage* which, along with the omission of 2 S 1–4, permitted him to interpret the passages in a very different way.

(2) 1 C 14:1–7//2 S 5:11–16/25/

(a) 2 S 5:11

4QSam^a: [וח]רשי עץ וחרשי קיר

M: וחרשי עץ וחרשי אבן קיר

B: και τεκτονας ξυλων και τεκτονας λιθων

L(-b),OL: και τεκτονας ξυλων και τεκτονας τοιχου

1 C 14:1

M,L: וחרשי קיר וחרשי עצים

B: και οικοδομους και τεκτονας ξυλων

A,rell: και οικοδομους τοιχων και τεκτονας ξυλων

4QSam[a], L, and OL agree with C[M] in reading וחרשי קיר, thus placing this reading solidly in the Palestinian tradition. The Egyptian tradition as indicated by B (S) probably read וחרשי אבן(ים). S[M] has conflated the two variants./26/

(b) 2 S 5:12

[4QSam[a]], M: נשא ממלכתו

B: επηρθη η βασιλεια αυτου

L: επηρται η βασιλεια αυτου

1 C 14:2 M,G: נשאת למעלה מלכותו

Spatial considerations make it unlikely that למעלה was in 4QSam[a]. Its presence would result in a line 59 spaces long where the average is 51. It is probably a minor expansion in C. However, נשאת appears to be supported by επηρθη (B), and επηρται (L).

(c) 2 S 5:13

4QSam[a]: פיל[ג]שׁים ו[נשׁים]

M: פלגשׁים ונשׁים

B: γυναικας και παλλακας

1 C 14:3 M,G: נשׁים

Some have suggested that Chr omitted the reference to concubines to preserve the pedigree of the royal line or to avoid a practice no longer acceptable in his day./27/ These do not, however, represent particularly convincing or consistent interests in C. פלגשׁים may have been lost by haplography in C as the result of homoioteleuton. This presupposes that the order of elements before the haplography was נשׁים ופלגשׁים, which is certainly possible in the light of the reading of B.

(d) 2 S 5:13

[4QSam[a]], M,G: אחרי באו מחברון (B: εις Χεβρων = לחברון)

1 C 14:3 M,G: omit

This reading or something like it was present in 4QSam[a]./28/ Still, the phrase appears expansionistic. Rudolph argues that Chr has omitted the reference to David's coming from Hebron in line with his stress on David as king of all Israel as in 11:1–3./29/ However, one must ask why Chr would omit the reference to Hebron here and include it in 11:1–3.

(e) 2 S 5:13

4QSam[a]: [ויולד]ו לדויד עוד

M: ויולדו עוד לעוד

G: και εγενοντο τω Δαυειδ ετι = ויולדו לדוד עוד

1 C 14:3

M,B: ויולד דויד עוד (και ετεχθησαν Δαυειδ ετι)

L: και ετεχθησαν αυτω

The hiphil in C instead of niphal as in S is clearly a difference due to scribal transmission. It is impossible to know which is original. The agreement of 4QSam^a and S^G with C in reading the order לדויד עוד against S^M follows the divisions of textual families and shows that C^M's order existed already in its *Vorlage*.

In 1 C 14:1-7 C^M agrees with 4QSam^a against S^M only twice (a [חרשי קיר] and e [לדויד עוד]). In both of these readings C is aligned with other Palestinian witnesses, showing that its variant reading was in its *Vorlage*. In the other examples the differences are probably the result of scribal transmission. Two passages (c, d) have been alleged to display biases on the part of Chr, but I have argued that this is not the case.

(3) 1 C 13:6-11//2 S 6:2-9/30/

(a) 2 S 6:2

4QSam^a: [וכול העם אשר] אתו

M,G: וכל העם אשר אתו

1 C 13:6

M,B: וכל ישראל

L: και πας ανηρ Ισραηλ

C's reading here is the result of Chr's pan-Israel interest. The S witnesses are unanimous in reading וכל העם אשר אתו, probably being a reference to David's army. Chr changed the text to read וכל ישראל. The reading of L (C) is probably an expansion of C^M.

(b) 2 S 6:2

4QSam^a: [בעלה היא קרית יערים אשר ליה]רה^(sic)ו

M: מבעלי יהודה

B, L: απο των αρχοντων Ιουδα εν (L:+τν) αναβασει

1 C 13:6 M: בעלתה אל קרית יערים אשר ליהודה

It is difficult to reconstruct the original reading here./31/ It may have been בעל יהודה. In that case S^M and 4QSam^a reflect interpretations with their respective additions of the preposition ל and the directive ה. The construct plural, בעלי, in S^M may be due to dittography of the *yod* of יהודה. C^M has apparently understood בעלה as the place name and has added an additional ה directive. The phrase אל קרית יערים אשר ליהודה in C^M is a gloss (cf. Josh 18:14). S^G apparently conflates the readings (מבעלי)ם

($=\alpha\pi o$ $\tau\omega\nu$ $\alpha\rho\chi o\nu\tau\omega\nu$) and בעלה ($=\epsilon\nu$ $\alpha\nu\alpha\beta\alpha\sigma\epsilon\iota$). In any case, it is clear from C's agreement with 4QSam[a] that C has followed its *Vorlage*.

(c) 2 S 6:2

4QSam[a]: את אשר נ[קרא שם יהוה יו[שב הכרוב]ים]

M: אשר נקרא שם שם יהוה צבאות ישב הכרבים

1 C 13:6 M: שם יהוה יושב הכרובים אשר נקרא

Spatial considerations between the נ of נקרא and the שב of יושב preclude the possibility the 4QSam[a] included the צבאות and שם (2) of S[M]. The two elements of this clause are reversed in C vis-à-vis 4QSam[a], but otherwise they agree against S[M].

(d) 2 S 6:3–4

4QSam[a]:   [וישאוהו] מבית א[בינדב אשר בגבעה ועזא ואחיו בני
אבינדב] נהגים א[ת] העגלה /32/ [ואחיו הולך לפני ה]ארון

M: וישאהו מבית אבינדב אשר בגבעה ועזה ואחיו בני אבינדב נהגים
את העגלה חדשה וישאהו מבית אבינדב אשר בגבעה עם ארון האלהים
ואחיו הלך לפני הארון

1 C 13:7 M: מבית אבינדב ועזה ואחיו נהגים בעגלה

The phrase וישאהו . . . בגבעה occurs twice in S[M] by dittography. The following words and phrases are lacking in C as compared with 4QSam[a]: (?) . . . הארון, בני יבנדב, אשר בגבעה, וישאוהו (see n. 32). These words and phrases can all probably be regarded as expansions./33/ Thus, C appears to contain the most pristine text in this passage.

(e) 2 S 6:5

4QSam[a]: [וכול] בני ישראל

M: וכל בית ישראל

B: $\kappa\alpha\iota$ $o\iota$ $\upsilon\iota o\iota$ $I\sigma\rho\alpha\eta\lambda$

L: $\kappa\alpha\iota$ $\pi\alpha\nu\tau\epsilon\varsigma$ $o\iota$ $\upsilon\iota o\iota$ $I\sigma\rho\alpha\eta\lambda$

1 C 13:8 M,G: וכל ישראל

C's reading here may be another example of his pan-Israel interest. However, in view of the variation among the witnesses it is better to conclude that independent expansions have occurred in several of the other witnesses. Again C's reading is pristine.

(f) 2 S 6:5

4QSam[a]: [בכול עוז ו]בשירים]

M: בכל עצי ברושים

G: $\epsilon\nu$ $o\rho\gamma\alpha\nu o\iota\varsigma$ $\eta\rho\mu o\sigma\mu\epsilon\nu o\iota\varsigma$ $\epsilon\nu$ $\iota\sigma\chi\upsilon\iota$ $\kappa\alpha\iota$ $\epsilon\nu$ $\omega\delta\alpha\iota\varsigma$

1 C 13:8 M,G: בכל עז ובשירים

S^M is obviously corrupt. S^G seems to be conflate. εν οργανοις ηρμοσμενοις seems to represent בכלי עז (cf. 6:14), but εν ισχυι και εν ωδαις reflects a reading similar to the one found in 4QSam^a and C.

(g) 2 S 6:6

4QSam^a: וישלח עזא [את] ידו אל ארון ה[אלוהים]

M: וישלח עזה אל ארון האלהים ויאחז בו

G: και εξετεινεν Οζα την χειρα αυτου επι (L: προς) την κιβωτον του θεου κατασχειν αυτην και εκρατησεν (L: εκραταιωσεν) αυτην

1 C 13:9 M,G: וישלח עזה את ידו לאחז את הארון

4QSam^a and C agree against S^M in reading את ידו. For the reading לאחז or ויאחז 4QSam^a is not extant. It has been argued that Chr substituted the infinitive here for the finite verb because for Chr just the attempt to touch the ark was enough to incur the wrath of God./34/ However, the very fact that the G witnesses to S conflate the infinitive (κατασχειν) and the finite verb (και εκρατησεν/εκραταιωσεν) is enough to suggest that Chr had the infinitive in his *Vorlage*. Furthermore, Ulrich has gathered evidence pointing to the infinitive as the OG reading./35/ Chr, therefore, has probably simply copied his *Vorlage* in this reading.

(h) 2 S 6:7

4QSam^a: [ו] יכהו שם אלוהי[ם]

M,G: ויכהו שם האלהים

1 C 13:10

M: ויכהו

G: και επαταξεν αυτον εκει

All witnesses except C^M contain expansions here.

(i) 2 S 6:7

4QSam^a: [על אשר שלח ידו] אל [ה]ארון]

M: על השל

B: omit

L: επι τη προπετεια

1 C 13:10 M,G: על אשר שלח ידו על הארון

S^M is clearly corrupt here. L probably contains an interpretation.

(j) 2 S 6:7

4QSam^a: ל[פני הא[ל[ו]ה]ים]

M: עם ארון האלהים

G: παρα την κιβωτον του κυριου ενωπιον του θεου

1 C 13:10

M: לפני אלהים

G: απεναντι του θεου

The reading of 4QSam^a and the conflation in S^G show that Chr followed his *Vorlage*. The variant in C comes from the text type of S used by Chr, not from his bias./36/

Of the ten examples surveyed, 4QSam^a is closer to C^M than to S^M in six cases (b, d, f, g, i, j). Chr's pan-Israel interest is responsible for only one variant (a). The other variations are due to textual phenomena. It is clear that Chr has generally followed his *Vorlage* closely in this passage.

   (4) 1 C 15:25–16:2//2 S 6:12–18

      (a) 2 S 6:13

4QSam^a: [ויזבח]ו שב[עה] פר[י]ם ושבע]ה אילים

M: ויהי כי צעדו נשאי ארון יהוה ששה צעדים ויזבח שור ומריא

G: και ησαν μετ᾽ αυτων (L: οι) αιρουντες την κιβωτον επτα χοροι και θυμα μοσχος (L: μοσχου) και αρνα (L: αρνος)

1 C 15:16 M,B: ויהי בעזר האלהים את הלוים נשאי ארון ברית יהוה ויזבחו שבעה פרים ושבעה אילים

Josephus also mentions the "seven choirs" (*Ant* VII. 85). 4QSam^a is incomplete here, but the C^M reading in the first half of the verse is too long for the space available on its leather./37/ C's reference to God helping the Levites, the "ark bearers," is probably Chr's own addition. It fits with his interest in the Levites and their cultic functions. In the second half of the verse the reading of 4QSam^a not only shows that C^M's reading comes from its *Vorlage* but also illustrates how extensively textual families may differ.

      (b) 2 S 6:14

4QSam^a, M,G: omit

1 C 15:27

M: וכל הלוים הנשאים את הארון והמשררים וכנניה השר המשא המשררים

This phrase is an addition of Chr. It obviously accords with his interest in the Levites and their divisions.

      (c) 2 S 6:15

4QSam^a: [ודו]יד וכל בית ישראל

M,B: ודוד וכל בית ישראל

L: και Δαυειδ και πας Ισραηλ

1 C 15:28 M,G: וכל ישראל

That the differences in this reading are probably expansions in the texts of 4QSam^a and S^M rather than the results of C's pan-Israel interest is evident from the reading of L which agrees with C^M in reading וכל ישראל but expands by adding the name of David.

(d) 2 S 6:15

4QSam^a, M,G: omit

1 C 15:28 M: ובחצצרות ובמצלתים משמעים בנבלים וכנרות

This expansion may be the result of Chr's interest in the cult. Such lists of instruments are especially susceptible to expansion and corruption and tend to vary in different witnesses./38/ However, the expansion here is extensive and fits well with Chr's interest in the cult.

(e) 2 S 6:17

4QSam^a: ויעל דויד ע[לות]

M,L: ויעל דוד עלות

B: και ανηνεγκεν αυτη ολοκαυτωματα

1 C 16:1 M,G: ויקריבו עלות (και προσηνεγκαν ολοκαυτωματα

ויעל and ויקריבו are lexical variants. ויעל is probably original. The expression הקריב עלה is found elsewhere in C (16:1), Ezra (8:35), Ezekiel (46:4), and P material. But it is not used in DH./39/ It is doubtful that this change in verbs in C is tendentious. Chr has probably simply utilized an expression that is more familiar to him and probably more common in his day. The reading αυτη in place of Δαυειδ occurs only in B (S). It is probably the result of scribal error. The similar sequence, αυτη Δαυειδ, earlier in the verse may have contributed to the error.

Within the five passages surveyed in (4) there is one example where 4QSam^a and C^M agree against S^M (a). But Chr has also made an addition to his *Vorlage* in (a). His additions are also apparent in (b) and probably in (d) and (e).

(5) 1 C 17:20–27//2 S 7:22–29

(a) 2 S 7:23/40/

4QSam^a, G: ואהלים (και σκηνωματα)

M: ואלהיו

1 C 17:21 M,G: omit

4QSam^a and S^G agree in an obvious error, making it clear that the latter's *Vorlage* was not M. Since Chr's *Vorlage* was also Palestinian, he may have omitted the corruption, but one cannot be certain.

(b) 2 S 7:26

4QSam^a: [יהוה צבא[ות אלוהים על י[שראל] (not in Ulrich)

M: יהוה צבאות אלהים על ישראל

L: Ks παντοκρατωρ ο θεος επι τον Ισραηλ

B: omit (see n. 41)

1 C 17:24 M: יהוה צבאות אלהי ישראל אלהים לישראל

C^M attests a conflation of the variants אלהי ישראל and אלהים
(ע(ל ישראל).

(c) 2 S 7:27

4QSam^a: [כי אתה יהוה] צבאות אלוהי יש[ראל] (not in Ulrich)

M,L: כי אתה יהוה צבאות אלהי ישראל

B: κυριε παντοκρατωρ θεος Ισραηλ

1 C 17:25 M: כי אתה אלהי

G: οτι συ

The text of C^G is the least expansionistic and may well be
original. It is clear, at any rate, that 4QSam^a and S^M contain
expansions which were probably motivated by the title in the
previous verse./41/

(d) 2 S 7:27

4QSam^a, M,G: את לבו (not in Ulrich)

1 C 17:25: omit

The syntax of C is unusual and probably represents a simple
omission.

(e) 2 S 7:28

4QSam^a: ודברך [יהיה אמת] (not in Ulrich)

M,G: ודבריך יהיו אמת

1 C 17:26 M,G: omit

C's minus is probably due to haplography triggered by the
sequence of the letters דבר in דבר(י)ך and תדבר.

(f) 2 S 7:29

4QSam^a: ה[ו]א[ל וברך (not in Ulrich)

M: הואל וברך

1 C 17:27 M: הואלת לברך

In the light of the other differences in this passage which are
clearly due to textual transmission the minor difference here
cannot be ascribed to Chr's *Tendenz*./42/

(g) 2 S 7:29

4QSam^a: [דברת ומ[ברכתך [יברך בית עבדך לעולם] (not in
Ulrich)

M: דברת מברכתך יברך בית עבדך לעולם

1 C 17:27 M: ברכת ומברך לעולם

B: ευλογησας και ευλογησον εις τον αιωνα

L: ευλογησας και ευλογηται εις τον αιωνα

C^M's reading is probably the result of haplography caused by the similarity of ברכ in ומברכתך and ברכ in עבדך. The readings in the Greek witnesses of C apparently represent attempts to understand C^M's corrupt text. The differences in the passages treated in (5) are due, without exception, to textual transmission. There is no reason in any of these cases to suspect tendentious change in C.

    (6) 1 C 18:2–8//2 S 8:2–8

        (a) 2 S 8:3

    4QSam^a,M,G: בן רחב (Not in Ulrich)

    1 C 18:3 M,G: omit

This appears to be a minor expansion in 4QSam^a and S^M perhaps on the basis of 8:12.

        (b) 2 S 8:4

    4QSam^a: [וילכוד] דויד אלף ר[כב] /43/

    M: וילכד דוד ממנו אלף

    G: και προκατελαβετο Δαυειδ των αυτου χιλια αρματα

    1 C 18:4

    M: וילכד דויד ממנו אלף רכב

    G: και προκατελαβετο Δαυειδ αυτων χιλια αρματα

S^M and C^M reflect the expansion ממנו. However, C agrees with 4QSam^a in reading רכב where S lacks it. Thus, C, S^G, and 4QSam^a report that David captured 1,000 chariots and 7,000 steeds while S^M reports that he captured 1,700 steeds. Clearly Chr has not invented his reading.

        (c) 2 S 8:7

    4QSam^a:[גם] אותם [לקח שושק מלך מצרים ב[עלותו אל יר[ושלים]

    M: omit

    G: και ελαβεν αυτα Σουσακειμ βασιλευς Αιγυπτου εν τω αναβηναι αυτου εις Ιερουσαλημ εν ημεραις Ιεροβοαμ υιου Σαλομωντος

    OL(S): haec accepit postea Susac in diebus Roboam filii Salomonis cum ascendisset in Ierusalem

    1 C 18:7 M,G: omit

Josephus also presupposes the reading in 4QSam^a and S^G (*Ant* VII. 104). This reading is the first of two pluses in this context to be found in the Palestinian witnesses. It is an expansion based on 1 K 14:25–26. Since the other Palestinian witnesses attest the plus, it is striking that C does not contain it. C is probably haplographic here. A mechanism for haplography exists in the reading of the OL(S) which reverses the clauses in the plus

and has ירושלים as the last word in the plus. If C had this same
order the plus could have been lost as a result of homoioteleuton.

(d) 2 S 8:8

4QSam[a], M,G: המלך דו(י)ד

1 C 18:8 M,G: דויד

המלך in 4QSam[a], S[M], and S[G] is probably an expansion.
Of the four examples surveyed in (6) 4QSam[a] and C[M] agree
against S[M] only in (b). Expansions in 4QSam[a] and S[M] (a, d) and a
probable haplography in C (c) account for the remaining cases
where C[M] and 4QSam[a] disagree. There is no evidence in this passage for Chr having rewritten his *Vorlage*. The available evidence
points in the opposite direction, that he followed it rather closely.

(7) 1 C 19:4–8, 18–19//2 S 10:4–7/44/

(a) 2 S 10:5

4QSam[a, g]: [על] האנשים

M: omit

1 C 19:5 M,G: על האנשים

The reading in S[M] is probably primitive. The other witnesses
agree in expansion.

(b) 2 S 10:6

4QSam[a]: אלף ככר כסף

M,G: omit

1 C 19:6 M,G: אלף ככר כסף

Ant VII. 121: χιλια ταλαντα

The Palestinian witnesses are clearly aligned in including
this reading against witnesses to other text types.

(c) 2 S 10:6

4QSam[a]: רכב ופרשים

M,G: omit

1 C 19:6 M: רכב ופרשים

Again 4QSam[a] and C[M] agree as Palestinian witnesses against
S[M]

(d) 2 S 10:6

4QSam[a]: [שנים ושלושי[ם אלף רכ]ב]

M,G: עשרים אלף רגלי . . . שנים עשר אלף איש

1 C 19:7 M,G: שנים ושלשים אלף רכב

The agreement of 4QSam[a] with C at this point means that
Chr is not guilty of inflating the number of chariots in order to
make David's victory more impressive.

(e) 2 S 10:6

4QSam[a]: [ואת מלך מעכה ואת א[ישטוב]

ואת מלך מעכה אלף איש ואיש טוב :M

ואת מלך מעכה ואת עמו :1 C 19:7 M,G

4QSam[a] and S[M,G] agree against C[M,G] in referring to איש טוב
although 4QSam[a] understands this reference as a proper name
and S does not. However, 4QSam[a] disagrees with S[M] by not
reading אלף איש after מעכה. This is an expansion, influenced by
the occurrence of the same two words at the end of the verse.

(f) 2 S 10:6

4QSam[a]: [ובני] עמון נאספו מן ה[ערים]

M,G: omit

1 C 19:7 M,G: ובני עמון נאספו מעריהם

4QSam[a] and C agree against S, and the fact that they are
not exactly the same indicates that their agreement is not due to
one borrowing from the other but to their dependence on a
common text type.

(g) 2 S 10:18

4QSam[a], M,G: הכה וימות שם (not in Ulrich)

1 C 19:18 M: המית

The origin of this variation is uncertain, but C should probably be preferred as the shorter reading.

Examples (b)–(f) are actually parts of one long reading in
which 4QSam[a] and C substantially agree. Their agreement furnishes strong evidence for their dependence on *Vorlagen* of a
text type different from S[M]. C's plus here, therefore, is not due
to his altering his *Vorlage* but to his following it closely.

(8) 1 C 21:15–21//2 S 24:16–20

(a) 2 S 24:16

4QSam[a]: עומד

M,B: היה ($\eta\nu$)

L: $\eta\nu$ $\epsilon\sigma\tau\eta\kappa\omega\varsigma$

1 C 21:15 M,G: עמד ($\epsilon\sigma\tau\omega\varsigma$)

The Palestinian witnesses agree, though L conflates.

(b) 2 S 24:16

4QSam[a]: וישא [דויד את עיניו וירא את מלאך יהוה עומד בין]
הארץ ובין [הש]מ[י]ם וחר[ב]ו שלופה בידו [נטויה על ירושלים
ויפל דויד והזקנים על פנ]יהם מתכ[סים] בשקים

M,G: omit

1 C 21:16 M: וישא דויד את עיניו וירא את מלאך יהוה עמד בין
הארץ ובין השמים וחרבו שלופה בידו נטויה על ירושלם ויפל דויד
והזקנים מכסים בשקים על פניהם

Ant VII. 327: $\alpha\nu\alpha\beta\lambda\epsilon\psi\alpha\varsigma$ δ' $\epsilon\iota\varsigma$ $\tau o\nu$ $\alpha\epsilon\rho\alpha$ o $\beta\alpha\sigma\iota\lambda\epsilon\upsilon\varsigma$ $\kappa\alpha\iota$

θεασαμενος τον αγγελον δι᾽ αυτου φερομενον επι τα
Ιεροσολυμα α και μαχαιραν εσπασμενον

Obviously 4QSamᵃ and Cᴹ agree against S in including this
reading. However, there are two important differences between
them which make it clear that 4QSamᵃ did not borrow the passage from C: 1) the transposition of the phrases כסים בשקים(ת)מ
and על פניהם ;2) מתכסים (4QSamᵃ) vs. מכסים (Cᴹ). Thus, 4QSamᵃ
and Cᴹ have copied the reading from independent *Vorlagen* of
the same text type. Chr's reading here cannot, then, be viewed
as tendentious. Furthermore, the mention of the angel in the
other witnesses disproves the notion that Chr introduces an
advanced form of angelology into the passage./45/ The minus in
S is apparently the result of haplography motivated by homoioarchton, ויאמר דויד . . . וישא דויד./46/

(c) 2 S 24:17

4QSamᵃ: [וא[נכי הרעה הרעתי

M: ואנכי העויתי

B (text): ηδικησα
    (margin of Ba,b): και εγω ειμι ο ποιμην

L: ημαρτηκον και εγω (e₂: ειμι) ο ποιμην εκακοποιησα

1 C 21:17

M: והרע הרעותי

G: κακοποιων εκακοποιησα

Ant VII. 328: αυτος ειη κολαοθηναι δικαιος ο ποιμην

Cᴹ is obviously closer to 4QSamᵃ than is Sᴹ. However, it is
obvious from their differences and from the other witnesses that
4QSamᵃ did not borrow this reading from C. It is also clear that
Josephus got his reading from a Greek text of S, since no C witness has "shepherd." The primitive reading,הרעתי, has given rise
to the reading of Sᴹ,העויתי, through a process begun by graphic
confusion of *waw* and *resh* in the script of the third
century./47/

(d) 2 S 24:18

4QSamᵃ: [ויבוא גד אל דויד ביו[ם ההוא ויאמר עלה ה[קם

M: ויבא גד אל דוד ביום ההוא ויאמר לו עלה הקם

G: και ηλθεν Γαδ προς Δαυειδ εν τη ημερα εκεινη και
ειπεν αυτω (L: omit αυτω) αναβηθι και στησον

1 C 21:18

M: ומלאך יהוה אמר אל גד לאמר לדויד כי יעלה דויד להקים

G: και αγγελος Κυριου ειπεν τω Γαδ του ειπεν προς
Δαυειδ ινα αναβη του στησαι

The only possible bias on the part of Chr in this reading is the mention of the angel. But since it has been seen that references to the angel in this context occur in C's other witnesses, C's variant reading cannot be regarded as the result of Chr's interests. It appears expansionistic. The second "David" is certainly an expansion, since it does not occur even in C^G.

(e) 2 S 24:19

4QSam^a, M: צוה יהוה

1 C 21:19 M: דבר בשם יהוה

דבר and צוה are unimportant variants. בשם in C is a minor expansion.

(f) 2 S 24:20

4QSam^a: וישקף [ארנא וירא את המלך ואת עבדיו עברים עליו
מתכסים] בשקים וארנא דש חטים

M,G: וישקף ארונה וירא את המלך ואת עבדיו עברים עליו

1 C 21:20 M: וישב ארנן וירא את המלאך וארבעת בניו עמו
מתחבאים וארנן דש חטים

Ant VII. 330: Ορουνας δε του σιτου αλοων επει του βασιλεα προσιοντα και τους παιδας αυτου ταυτας εθεασατο

C's unusual reading seems to be a corruption of the text reflected in 4QSam^a: המלאך for המלך, וארבעת בניו for את עבדיו, עברים, and מתחבאים for מתכסים. Since 4QSam^a and Josephus do not contain this corruption, it is evident that they do not depend on C for their reading here. Thus, the fact that 4QSam^a, Josephus, and C^M all agree against S^{M,G} in including the phrase ארנא דש חטים establishes that phrase in the Palestinian tradition.

(g) 2 S 24:20

4QSam^a, M,G: omit

1 C 21:21

M: ויבא דויד עד ארנן ויבט ארנן וירא את דויד

B: και ηλθεν Δαυειδ προς Ορναν

C^M's text here is conflationary. The phrase ... דויד ויבט is suspiciously similar to an earlier phrase ... המלאך וישב (sic) in v 20. The repetition of the notice that Ornan (sic) saw David is superfluous, and ויבט ... דויד is probably a doublet. Similarly, the line ויבא ... ארנן, which is also attested in C^G, may be a doublet of the later line, ויצא מן הגרן. There is clearly confusion here. Does David come to Ornan or does Ornan go out too David? C's text is corrupt.

Of the six examples surveyed in (8) C^M agrees with 4QSam^a against S^M four times: (a, b, c, and f [in the final phrase]). Two

of these cases, (b) and (f), show that 4QSam^a did not get its reading from C. The three cases where 4QSam^a and C^M disagree are
attributable largely to corruption in the witnesses. In no case is
there any reason for supposing that Chr has rewritten his *Vorlage* in order to display his own interests. In fact, the agreements
of C and 4QSam^a especially in (b) indicate that C has followed
his *Vorlage* closely.

In the preceding survey of the passages where C and S contain parallel accounts and 4QSam^a is extant only six examples
have been found in which the different reading in C^M can definitely be attributed to an interest on the part of Chr: (1a, f; 3a;
4a, b, d). Aside from these cases there is no reason for ascribing
the differences in C in the material surveyed to tendentious
change. The majority of C^M's variant readings from S^M can be
shown to have existed in C's *Vorlage* or to be the result of textual transmission and corruption in the witnesses. The textual
evidence in the above passages, then, points to the conclusion
that Chr generally followed his *Vorlage* closely. What is more,
the 10 percent of S which is extant in 4QSam^a must be regarded
as representative, since the fragments which make up that 10
percent are the remains after the natural processes of corrosion.
The remainder of this chapter will survey those passages which
are parallel in 2 S and 1 C where 4QSam^a is not extant but
where the differences are particularly significant or C has been
alleged to contain a tendentious reading.

B. *Passages where 4QSam^a is not extant*

(1) 1 C 10 // 1 S 31
(a) 1 S 31:6
M: וימת שאול ושלשת בניו ונשא כליו גם כל אנשיו ביום ההוא יחדו

B: και απεθανεν Σαουλ και οι τρεις υιοι αυτου και ο αιρων
τα σκευη αυτου εν τη ημερα εκεινη κατα το αυτο

L: και απεθανεν Σαουλ και οι τρεις υιοι αυτου και ο αιρων
τα σκευη αυτου και παντες οι ανδρες αυτου εν τη ημερα εκεινη
κατα το αυτο

1 C 10:6
M: וימת שאול ושלשת בניו וכל ביתו יחדו מתו

McCarter may be correct in suggesting that the original
reading was וימת שאול ושלבת בניו יחדו ./48/ In any case, each of
the witnesses attests an expanded text, though C^M's text is the

least expansionistic. It is doubtful, therefore, that the reference to all of Saul's house dying in C can be considered tendentious, as some have argued./49/

(b) 1 S 31:7

M: ויראו אנשי ישראל אשר בעבר העמק ואשר בעבר הירדן כי נסו אנשי ישראל וכי מתו שאול ובניו ויעזבו את הערים וינסו ויבאו פלשתים וישבו בהן

1 C 10:7

M: ויראו כל איש ישראל אשר בעמק כי נסו וכי מתו שאול ובניו ויעזבו עריהם וינסו ויבאו פלשתים וישבו בהם

I agree with McCarter that the pluses in S are probably expansions./50/ Thus, C^M attests a more primitive text.

(c) 1 S 31:10

M: וישמו את כליו בית עשתרות ואת גויתו תקעו בחומת בית שן

1 C 10:10

M: וישימו את כליו בית אלהיהם ואת גלגלתו תקעו בית דגון

Commentators have argued that Chr omitted the reference to the Aštarôt as offensive and that he omitted the reference to Saul's body being nailed to the wall at Beth Shan because of the injuction in Deut 21:22–23 against leaving the body of a hanged man over night./51/ However, it is difficult to believe that Chr omitted the reference to the Aštarôt for tendentious reasons but included the mention of Dagon in the same verse. He also mentions Asherah in 2 C 15:16. It is also doubtful that Deut 21:22–23 would have influenced Chr to make a tendentious change since the situation it addresses is so different from that of Saul. Deut 21:22–23 concerns criminals who have been hanged. Saul is not a criminal, nor was he hanged since his head had been detached from his body. Furthermore, it was not the Israelites who desecrated Saul's body, but the Philistines who were not subject to the law of Deuteronomy. The difference in readings here may be due to textual corruption./52/

(d) 1 S 31:12

M: ויקומו כל איש חיל וילכו כל הלילה ויקחו את גוית שאול ואת גוית בניו מחומת בית שן ויבאו יבשה וישרפו אתם שם

1 C 10:12a

M: ויקומו כל איש חיל וישאו את גופת שאול ואת גופת בניו ויביאום יבישה

Several commentators state that Chr omitted the reference to burning the bodies of Saul and his sons because such treatment was limited under the law to criminals (Lev 20:14, 21:19;

Josh 7:25)./53/ Again there are problems with such a view. The
three passages cited as the legal basis for Chr's alleged bias all
describe burning as a form of execution. In the case of 1 C
10:12//2 S 31:12, it is not execution but disposal of the corpses
that it described. Indeed why would the S writer, who was
surely familiar with the legal traditions, include the reference to
burning the bodies if it were a violation of the law code. Clearly
he pictures the men of Jabesh Gilead as wishing to honor Saul by
their actions, not dishonor him. The reference to burning the
bodies is actually one of several pluses in S^M in this verse including ‏וילכו כל הלילה‎ and ‏שן בית מחומת‎. These minuses in C are best
attributed to Chr's having used a different, and perhaps less
expansionistic, text of S.

(2) 1 C 11 // 2 S 23

(a) 1 C 11:10 //—

C^M: ‏ואלה ראשי הגבורים אשר לדויד המתחזקים עמו במלכותו עם כל‎
‏ישראל להמליכו כדבר יהוה על ישראל‎

Chr probably composed this verse as an introduction to the
list of warriors that follows. None of the S witnesses includes the
reading, and the verse displays Chr's pan-Israel interest.

(b) 2 S 23:10–11a//—

S^M: ‏הוא קם ויך בפלשתים עד כי יגעה ידו ותדבק ידו אל החרב‎
‏ויעש יהוה תשועה גדולה ביום ההוא והעם ישבו אחריו אך לפשט‎
‏ואחרו שמא בן אגא הררי ויאספו פלשתים לחיה‎

C is probably haplographic here, though the mechanism is
not exact. The last phrase before the omission in 1 C 11:13 is
‏והפלשתים נאספו שם למלחמה‎. The last phrase of the omitted material in S^M is ‏ויאספו הפלשתים לחיה‎. The similarity between the two
lines is evident. If C's *Vorlage* had a variant form of the line
which was closer to the line in 1 C 11:13 a haplography would
have been more likely to occur. For example, the variant
‏למלחמה‎ for ‏לחיה‎ would facilitate such a haplography.

(c) 2 S 23:21

M: ‏והוא הכה את איש מצרי אשר מראה וביד המצרי חנית‎

B: αυτος επαταξεν τον ανδρα τον Αιγυπτιον ανδρα ορατον
εν δε τη χειρι του Αιγυπτιον δορυ ως ξυλον διαβαθρας

L: και ουτος επαταξεν τον Αιγυπτιον ανδρα ορατον ανδρα
και εν τη χειρι του Αιγυπτιον δορυ ως ξυλον διαβαθρας

1 C 11:23

M: ‏והוא הכה את האיש המצרי איש מדה חמש באמה וביד המצרי חנית‎
‏כמנור ארגים‎

The readings חמש באמה and כמנור ארגים appear to be expansions occasioned perhaps by the descriptions of noteworthy opponents elsewhere (cf. 1 S 17:4–7; 2 S 21:19; 1 C 20:5). The expansions were already in C's Palestinian *Vorlage*, as is clear from the fact that B and L attest them. C stands alone in reading מדה. However *Ant* VII. 315 also refers to the Egyptian's extraordinary size. The difference between מראה and מדה is clearly the result of graphic confusion. There is no bias here on the part of Chr.

(3) 2 S 6:1–2a

M: ויסף עוד דוד את כל בחור בישראל שלשים אלף ויקם וילך
דוד וכל העם אשר אתו מבעלי יהודה

1 C 13:5–6a

M: ויקהל דויד את כל ישראל מן שיחור מצרים ועד
לבוא חמת להביא את ארון האלהים מקרית יערים (6) ויעל דויד
וכל ישראל בעלתה אל קראת יערים אשר ליהודה

Chr's pan-Israel interest is quite strong here, and there is no textual support to indicate that C's reading stems from its *Vorlage*./54/ The bringing up of the ark is an extremely important juncture for Chr. Chr makes explicit with the plus מן שיחור מצרים ועד לבוא חמת that he interprets "Israel" to refer to both Northern and Southern tribes. "Israel" in S may also refer to both North and South at this point, but Chr stresses the pan-Israelite nature of the event.

(4) 1 C 14:8–12 // 2 S 5:17–21

(a) 2 S 5:17

M: וישמעו פלשתים כי משחו את דוד למלך על ישראל ויעלו כל
פלשתים לבקש את דוד וישמע דוד וירד אל המצודה

1 C 14:8

M: וישמעו פלשתים כי נמשח דויד למלך על כל ישראל ויעלו
כל פלשתים לבקש את דויד וישמע דויד ויצא לפניהם

The reading כל ישראל in C probably represents another example of his pan-Israel interest. However, the argument that ויצא לפניהם in C is a tendentious change motivated by Chr's attempt to protect David from the charge of cowardice at fleeing to the fortress cannot be accepted./55/ In the first place, it is not clear what is meant by המצודה. Most commentators think it is Adullam./56/ It is certainly not Jerusalem. The reading in C may represent an attempt to clarify the S reading./57/ In any case, the meaning in both accounts is the same. David is not pictured in S as fleeing from the Philistines. Rather he goes to the fortress to prepare for battle.

(b) 2 S 5:21

M: ויעזבו שם את עצביהם וישאם דוד ואנשיו

L: και καταλειπουσιν εκει οι αλλοφυλοι τους θεους αυτων
και λαμβανουσιν αυτους Δαυειδ και οι ανδρες αυτου και λεγει
Δαδ κατακαυσατε (e2̤: -σετε) αυτους εν πυρι

1 C 14:12

M: ויעזבו שם את אלהיהם ויאמר דויד וישרפו באש

The attempts to find here a tendentious addition by Chr
which would portray David as piously following the law (Deut.
7:25) by burning the idols/58/ must be dismissed because of the
reading of L which conflates the two variants./59/ Thus, C's
reading existed already in its *Vorlage*.

(5) 1 C 15:1–16:3 // 2 S 6:12–19

(a) — // 2 S 6:12

M: ויגד למלך דוד לאמר ברך יהוה את בית עבד אדם ואת כל אשר לו
בעבור ארון האלהים

It is not clear why this verse is lacking in C. There is no
reason to suspect haplography. It is possible, as Lemke has suggested, that Chr accidentally omitted the verse when he
returned at this point to his *Vorlage*./60/ It has been suggested
that Chr omitted this verse because it attributed to David an
unworthy motive for wanting to bring the ark up to Jerusalem./61/ However, it is unclear that the desire for blessing
would really have been regarded by Chr as an improper motive.
1 C 13:14 connects Yahweh's blessing of Obed Edom with the
ark's residing in his house. Thus, while the precise reason for
omission is uncertain, it is unlikely that it is due to Chr's bias.

(b) 1 C 15:25a//—

M: ויהי דויד וזקני ישראל ושרי האלפים ההלכים

This verse's reference to the elders of Israel gathering for the
bringing of the ark to Jerusalem fits with Chr's pan-Israel interest and is probably best viewed as his addition. The same may
be true with regard to the commanders of thousands. They are
also mentioned in 1 C 13:1 as David's advisors in the context of
the first attempt to bring up the ark and apparently represent
the leadership of the entire people.

(c) 2 S 6:14

4QSam[a]: דויד חגור אפוד בד

M: ודוד מכרכר בכל עז לפני יהוה ודוד חגור אפוד בד

B: και Δαυειδ ανεκρουετο εν οργανοις ηρμοσμενοις ενωπιον
Κυριου και ο Δαυειδ ενδεδυκως στολην εξαλλον

1 C 15:27

M: ודויד מכרבל במעיל בוץ וכל הלוים הנשאים את הארון

והמשררים וכנניה השר המשא המשררים ועל דויד אפוד בד

Opinion varies widely and is even contradictory as to the nature of Chr's *Tendenz* in the first line of this verse where C^M reads ודוד מכרבל במעיל בוץ./62/ No convincing explanation of C's bias here has been offered. In addition, the textual evidence for the first line is uncertain. The different text types vary widely in this context as has been seen in the study of the previous verse. Furthermore, it is possible that the line ודוד מכרבל במעיל בוץ in C is corrupt. It seems to be a doublet of the later phrase ועל דויד אפוד בד, and it is similar enough to the S^M parallel, ודויד מכרכר בכל עז, to have developed as a corruption of it. The later reference to אפוד may have influenced the corruption in the direction of a description of David's clothing. However, the rest of the verse is clearly Chr's addition and attests his interest in the Levites.

(6) 1 C 17 // 2 S 7

(a) 2 S 7:1

M: ויהי כי ישב המלך בביתו ויהוה הניח לו מסביב מכל איביו

1 C 17:1a

M: ויהי כאשר ישב דויד בביתו

There is no evident textual reason for the lack of the phrase ויהוה הניח לו מסביב מכל איביו in C. Some have proposed that Chr omitted the phrase because the next two chapters in C recount some of David's wars/63/ or that he wished to make a direct connection between the bringing up of the ark and the building of the Temple./64/ A better explanation of the difference here, however, is that S^M is expansionistic. The expression (להניח מכל אויב מסביב) is a common Deuteronomistic idiom./65/

(b) 2 S 7:14

M: אני אהיה לו לאב והוא יהיה לי לבן אשר בהעותו והכחתיו

בשבט אנשים ובנגעי בני אדם

1 C 17:13a

M: אני אהיה לו לאב והוא יהיה לי לבן

C lacks the reference to punishing with the rod of men. There is no textual ambiguity and no apparent trigger for haplography. Thus, those who suggest that Chr has omitted the reference to punishment because of his idealized view of Solomon are probably correct./66/

(c) 2 S 7:16

M: ונאמן ביתך וממלכתך עד עולם לפניך כסאך יהיה נכון עד עולם

G: και πιστωθησεται ο οικος αυτου και η βασιλεια αυτου
εως αιωνος ενωπιον εμου και ο θρονος αυτου εσται ανωρθωμενος
εις τον αιωνα

1 C 17:14

M: והעמדתיהו בביתי ובמלכותי עד העולם וכסאו יהיה נכון עד עולם

G: και πιστωσω αυτον εν οικω μου και εν βασιλεια αυτου
εως αιωνος και θρονος αυτου εσται ανωρθωμενος εως αιωνος

Several scholars argue that Chr's theology surfaces here in
the suffixes he employs./67/ Chr constantly refers to Yahweh's
house (Temple) or Yahweh's kingdom rather than David's house
(dynasty). The evidence for this suggestion is found mostly in
Chr's consistent reference to the kingdom as Yahweh's outside of
this verse./68/ Certainly Chr views the kingdom as Yahweh's
and refers to it as such. However, the textual evidence is simply
too diverse to allow the variant suffixes in this verse to be
explained as the result of theological bias. In this verse there is a
great deal of confusion within the witnesses as to the correct
suffixes. No two of the above witnesses agree completely on the
suffixes they reflect. What is more, suffixes are especially susceptible to scribal error. This is particularly true with regard to first
and third person suffixes, since *yod* and *waw* are so easily confused. Of the four cases in the verse where the suffixes vary in
the witnesses, two have to do in part with variation between first
and third person; (1) ביתך (S^M), בביתי (C^{M,G}), ביתו (S^G) and (2)
וממלכתך (S^M), ובמלכותי (C^M), η/εν βασιλεια αυτου (S^G,C^G).

(7) 1 C 18 // 2 S 8

(a) 2 S 8:2

M: ויך את מואב וימדדם בחבל השכב אותם ארצה וימדד שני חבלים
להמית ומלא החבל להחיות ותהי מואב לדוד לעבדים נשאי מנחה

1 C 18:2

M,G: ויך את מואב ויהיו מואב עבדים לדויד נשאי מנחה

It could be argued that Chr omitted this detail because it
did not fit his idealized picture of David. However, Chr's own
explanation of why David did not build the Temple is that he
shed too much blood (1 C 22:8; 28:3). For this reason, I would
suggest that this minus is the result of haplography in C. Unfortunately the mechanism for haplography is inexact./69/

(b) 2 S 8:8

M: omit

G: εν αυτω εποιησεν Σαλωμων την θαλασσαν την χαλκην
και τους στυλους και τους λουτηρας και παντα τα σκευη
1 C 18:8
M: בה עשה שלמה את ים הנחשת ואת העמודים ואת כלי הנחשת
G: εξ αυτου εποιησεν Σαλωμων την θαλασσαν την χαλκην
και τους στυλους και τα σκευη τα χαλκα
Ant VII. 106: εξ ου και Σολομων το μεγα σκευος θαλασσαν
δε καλουμενον εποιησε και τους καλλιστους εκεινους λουτηρας

This is the second major plus attested by the Palestinian
witnesses in this context (see p. 53). It is clear that C's reading is
the result of Chr's following his Palestinian *Vorlage*. This is
particularly striking because without the other witnesses one
would suspect that Chr had composed the plus in order to introduce his interest in the Temple and the cult./70/ The evidence
is also important because Josephus' agreement with S[G] in reading λουτηρας contra C[G] indicates that Josephus' account is
derived from a Greek version of S, not C.

(c) 2 S 8:18b
M: ובני דוד כהנים היו
G: (L: και) υιοι Δαυειδ αυλαρχαι ησαν
1 C 18:17b
M: ובני דויד הראשנים ליד המלך
G: και (L: οι) υιοι Δαυειδ οι πρωτοι διαδοχοι του βασιλεως

C's reading appears to represent a tendentious change,
removing the reference to David's sons as priests. Such a change
would accord with Chr's interest in the priests and Levites as
cultic functionaries. The word αυλαρχαι in S[G] is a *hapax*, but it
apparently refers to some sort of palace official. Its Hebrew
antecedent is uncertain. Similarly, the antecedent of C[G]'s
διαδοχοι is unclear. Both of these words probably reflect
attempts on the part of the translators to get around the difficulty of David's sons being priests.

(8) 2 S 12:26–29
M: וישלח (27) וילחם יואב ברבת בני עמון וילכד את עיר המלוכה
יואב מלאכים אל דוד ויאמר נלחמתי ברבה גם לכדתי את עיר המים
(28) ועתה אסף את יתר העם וחנה על העיר ולכדה פן אלכד אני את
העיר ונקרא שמי עליה (29) ויאסף דוד את כל העם וילך רבתה
וילחם בה וילכדה

B: και επολεμησεν Ιωαβ εν Ραββαθ υιων Αμμων και
κατελαβεν την πολιν της βασιλειας (27) και απεστειλεν Ιωαβ
αγγελους προς Δαυειδ και ειπεν επολεμησα εν Ραββαθ και

κατελαβομην την πολιν των υδατων (28) και νυν συναγαγε το
καταλοιπον του λαου και παρεμβαλε επι την πολιν και
προκαταλαβου αυτην ινα μη προκαταλαβωμαι εγω την πολιν
και κληθη το ονομα μου επ᾽ αυτην (29) και συνηγαγεν Δανειδ
παντα τον λαον και επορευθη εις Ραββαθ και επολεμησεν εν
αυτη και κατελαβετο αυτην

1 C 20:1b

M: ויך יואב את רבה ויהרסה

G^G(i, y): και επαταξεν την ραββα και απεστειλεν ιωαβ
αγγελους προς δαδ λεγων ελθων προκαταλαβου την παββα συ
οπως μη προκαταλαβωμαι αυτην εγω και κληθη το ονομα μου
επ᾽ αυτην και συνηγαγε δαδ τον λαον και επορευθη εις ραββα
και προκαταλαβετο αυτην

C^G(g): και επαταξεν την ραββαθ και κατεσκαψεν αυτην
διερθειρεν αυτην και απεστειλεν ιωαβ προς δαδ λεγων ελθων
προκαταλαβου την ραβαθ οπερ μη προκαταλαβωμε αυτην εγω
και κληθει το ονομα μου επ᾽ αυτην και συναγαγεν δαδ τον λαον
και επορευθη εις ραββαθ και προκατελαβετω αυτην

1 C 20:1 is a fascinating verse. By relating in this verse only
the battle of Joab against Rabbah, Chr is able to omit entirely
the narrative of David's sin with Bathsheba. However, the end
of the account of Joab's battle may have been omitted accidentally from C^M. The miniscules (g, i, and y), attest a reading very
similar to that found in 2 S 12:26 29./71/ However, their read-
ings differ from both S^M and S^G indicating that their *Vorlage*
was not S^M or S^G. In addition, as Rudolph has observed, there is
a possible mechanism for haplography in the name Rabbah
which occurs near the end of v 1 in C^M and near the end of the
plus in the miniscules (i and y)./72/ Unfortunately, the textual
evidence for the plus is not exceptionally strong, and the mechanism for haplography is not exact. The strongest argument for
the plus is the text of C^M itself. In 20:1 David is in Jerusalem. In
20:2 he takes Rabbah, and there is no transition from one verse
to the other. In addition, the omission in C^M cannot be ascribed
to *Tendenz*. It could be argued that the episode detracts from
David's stature as a warrior. However, it is still apparent in C^M's
account that Joab really defeats the city and David simply shows
up for the final coup. The only real difference is that C^M lacks
the transition provided by 2 S 12:26–29.

(9) 2 S 21:19

M: ותיהי עוד המלחמה בגוב עם פלשתים ויך אלחנן בן יערי ארגים

בית הלחמי את גלית הגתי ועץ חניתו כמנור ארגים

1 C 20:5

M: ותהי עוד מלחמה את פלשתים ויך אלחנן בן יעור את

לחמי אחי גלית הגתי ועץ לניתו כמנור ארגים

In S Elhanan is called a Bethlehemite, with הלחמי being an element of the name Bethlehem. In C לחמי is made the name of Goliath's brother whom Elhanan is credited with slaying. The change was intentional and was motivated by the fact that in the well known tradition accounted in 1 S 17 David is Goliath's slayer. There is no evidence, however, that Chr is responsible for the change. It could be the work of a later editor of C or of a pious scribe.

(10) 1 C 21 // 2 S 24

(a) 2 S 24:1

M: ויסף אף יהוה לחרות בישראל ויסת את דוד בהם לאמר לך

מנה את ישראל ואת יהודה

1 C 21:1

M: ויעמד שטן על ישראל ויסת את דויד למנות את ישראל

The reference to Satan has clearly been added to C to preserve the view that Yahweh is holy and transcendent. It may be the work of Chr. Again, however, it could be a pious gloss of a later editor or copyist. David's order to count "Israel" in C refers to the entire nation. In S, he orders his servants to count "Israel" and "Judah." Chr's pan-Israel interest is obvious.

(b) 2 S 24:2

M: ויאמר המלך אל יואב שר החיל אשר אתו שוט נא בכל שבטי ישראל

מדן ועד באר שבע ופקדו את העם וידעתי את מספר העם

L: και ειπεν ο βασιλευς προς Ιωαβ και προς τους αρχοντας των δυναμεων των μετ' αυτου εν Ιλημ περιελθατε δη εις παντα τον φυλον Ισραηλ και Ιουδαν απο Δαν και εως βηρσαβεαι και επισκεψασθε τον λαον και ενεγκατε προς με

1 C 21:2

M: ויאמר דויד אל יואב ואל שרי העם לכו ספרו את ישראל מבאר

שבע ועד דן והביאו אלי ואדעה את מספרם

At first glance these two accounts appear to be very different. However, most of the differences are probably due to different text types. This is illustrated by the reading of L (S) which twice appears to conflate variants found in S^M and C^M. και προς τους αρχοντας των δυναμεων conflates (העם) ואל שרי (C^M) and

שׂר החיל (S^M), and ἐπισκέψασθε τον λαον και ἐνεγκατε προς με
conflates ופקדו את העם (S^M) and והביאו אלי (C^M). Thus, Chr clearly
follows his *Vorlage*. The one exception may be C's reading
את ישראל where S^M has בכל שבטי ישראל. Even here, though,
both accounts have the same meaning as is obvious from their
modifying phrase "from Dan to Beer Sheba" (reversed in
C^M)./73/

(c) 2 S 24:3

M: ויאמר יואב אל המלך ויוסף יהוה אלהיך אל העם כהם וכהם מאה
          פעמים ועיני אדני המלך ראות ואדני המלך למה הפץ בדבר הזה

1 C 21:3

M: ויאמר יואב יוסף יהוה על עמו כהם מאה פעמים הלא אדני המלך
          כלם לאדני לעבדים למה יבקש זאת אדני למה יהיה לאשמה לישראל

S^M contains several minor expansions which are obvious in
comparison with C^M: אל המלך, אלהיך, and וכהם. The readings
כלם לאדני לעבדים (C^M) and ועיני אדני המלך ראות (S^M) are both
reflected in C^G and are best regarded as variants in different
text types. There is no tendentious reason for C's different readings in this verse.

(d) 2 S 24:4–8//1 C 21:4

Lemke argues that Chr omitted Joab's itinerary because it
lay outside of his purposes, and it is hard to find a better explanation for the minus./74/ Chr apparently summarizes the itinerary with the phrase ויתהלך בכל ישראל. *Ant* VII. 319–20 also
omits the itinerary, but it does mention that the census took nine
months and twenty days to complete, a datum found only in 1 S
24:8. There is certainly nothing in the itinerary which Chr
would have found offensive or adverse to his purpose.

(e) 1 C 21:6–7//—

M: ולוי ובנימן לא פקד בתוכם כי נתעב דבר המלך את יואב
          וירע בעיני האלהים על דבר הזה ויך את ישראל

Several scholars argue that this verse is tendentious./75/
According to them, Levi is excluded from the census because of
the prohibition against numbering Levi in Num. 1:49. The exclusion of Benjamin is also cited as the reason for the different figures
in the previous verse. C has 470,000 for the population in Judah
while S has 500,000 because Chr has excluded the 30,000 of
Benjamin. The major difficulty with this view is that there is no
satisfactory reason for the exclusion of Benjamin. The difference
between the two accounts with regard to the population figures for
Judah can hardly be ascribed to the exclusion of Benjamin in C.

Numbers are especially susceptible to corruption and change in textual transmission, and there is nothing in C's account to connect its lower figure with the exclusion of Benjamin. In addition, *Ant* VII, 320 also mentions that Levi and Benjamin were not counted. It states that Joab did not have time to count them. Thus, C's reading may be a Palestinian reading. Finally, the end of 2 S 24:9 appears incomplete. One expects something like חרב שלף. Something may have fallen out of S^M at this point.

(f) 2 S 24:13

M: התבוא לך שבע שנים רעב בארצך ואם שלשה חדשים נסך לפני צריך
והוא רדפך ואם היות שלשת ימים דבר בארצך עתה דע וראה מה אשיב
שלחי דבר

1 C 21:12

M: אם שלוש שנים רעב ואם שלשה חדשים נספה מפני צריך וחרב אויבך
למשגת ואם שלשת ימים חרב יהוה ודבר בארץ ומלאך יהוה משחית בכל
גבול ישראל ועתה ראה מה אשיב את שלחי דבר

Most of the differences here are minor. S^G agrees with C^M in reading "three" against S^M's "seven" for the number of years of famine, and since "seven years of famine" was the cliché (Gen 41), "three" here is probably primitive. נספה in C^M appears to be a corruption of נוס. Similarly, למשגת also appears corrupt. The major difference between the two accounts is the additional phrase in C: ומלאך יהוה משחית בכל גבול ישראל. As has been seen, the 4QSam^a fragment for vv 16–20 renders untenable the notion that C contains an advanced angelology. Thus, this plus was probably already in C's *Vorlage*.

(g) 2 S 24:15

M: ויתן יהוה דבר בישראל מהבקר ועד עת מועד וימת מן העם מדן
ועד באר שבע שבעים אלף איש

G: και εξελεξατο εαυτω Δαυειδ τον θανατον και ημεραι θερισμου πυρων και εδωκεν Κυριος εν Ισραηλ θανατον (L: θανατον εν τω Ιηλ) απο πρωιθεν (L: και) εως ωρας αριστου και ηρξατο η θραυσις εν τω λαω και απεθανεν (L: -νον) εκ του λαου απο Δαν και εως βηρσαβεε (L: -βεαι) εβδομηκοντα χιλιαδες ανδρων

1 C 21:14

M: ויתן יהוה דבר בישראל ויפל בישראל שבעים אלף איש

The phrases מדן ועד באר שבע and מהבקר ועד עת מועד as well as the number 77,000 are expansions in S. S^G contains two additional expansions: εξελεξατο εαυτω Δαυειδ τον θανατον και ημεραι θερισμου πυρων and και ηρξατο η θραυσις εν τω λαω. C's

shorter reading is to be preferred, and there is every indication
that Chr followed his *Vorlage* closely here.

(h) 2 S 24:22b–23aa

ראה הבקר לעלה והמרגים וכלי הבקר לעצים (23) הכל נתן :M

1 C 21:23b

ראה נתתי הבקר לעלות והמורגים לעצים והחטים למנחה הכל נתתי :M

Some scholars argue that Chr introduced the reference to מנחה
in order to conform with regulations such as Num 15:1–10 and
Exod 29:38–46 about offering the מנחה with a burnt offering./76/
However, in both Num 15 and Exod 29 the מנחה consists not of
wheat, but of "fine flour" (סלת). The language is different.
Furthermore, the alleged bias is not consistently represented in C.
C shows no attempt to adhere to such regulations./77/ The
differences here are best ascribed to textual transmission,
particularly in view of the broad differences in the text types
represented by C^M and S^M in this chapter./78/

(i) 2 S 24:24b

ויקן דוד את הגרן ואת הבקר בכסף שקלים חמשים :M

1 C 21:25

ויתן דויד לארנן במקום שקלי זהב משקל שש מאות :M

The major difference here is the price paid for the
threshing-floor. Numbers are especially subject to change and
corruption in textual transmission. However, in this case the
figure is so much larger in C than in S and the value of the
amount in C is increased even more by the fact that the element
of exchange is gold not silver. This is more than simple inflation
of numbers. Lemke may well be correct in suggesting that both
C^M and S^M are corrupt./79/ The three verbs ויקן, ויתן, and ויבן
appear alike enough to have triggered a haplography if they
stood at one time in the same text. Also, the figure of 50 shekels
of silver for the cattle and the threshing floor as reported in S is
extremely low. Abraham paid 400 shekels of silver for his burial
cave (Gen 23) and Omri paid two talents of silver or 720 shekels
for the hill of Samaria (1 K 16:24). 50 shekels may have originally been the cost of the cattle alone. The figure of 600 shekels
of gold may still be an inflated one. Chr, with his interest in the
Temple and its cult, might have increased its sale price. But
tendentious change on the part of Chr can only be suggested
tentatively as an explanation for some of the differences between
S and C in this verse. It is possible that Chr has merely recorded
an oral tradition in which the cost of David's purchases had

become inflated, and there is also good reason to suspect that both S^M and C^M have experienced textual corruption here.

(j) 1 S 24:25

M: ויבן שם דוד מזבח ליהוה ויעל עלות ושלמים ויעתר יהוה לארץ
ותעצר המגפה מעל ישראל

1 C 21:26

M: ויבן שם דויד מזבח ליהוה ויעל עלות ושלמים ויקרא אל יהוה
ויענהו באש מן השמים על מזבח העלה

The unique ending to 1 C in 21:27–22:1 betrays Chr's interests and clarifies his reason for including the account of the census. This special ending could actually be viewed as beginning with 21:26b. The devouring of the offering by fire from heaven is a traditional *topos* which Chr has appropriated to stress the importance for him of Jerusalem and its Temple as the place of true worship to Yahweh. This is particularly clear in view of 2 C 7:1 where Solomon's prayer of dedication for the temple is also answered by fire from heaven.

To summarize the results of this investigation of synoptic passages where 4QSam^a is not extant, of 31 examples there were nine passages where tendentious change on the part of Chr is relatively certain (2a, 3, 4a, 5b, c, 6b, 7c, 10a, j). Of these, five display a pan-Israel interest (2a, 3, 4a, 5b, 10a); one has to do with Chr's idealized view of Solomon (6b); two show Chr's interest in the Levites and the site of the Temple (5c. 10j; compare 7c). In three cases (9, 10a–Satan, 10i) a change has clearly been made, but it is uncertain that Chr is responsible. It is important that the passages treated are those which scholars have alleged to reflect Chr's *Tendenz* and/or which show the greatest divergence from S^M. The parallel accounts in the remainder of 1 C//2 S are very close. Thus, the number of tendentious changes by Chr in the synoptic portions of his account is very small indeed.

IV. *Conclusions to Chapter 3*

We may now address the dual question regarding the extent and the ways in which Chr made use of his DH source. It is obvious that S was Chr's major source for the account of David's kingship. Chr probably had some other sources available to him for this period. However, if the independent material in 1 C is any indication (see section II of this chapter), his other sources were mainly lists: genealogical (1 C 1–9), military (1 C 12; 13:1–5) and Levitical (1 C 15:1–25a; 23:26). With very few exceptions the narrative material about David in 1 C has all been borrowed from S, though oral tradition may have occasionally influenced Chr's account.

In regard to the ways in which Chr has used his S source the preceding study allows us to draw the following conclusion. Chr used S selectively, but where he did borrow from S he generally followed it closely. The appearance of the 4QSam^a fragments has shown that the evidence for tendentious change on the part of Chr in the synoptic passages is very slight. The notion that Chr has tendentiously and extensively rewritten his S source must be abandoned. The available textual evidence points in the opposite direction, that Chr has generally followed his S *Vorlage* quite closely in the synoptic passages.

This conclusion does not mean that Chr did not introduce his own interests. His interests are visible to some extent in the synoptic material. There are a few places where Chr has made minor changes in the narrative introducing particularly his pan-Israel interest, his idealized view of David and Solomon, or his interest in the Levites and the cult. To a much greater extent Chr's interests are apparent in his omissions and his independent material. The omission of 2 S 11–21 is astounding. As a result David appears blameless and his reign trouble free. The lengthy independent sections in 1 C 1–9 and 22–29 similarly contain clear indications of Chr's interests. By means of the omissions from his S *Vorlage* combined with the addition of material not found in S, Chr is able to structure his history of David in a way which presents his own viewpoint forcefully. After the genealogies (1–9), Chr begins his history of David with his being chosen by Yahweh and anointed by all Israel as king and with David's immediate conquest of Jerusalem (10–12). As soon as David has taken Jerusalem he concerns himself with bringing up the ark (13–16) and immediately thereafter, with planning a temple for Yahweh (17). The account of David's wars in chaps. 18–20 follows and seems unusual at first in light of Chr's concerns. However, in the account of David's preparations for the Temple (22–28) one learns that David was not allowed to build the Temple because he was a man of blood, which suggests a reason for Chr's inclusion of David's wars.

Chr's techniques of composition, then, are a good deal more

sophisticated than he has usually received credit for. Perhaps the clearest illustration of his use of the techniques described above to convey his own viewpoint is found in 11:1-3. By omitting the material found in 2 S 1-4 Chr has been able to structure 11:1-3 immediately following the death of Saul. Also, he has thus omitted the account about civil war between David and Ish-baal. In addition, he has omitted the word שבטי in 11:1 (cf. 2 S 6:1), thus allowing his pan-Israel interest to surface. By means of these techniques he has given an entirely different meaning to his history than that found in the parallel S account. Yahweh chooses David as king. His choice is confirmed immediately by all the people upon Saul's death, and the transition from Saul's reign to David's is smooth. The quantitative change within the synoptic passage is minor, but the qualitative change in meaning which Chr has accomplished through selectivity and structuring is enormous.

NOTES

/1/ See Cross's articles cited in Chapter 2, n. 42. See also "The Evolution of a Theory of Local Texts," *Qumran and the History of the Biblical Text* (ed. F. M. Cross and S. Talmon; Cambridge: Harvard, 1975) 308-20. For a summary of further work done in different books of the Bible in support of Cross's theory see E. C. Ulrich, *The Qumran Text of Samuel and Josephus* (HSM 19; Missoula, MT: Scholars Press, 1978) 33-35. Cross's theory represents an extensive development of seminal proposals made by W. F. Albright, "New Light on Early Recensions of the Hebrew Bible," *BASOR* 140 (1955): 27-33.

/2/ *Les devanciers d'Aquila* (VT Sup 10; Leiden: E. J. Brill, 1963) especially 91-143. For Cross's additional work see his articles referred to in the previous note. Also see Ulrich's discussion of the history of the problem in *Qumran Text*, 15-33, and especially the summary of J. D. Shenkel, *Chronology and Recensional Development in the Greek Text of Kings* (HSM 1: Cambridge, MA: Harvard, 1968) 5-21.

/3/ Shenkel presented evidence to the effect that 2 S 10 in B also belongs to the *kaige* recension in *Chronology*, 117-20.

/4/ See E. C. Ulrich, "The Old Latin Translation of LXX and the Hebrew Scrolls from Qumran," *The Hebrew and Greek Texts of Samuel*, 1980 Proceedings IOSCS (ed. E. Tov; Jerusalem: Academon, 1980) 121-65. One should also remark here about the evidence of C^G. In his

"Studies in the Greek Texts" Klein concludes that "G reflects a text of
the same type as MT although it is not identical with the latter" (308).
He further states that "while G and MT are not identical, their resem-
blance is very close. Most differences between the two, in fact, are
explainable as earlier and later stages in a single textual history" (322).
Compare the similar conclusions of L. C. Allen *The Greek Chronicles
II, Textual Criticism* (VT Sup 27; Leiden: E. J. Brill, 1974) 166. The
studies of Klein and Allen point out the general unreliability of C^G as a
textual witness. It betrays a good deal of assimilation and revision to
other witnesses. For these reasons it cannot be counted on to furnish
independent readings, and I have not made extensive use of it in the
present study.

/5/   *Qumran   Text*,   especially   pp. 223–59.   The   proto-Lucianic
recension obviously fits this description, but Ulrich is judiciously
cautious about using that designation.

/6/   Klein (*Textual Criticism of the Old Testament* [Philadelphia: Fortress, 1974] 45) in his discussion of 1 C 21:16 states, "We must conclude
that Josephus needs to be checked for important old Samuel readings
elsewhere since they may be lost in other Greek and Hebrew witnesses."
Similarly, Lemke ("The Synoptic Problem," 357, note) writes, "This, of
course, greatly enhances the value of the latter (Josephus) for textual
criticism in the historical books of the OT. Consequently, whenever
Josephus agrees with the Chronicler against the text of Samuel . . . we
can no longer automatically assume that he was simply following the
Chronicler, but we must seriously entertain the possibility that the text of
Samuel at his disposal contained, in fact, such a reading," Compare the
conclusions of Mez, *Die Bibel des Josephus untersucht für Buch V-VII
der Archäologie* (Basel: Jaeger Kober, 1895) 80, and Thackeray, *Josephus, the Man and the Historian* (New York: Jewish Institute of Religion,
1929) 83.

/7/   Ulrich, *Qumran Text*, 163–64.

/8/   The word "theocracy" has often been used to describe Chr's paradigmatic presentation of David's reign. I have attempted to avoid the
term because of its lack of precision. In fact, no single term incorpo-
rates all the various aspects of Chr's concept of the ideal monarchy. It
is best described in detail. Succinctly put, Chr envisions in David a
pious king who puts his trust always and only in Yahweh and places the
performance of the cult as the first priority of his kingdom. As a result,
his reign is blessed with prosperity and tranquility.

/9/   The real importance of Chr's "pan-Israel" theme is only now
being fully understood. Von Rad's view that Chr intended to exclude

the Northern tribes has long predominated but is incorrect. See his *Das Geschichtsbild des chronistischen Werkes* (Stuttgart: W. Kohlhammer, 1930) 25–37. Chr's intention, rather, is to persuade the Northern Israelites to take part in the restoration of the true monarchy and cult. Williamson's (*Israel*, 87–131) recent treatment of this theme is good, though in my view he fails to perceive correctly the original setting and purpose of Chr's work.

/10/ For a summary of various explanations see Myers, *I Chronicles*, 81.

/11/ I cannot agree with Noth's attempt to downplay Chr's interest in the Levites and their cultic functions (*ÜS*, 174) which has caused him to deny to Chr most of the material about David's organization of them in this chapter and in 1 C 23–27 (*ÜS*, 112–16). Rudolph and Willi have followed Noth in this basic position. See Rudolph, *Chronikbücher* (HAT 21; Tübingen: J.C.B. Mohr, 1955) xvi and his chart on pp. 1–5; "Problems of the Books of Chronicles," *VT* 4 (1954): 407; and Willi, *Die Chronik*, 194–204. Chr's interest in the Levites and their functional divisions fits perfectly with his work as a program for the restoration of the Temple cult and the Davidic monarchy. The concern for the Levites in C is simply too important and too pervasive to be diminished. The importance of the Levites in C is supported by Petersen's recent study, *Late Israelite Prophecy*, 55–87.

/12/ Compare the list of Deuteronomistic expressions in 2 S 7 given by Cross, *CMHE*, 252–54, and the list of Deuteronomic phraseology in Weinfeld, *DDS*, 320–65. On the basis of these expressions some have arged that Chr patterns his account of Solomon's accession on the report in Josh 1 of the transfer of leadership from Moses to Joshua. See R. Braun, "Solomon, the Chosen Temple Builder: The Significance of 1 Chronicles 22, 28, and 29 for the Theology of Chronicles," *JBL* 95 (1976): 581–90, and Williamson, "The Accession of Solomon in the Books of Chronicles," *VT* 26 (1976): 351–61. While there is some similarity between Josh 1 and David's speeches in 1 C 22 and 29, Braun and Williamson have overlooked the greater similarity of the latter with the Nathan oracle and Solomon's Temple dedication speech.

/13/ See the discussion of Lemke ("Synoptic Studies," 86, n. 18) who cites the well known statement of Thucydides (*History of the Peloponnesian War*, I. 22) regarding his methods of historiography. Cf. O. Plöger, "Reden und Gebete im deuteronomistischen und chronistischen Geschichtwerk," *Festschrift für Gunther Dehn* (Neukirchen, 1957) 35–49.

/14/ Cf. M. Cogan, "Tendentious Chronology in the Book of Chronicles," *Zion* 45 (1980): 165–72.

/15/ Lemke, "Synoptic Studies," 21.

/16/ There are three passages extant in 4QSamᵃ with parallels in C
which are not included in this section. The first is 2 S 3:2–5//1 C 3:1–4.
I have omitted this passage and the other brief synoptic passages within
1 C 1–9 because of the overall uniqueness of these chapters in comparison to 2 S. While the information found in both genealogies is basically
the same, their styles are different, and because of the nature of genealogies it is not certain that C relies on S for its version of the geneal-
ogy. The second passage not included is 2 S 12:30–31//1 C 20:1–3.
There are only parts of three words from 2 S 12:31 actually visible on
the leather of the fragment, and all three words are found in both S
and C, so that the fragment is of no help in evaluating their respective
readings. The third such passsage is 1 C 10:2–4//1 S 31:2–4 where
there is no significant variation among the witnesses. I would like to
thank Prof. F. M. Cross who allowed me access to the photographs of
4QSamᵃ and who helped to clarify several readings. The readings given
for 4QSamᵃ are generally taken from Ulrich's *Qumran Text* except for
minor corrections based on Cross's most recent examination of the scroll
itself. Insignificant differences such as lexical and orthographic variants
are excluded from consideration.

/17/ Cf. Rudolph *Chronikbücher*, 97.

/18/ See Ulrich, *Qumran Text*, 65–66. The term "Rabbinic text" refers
to the Hebrew text fixed by Pharisaic scholars in the first century A.D.
It is a more accurate designation for the *textus receptus* at this point in
history than is the more common term, "Masoretic text," which refers
to the medieval recension of the *textus receptus*. See Cross, "Problems
of Method in the Textual Criticism of the Hebrew Bible," *The Critical
Study of Sacred Texts* (ed. W. D. O'Flaherty; Berkeley: Graduate Theological Union, 1979) 38–40.

/19/ The average number of letter spaces per line in this fragment is
51. With the above phrase the first line of the fragment would have 75
spaces.

/20/ On the readings of 4QSamᵃ and Josephus see Ulrich, *Qumran
Text*, 60–61.

/21/ Ibid., 62, 193–221.

/22/ Rudolph (*Chronikbücher*, 99) argues that Chr wished to create a
place for Joab since he was Zeruiah's most famous son. Joab's prominent place in S is due to his murder of Abner. Chr replaces that with
Joab's conquest of Jerusalem. This view cannot be accepted not only
because it is not a consistent concern of C (Joab plays a very minor role

in 1 C) but also because the text of 2 S 5:8 appears corrupt in S^M and may well be incomplete.

/23/ Ulrich (*Qumran Text*, 70) is incorrect in citing Josephus as support for the reading עיר here. *Ant* VII. 65 reads και αυτος ανοικοδομησας τα Ιεροσολυμα πολιν αυτην Δαυιδου προσηγορευσε. The עיר reflected in this sentence is the one in the previous line of the Hebrew text, ויקרא לה עיר דוד.

/24/ Rudolph (*Chronikbücher*, 84) is probably correct in arguing that the line απο της ακρας και εως του κυκλου is missing from B(C) as a result of haplography brought on by homoioteleuton. Allen (*Greek Chronicles*, I 129) attempts to derive the phrase και επολεμησεν και ελαβεν την πολιν from a misreading of a defective Hebrew manuscript. While his explanation is too ad hoc to be convincing, he may be correct in attempting to see this phrase as interpreting a corrupt Hebrew text.

/25/ This is actually a continuation of the 4QSam^a fragment in Section (1) above. I have divided it from the previous section for the sake of manageability and because the location of the C parallel changes from chap. 11 to chap. 14.

/26/ Cf. Cross, "History of the Biblical Text," 293; Talmon, "Double Readings in the Masoretic Text," *Textus I* (1960) 167; and Ulrich, *Qumran Text*, 99–100. The other variants in the verse should be mentioned but are not especially significant. First, the C tradition displays a scribal transposition of the elements חרשי קיר and חרשי עצ(ים). Secondly, whether the original reading was עץ or עצים the Greek witnesses to S indicate that the plural was in C's *Vorlage*. Finally, the reading of B(C) simply attests the loss from the Greek text of the word τοιχου.

/27/ Cf. E. L. Curtis and A. A. Madsen, *The Books of Chronicles* (ICC; Edinburgh: T. & T. Clark, 1910) 208, and Ulrich, *Qumran Text*, 163.

/28/ Without such a phrase the line in 4QSam^a would have fewer than 40 spaces in a section where the average line is 51 spaces long.

29 ". . . dass dabei der Hinweis auf die Hebroner Zeit (2 Sam 5:13) vermeiden wird, entspricht dem Verfahren des Chr. in 11:1–3" (*Chronikbücher*, 113).

/30/ On 2 S 6 as a whole see Ulrich, *Qumran Text*, 193–221.

/31/ See the discussions of Ulrich (*Qumran Text*, 198–99), J. Wellhausen (*Der Text der Bucher Samuelis* [Göttingen: Vandenhoeck & Ruprecht, 1871] 166–67), and S. R. Driver (*Notes on the Hebrew*

Text of the Books of Samuel [Oxford: Clarendon, 1890] 203).

/32/ The reconstruction of 4QSam[a] here is uncertain. The ע of עם read by Ulrich (*Qumran Text*, 66) appears upon examination of the photograph to be a shadow on the leather rather than traces of a letter. Two possible readings are עם ארון היוה (עם האלוהים is too long) and עם ארון החדשה.

/33/ Ulrich, *Qumran Text*, 197, notes that 4QSam[a] contains a number of expansions in this chapter.

/34/ A. M. Brunet, "Le Chroniste et ses sources," *RB* 60 (1953): 500, and Ackroyd, *I & II Chronicles*, 57.

/35/ *Qumran Text*, 199–201. Ulrich is probably correct in reconstructing 4QSam[a]'s reading as לאחז on the basis of the OG.

/36/ See, for example, G. J. Botterweck ("Zur Eigenart der chronistischen Davidgeschichte," *TQ* 136 [1956] 414), who argues that Chr altered his *Vorlage* because of his belief that Yahweh's presence resided in or with the ark.

/37/ The average line length in this fragment seems to be about 58 spaces. ויהי, the first word in this verse, appears on the fragment almost directly above the second שבעה. The S reading for the first half of the verse fits perfectly into this space, yielding a line length of about 59 letter spaces, while the C reading yields a line length of some 68 letter spaces.

/38/ See Ulrich, *Qumran Text*, 217, note.

/39/ See *BDB*, 750.

/40/ This verse has experienced considerable disturbance. The original reading is not clear, nor is the reason for the disturbance. For a possible reconstruction see *NAB*'s textual notes. Also cf. Wellhausen, *Der Text*, 173–74.

/41/ The variants in (b) and (c) are related. The reading of S[M] and 4QSam[a] at the beginning of v 26 is probably original. As argued, the title at that point led to the expansion in v 27. The entire phrase,
לאמר יהוה צבאות אלהים על ישראל ובית עבדך דוד יהיה נכון לפניך
at the end of v 26 in S[M] is lacking in B. The minus is probably the result of haplography due to homoioarchton with the already expanded beginning of the next verse. Finally, an expanded title similar to the beginning of v 27 has been inserted into B or its *Vorlage* in v 25.

/42/ Botterweck ("Zur Eigenart," 423) argues that Chr uses the perfect here in order to express his firm belief in the fulfillment of Yahweh's promise.

/43/ The ר in רכב is badly damaged, but there is good reason to believe that the reading here is correct. See Ulrich, *Qumran Text*, 56.

/44/ There are four Qumran fragments which contain parts of these verses. One contains parts of vv 4–5; two are fragments of vv 6–7. A fourth contains parts of vv 18–19. For a reconstruction of the two fragments of vv 6–7 see Ulrich, *Qumran Text*, 152.

/45/ The idea that 1 C displays Chr's advanced angelology is found commonly in the commentaries. Cf. Rudolph (*Chronikbücher*, 145–47), Botterweck ("Zur Eigenart," 428), R. Kittel (*Die Bucher der Chronik und Esra, Nehemia und Esther* [HAT; Göttingen: Vandenhoeck & Ruprecht, 1902]) 80, and Curtis and Madsen (*Chronicles*, 251). Lemke, "Synoptic Studies," 67–73, has clearly shown the fallacy of this position.

/46/ See Cross, *ALQ*, 188, n. 40a. The verbs alone are not similar enough to provide a mechanism (contra Ulrich, *Qumran Text*, 157).

/47/ Cross, ibid.

/48/ *I Samuel* (AB; New York: Doubleday, 1980) 440–41.

/49/ So Rudolph, *Chronikbücher*, 95. This idea is especially hazardous since Chr clearly knows that Michal did not die at this time (1 C 15:29).

/50/ McCarter, *I Samuel*, 442.

/51/ Cf. Rudolph (*Chronikbücher*, 95) on the omission of Aštarôt and Botterweck ("Zur Eigenart," 406–7) on the nailing of Saul's body.

/52/ Cf. Wellhausen, *Der Text*, 148–49, and Rudolph, *Chronikbücher*, 92.

/53/ So Botterweck, "Zur Eigenart," 407–8; J. Myers, *I Chronicles*, 81; and Curtis and Madsen, *Chronicles*, 182.

/54/ Josephus' account agrees with C in a number of details, but it is likely that he borrowed them from C. See Ulrich, *Qumran Text*, 189, 213.

/55/ J. W. Rothstein and D. J. Hänel, *Das erste Buch der Chronik* (KAT; Leipzig: D. Werner Scholl, 1927) 270. Cf. R. J. Coggins, *The First and Second Books of the Chronicles* (Cambridge: Cambridge University, 1976) 81.

/56/ See Botterweck ("Zur Eigenart," 415) and his references there to other commentators.

/57/ So Rudolph, *Chronikbücher*, 114.

/58/ So Ackroyd, *I and II Chronicles*, 59; Coggins, *Chronicles*, 82; Rudolph, *Chronikbücher*, 115; and Curtis and Madsen, *Chronicles*, 209.

/59/ It is unlikely that the reading of L(S) represents a late conflation of S^M and C^M rather than an early conflation of readings in variant text types. L(S) consistently agrees with 4QSam[a] even where C is not extant. (See Ulrich, *Qumran Text* 100). Thus, to argue that it follows C here is to posit a unique case. Rather, it consistently follows the pattern of agreement with the Palestinian text type.

/60/ Lemke, "Synoptic Studies," 35–36.

/61/ Brunet, "Le Chroniste," 501.

/62/ The suggestions about *Tendenz* have to do with the mention in C of the מעיל בוץ. See Lemke ("Synoptic Studies," 38–39) for a summary of the proposals.

/63/ Brunet, "Le Chroniste," 505–6; cf. Curtis and Madsen, *Chronicles*, 226.

/64/ Cf. Ackroyd, *I and II Chronicles*, 67, and Rudolph, *Chronikbücher*, 129.

/65/ See Weinfeld, *DDS*, 343.

/66/ Coggins, *Chronicles*, 94–95. Cf. Ackroyd, *I and II Chronicles*, 67; Rudolph, *Chronikbücher*,4 135; and Curtis and Madsen, *Chronicles*, 227.

/67/ Lemke ("Synoptic Studies," 43–46) provides the most comprehensive arguments. Cf. Rudolph, *Chronikbücher*, 135 and Brunet, "Le Chroniste," 505.

/68/ See Lemke, "Synoptic Studies," 43–46.

/69/ C's verb in the construction ויהו מואב is ungrammatical. S correctly reads ותהי מואב. If the verison of the story in C's *Vorlage* began with ויהיו or the like, its similarity with ותהי could have triggered the haplography. The presence of מואב immediately before and after the material in question may have contributed to the error.

/70/ So Brunet "Le Chroniste," 506. Cf. Ackroyd, *I and II Chronicles*, 70.

/71/ These miniscules are classified as sub-Lucianic by P. Vannutelli (*Libri Synoptici Veteris Testament* [Rome: Pontifical Biblical Institute, 1931] vi).

/72/ *Chronikbücher*, 138. Cf. Botterweck, "Zur Eigenart," 426. It is also possible that the verb (ה)וילכד at the beginning and end of the omitted material may have contributed to the haplography (cf. the readings of S^M and S^G), although the miniscules (g, i, and y) do not attest the same verb in both these places.

/73/ Lemke ("Synoptic Studies," 62) argues that S^M probably had a reference to Judah, which has been lost, because of the fact that L(S) mentions both Israel and Judah. If this were the case, then "Israel" in S would refer only to the North while in C it clearly refers to both northern and southern tribes. Then, C's reading would clearly represent tendentious change. Lemke's proposal may well be correct. Heretofore, "Israel" in S usually refers to the North alone. Whether Chr found this reading in his *Vorlage* or introduced it himself, it certainly fits with his pan-Israel interest.

/74/ Lemke, "Synoptic Studies," 62–63.

/75/ Botterweck, "Zur Eigenart," 428; Myers, *I Chronicles*, 147; Rudolph, *Chronikbücher*, 144–45.

/76/ Rudolph, *Chronikbücher*, 147; Curtis and Madsen, *Chronicles*, 252.

/77/ See examples 1c, d, 4b above.

/78/ I would tentatively reconstruct the reading as follows:
ראה הבקר לעלות והמרגים לעצים.
למנחה והחטים could have been an expansion already in the Palestinian text. נתתי is an expansion in C, and וכלי בקר appears to be an expansion or a gloss in S.

/79/ "Synoptic Studies," 73–74, especially n. 107.

Chapter 4
2 CHRONICLES 1–28

I. *The Witnesses*

In this chapter I will investigate the material in 2 C 1–28 and its parallel in 1–2 K. The methodology will be similar to that used in the previous chapter. However, the condition of the extant textual witnesses for K and consequently our knowledge of K's textual history are far poorer than for S. The tremendous amount of work done on the history of the text of S has not yet been duplicated for K./1/ The work done on the textual history of S was prompted by the new evidence furnished by S fragments from Qumran. The importance of this evidence was made clear in the previous chapter. However, the evidence for the text of K from Qumran is far less extensive. It is diminished even further when one focuses on passages with parallels in C./2/

In addition to the paucity of Qumran material for K, the amount of independent textual evidence is further reduced by the observation of Barthélemy that the majority of B (1 K 1:1–2:11; 22:1–2 K 25:30) represents the *kaige* recension./3/ Since *kaige* material represents a revision of the Greek text toward a proto-Rabbinic text B has essentially lost its value as an independent witness to the OG in its *kaige* sections. The Lucianic recension remains a valuable resource for possible old Palestinian readings where the OG is extant (but see below).

Josephus must also be disqualified from furnishing any kind of independent textual evidence regarding which text type of K underlies 2 C. Because Josephus consistently contains parallels to C material that is unparalleled in K, it is clear that he had C before him. Since Josephus' style is very loose, and C and K are often very close, it is frequently impossible to determine whether Josephus' source for a given account is K or C. In fact, he often combines the two in his account.

The 4QSam[a] fragments have made it clear that Chr used a

text of S of a different type from S^M. However, it is important to recognize that the situation is not necessarily the same for the text of K used by Chr. In this respect Lemke errs. Influenced by the striking evidence of 4QSam^a, he automatically asssumes a similar set of circumstances for K vis-à-vis C as for S, without taking account of the complex relationship of the textual witnesses for K./4/ A thorough evaluation of the affiliation of the K witnesses lies outside of my immediate interests. However, the evidence presented in the excursus below shows clearly the textual affiliation between C^M and K^M and strongly indicates that Chr's *Vorlage* of K was of the same type as the *textus receptus*. If Chr's K *Vorlage* was in fact proto-Rabbinic, it has two important consequences for the remainder of this study. First, where K^M and C^M differ, the possibility of intentional change is perhaps stronger than where S^M and C^M differ. Textual alteration may still account for many of the different readings between the two texts, but we are now dealing with differences within a single textual family, not different families as in S//C. Secondly, the close similarity of C and K in synoptic passages facilitates the task of determining the extent to which Chr has used his K source. It will become obvious at what point Chr has ceased to use K.

II. *Omissions from 2 C vis-à-vis K*

A. *1 K 1:1–2:46a.* Except for the information about the length of David's reign in 1 K 2:10–12//1 C 29:26–28 this material is unparalleled in C. It continues the same sort of court history as that which dominates 2 S 13–21, which is also unparalleled in C. 1 K 1 tells of Adonijah's rivalry to Solomon for the throne of Israel. In C Solomon has no competition for the throne. There is never any doubt that he is to be David's successor. In 1 K 2 the story continues with Solomon eventually getting rid of his (and David's) enemies. This passage seems to cast some negative reflections on David and Solomon and is probably omitted for that reason.

B. *1 K 3:1–3.* It is difficult to find a reason for C's omission of the information in v 1 about Solomon's Egyptian wife, since 1 C 8:11 presumes that information. However, v 1 does place the building of Solomon's house before the building of the Temple, and in Chr's structuring of the material the building of the Temple is Solomon's first concern as king./5/ C also omits the reference in vv 2–3 to the people sacrificing at the high places. This is probably due to his idealized view of Solomon. It is true that Chr mentions the *bāmâ* in Gibeon (1:3), but he clearly views it as the only one allowed, in contrast to K, and he legitimizes it by stating that the *'ōhel mô'ēd* was there.

C. *1 K 3:16–5:14.* 3:16–28 contain a story illustrating Solomon's great wisdom. 4:1–5:14 consist mostly of lists of Solomon's officers and provisions, as well as further descriptions of his wisdom. By including at this point these summaries of the wealth and wisdom acheived by Solomon during his reign the K account seems to imply an interval between Solomon's becoming king and his beginning to build the Temple. Chr may have omitted this material in order to give the impression that Solomon's piety leads him to begin work on the Temple as his first act as king (see n. 5). No other reason for the omission of this material in C is immediately obvious.

D. *1 K 6:4–20.* This material is largely a continuation of the description of the interior of the Temple. There is a reiteration of the Davidic promise in vv 11–13. These verses have been secondarily inserted into K (see chap. 7) and may not have been in C's *Vorlage*. Only vv 19–20 have any kind of equivalent in C (cf. 2 C 3:8). C's description of the building of the Temple is substantially shorter than that of K and varies widely from it at points. It is possible that for part of the narrative Chr relies on a source other than K. However, it is also clear that Chr used K selectively. Lemke suggests that Chr is more interested in the selection of the Temple site than in the building itself./6/ The most that can be said for certain is that the omitted details of the Temple building lay somehow outside of Chr's interests.

E. *1 K 6:29–7:12.* 6:29–38 further describe the interior of the Temple, and the reason for omission from C is uncertain. It is easier to understand why 7:1–12 are omitted. These verses deal with Solomon's other building projects in which Chr was not particularly interested.

F. *1 K 7:27–37.* This passage describes the ten bronze stands inside the Temple. Again one can only observe that their description lay outside of Chr's interests.

G. *1 K 8:54–61.* This is the fifth part of Solomon's speech at the dedication of the Temple. Chr has altered the end of the fourth speech, inserting excerpts from Ps 132 in a different version from M. The net effect is to locate the source of Israel's hope in

Yahweh's promise to David and his concern for the Temple rather than in the covenant with Moses. This does not mean that Chr sees Moses and David or their respective covenants as somehow opposed to each other. The change here simply illustrates the importance that Chr attaches to the Davidic covenant.

H. *1 K 11:1-40*. This passage describes how Solomon's foreign wives led him to idolatry. The passage goes on to describe the adversaries whom Yahweh raised up against Solomon as a result of his sins. The passage is clearly omitted by Chr in accord with his idealized portrayal of Solomon.

I. *1 K 12:25-14:20*. 12:25-33 describe Jeroboam's establishment of the cultic sites at Dan and Bethel. Chapter 13 contains the story of the young and old prophets. 14:1-20 narrate the oracle of Ahijah regarding Jeroboam's ill son. It is Chr's custom to omit the information about the history of the North. However, the omission of this passage has a greater significance. As Cross has shown, this passage with its description of Jeroboam's sin and the *vaticinium ex eventu* about Josiah's destruction of the Bethel altar is a clear indication of Dtr 1's polemical theme of the unfaithfulness of the North./7/ Chr's omission of this passage is indicative of the overtures which he makes to the North throughout his work. Although he clearly regards the Northern monarchy as illegitimate and refuses to relate its history, he still regards the residents of the North as integral to Israel. His complete omission of DH's polemic against the North illustrates his concern to attract its inhabitants.

J. *1 K 15:3-5*. In contrast to K, C views Abijah as a pious king. This is clear from 2 C 15:3-21. Therefore, he omits 1 K 15:3 which applies the formulaic, Deuteronomistic condemnation of the kings to Abijah. The reference to Yahweh's faithfulness with regard to the *nîr* of David in 1 K 15:4-5 is unnecessary if Abijah is seen as pious. In addition, v 5 refers to David's sin against Uriah and has obviously been omitted by Chr because of his idealized view of David.

K. *1 K 15:25-21:29*. This material includes narratives about the Northern kings from Baasha through Ahab as well as stories about the Northern prophet, Elijah. As is his custom, Chr here omits the narrative history of the North.

L. *1 K 22:36-40*. Chr relates the story of Jehoshaphat's alliance with the king of Israel, but his interest is clearly in Judah's role in these events. Thus, he omits entirely the account of Ahab's death in vv 36-40.

M. *1 K 22:47–48*. Verse 47 tells of Jehoshaphat expelling the cult prostitutes left from the days of Asa. Verse 48 informs that in those days Edom had no king. It is easy to see how the information in v 48 might be omitted by C as lying outside of his interests. The reason for omitting v 47 is less clear. Possibly Chr believed this reference to be unnecessary in the light of the thoroughgoing reform which he ascribed to Asa. A better possibility has to do with Chr's sources here. Source notices like the one in 2 C 20:34 were clearly derived from a source other than K (cf. 1 K 22:40; see p. 174); 2 C 20:35–37 may also come from a source outside of K (pp. 109–10). Thus the omission of 1 K 22:47–48 may be due to Chr's use of another source.

N. *1 K 22:52–2 K 8:16*. All of this material deals with the Northern kingdom, the Northern prophet, Elijah, and their relationship with the kingdom of Aram. These narratives are omitted as lying outside of Chr's interests.

O. *2 K 9:1–10:36*. This is the account of Jehu's revolt. 2 C 22:7–8 summarizes the consequences of the revolt for Judah. However, since the story deals mostly with the North, it is, in effect, omitted by Chr.

P. *2 K 13*. This chapter covers the reigns of Jehoahaz and Jehoash, kings of Israel, and contains stories surrounding Elisha and Hazael, king of Aram. This material lies outside of Chr's chief interest in Judah.

Q. *2 K 14:15–16*. These two verses contain formulae regarding the death of Jehoash and the accession of Jeroboam II, both Northern kings, and therefore outside of Chr's concerns.

R. *2 K 14:23–29*. The information about the Northern king, Jeroboam II, has been omitted by Chr as is his custom in regard to the history of the North.

S. *2 K 15:8–31*. The Northern kings, Zechariah, Shallum, Menahem, Pekahiah, and Pekah are covered in these verses.

T. *2 K 17*. In accord with his practice of omitting the history of the North and Dtr 1's polemic against the North, Chr omits this lengthy peroration on the fall of the Northern kingdom.

This brief survey of the major passages omitted by Chr vis-à-vis his K source illustrates clearly some of his interests. Most obvious is his interest in the history of Judah alone, to the complete exclusion of Israel's history except where it overlaps with that of Judah. In addition to the omission of lengthy passages dealing with Israel, Chr also consistently omits the synchronisms

of the reigns of Judean kings with those of Israelite kings which
K provides. Chr's omission of the information about the North in
no way lessens his pan-Israel interest. He believes that the
Northern monarchy is guilty of apostasy, but the Northern tribes
are no less a part of true Israel. Chr stresses that the only God-
given dynasty is the Davidic line, and the only divinely accepted
cultic spot is that founded by David in Jerusalem. His omission
of Dtr 1's polemic against the North is the product of his desire
to attract the residents of the North. He calls them to return to
the Davidic monarchy and the Jerusalem cult.

The only other real interest of Chr that appears through his
omissions is his idealized view of Solomon. Chr pictures Solomon's reign as sinless and, as a result, trouble-free. This is particularly clear in the omission of 1 K 11:1–40. Chr also omits any
material which might detract from Solomon's character or kingdom, such as that found in 1 K 1:1–2:46a.

III. *Additions in 2 C vis-à-vis K*

A. *2 C 1:1–6.* Most of this material was probably composed by
Chr. Verse 2 displays his pan-Israel interest in Solomon's calling all
the people to Gibeon. In addition, as was mentioned above, the
reference to the *'ōhel mô'ēd* and the bronze altar being at Gibeon
may be attempts on the part of Chr to legitimize the *bāmâ* there.
However, it is doubtful that Chr would invent the idea of the high
place in Gibeon. Thus, he has used K or some other source as the
basis for his composition here.

B. *2 C 3:1–2.* Verse 1 specifies the location of the Temple as
the threshing floor of Ornan. Verse 2 dates the start of the work on
the Temple to the second month of Solomon's fourth year. The
information in v 2 is found in 1 K 6:1. However, the information in
v 1 is based on 1 C 21:28–22:1. Both verses are compositions of Chr
and express his interest in the location of the Temple.

C. *2 C 4:1.* Rudolph is correct in arguing that the parallel to
this verse in K has been lost thorugh haplography./8/ The
bronze altar is referred to in 1 K 8:22, 64; 2 K 16:14. The verses
which follow in 1 K 7:23–26//2 C 4:2–5 are nearly verbatim the
same in the two accounts. Also there is a good mechanism for
haplography in the word *wayya'aś* which occurs at the
beginning of 2 C 4:1, 2 and 1 K 7:23.

D. *2 C 4:7–9.* These verses describe the lampstands and

tables in the Temple as well as the court of the priests. These items are nowhere described in K, and C has probably taken their description from a different source.

E. *2 C 5:11b–13*. This parenthetical statement (beginning with כי) about the divisions of the priests and the music of the Levitical singers was clearly introduced by Chr and accords well with his interest in the cult and its priestly functionaries.

F. *2 C 6:5b–6a*. This material has fallen out of K by haplography. It was triggered by homoioteleuton in the words להיות שמי שם.

G. *2 C 6:13*. This minus in K is again the result of haplography caused by homoioteleuton in the words ויפרש כפיו (1 K 8:22; 2 C 6:12, 13).

H. *2 C 6:40–42*. As mentioned above, in this passage Chr alters the end of Solomon's fourth speech at the dedication of the Temple by inserting this material which is roughly equivalent to Ps 132:8–10. In this way he finds the basis of Israel's hope in the Davidic covenant. This fits well with the important place assigned by Chr to David.

I. *2 C 7:1b–3*. As mentioned in the previous chapter, this reference to fire from Yahweh is connected with 1 C 21:26. By means of this traditional *topos* for the dedication of a new altar Chr stresses the importance of the Temple and Yahweh's approval of the cult there.

J. *2 C 7:6*. This verse stands out because the accounts of K and C are so close elsewhere in this context. It clearly illustrates Chr's interest in David as the founder of the cult and its functionaries, and it is obviously Chr's addition.

K. *2 C 7:13–15*. As Lemke points out, the late usage of *ḥēn* to mean "if" in this passage indicates that it stems from Chr./9/ Nonetheless, Chr is obviously composing on the basis of the earlier speech of Solomon (2 C 6:26–31//1 K 8:35–40) which he has taken over nearly verbatim from Kings.

L. *2 C 8:13–16*. These verses deal with the performance of cultic activities in the Temple according to the Levitical divisions. They stem from Chr. Verses 14–15 strongly display Chr's interests, since they stress that the Levites are to follow the ordinances and divisions given by David.

M. *2 C 11:5–12:1*. Some of this material probably stems from other sources available to Chr, especially the building activities and fortifications of Rehoboam in 11:5–12 and the list of his

wives in 11:18-23. However, the account of the migration of the
Levites from North to South in 11:13-17 is probably the composition of Chr, though it too may based on other sources. It certainly corresponds to Chr's interest in the Levites. It also accords
with Chr's pan-Israel interest, since the fact that legitimate
priests came from the North to Jerusalem would be a significant
drawing point for the inhabitants of the North whom Chr hoped
to attract. The judgment of Rehoboam in 12:1 also comes from
Chr's hand. While it essentially agrees with the judgment given
in DH it also fits Chr's dogma of retribution. Rehoboam's
troubles begin in 2 C 12:1 when he forsakes Yahweh.

N. *2 C 12:2b-9, 12.* Verses 2b-4 give additional information
about Shishak's invasion, principally the components of his army.
The other verses contain an oracle of Shemaiah, the prophet,
announcing that Yahweh has abandoned Judah because they
abandoned him (v 5). As a result of his oracle, the leaders of the
people are humbled (v 6), and Yahweh announces through Shemaiah that he will mitigate the punishment (vv 7-8). In v 9 C
resumes the narrative of Shishak's invasion in parallel with K by a
near repetition of the phrase before the insertion. While the
information in this insertion may derive in part from other
sources, it betrays Chr's belief in the divine retribution for sin and
illustrates his prophecy-fulfillment schema.

O. *2 C 13:3-21.* This is the account of a battle between Abijah of Judah and Jeroboam of Israel. It contains a speech placed
by Chr into the mouth of Abijah. The speech is a significant
indication of Chr's theology. Through it Chr addresses the
Northern tribes. He recognizes the illegitimacy of the Northern
monarchy and cult and calls upon the Israelites to return to the
genuine monarchy and cult in Jerusalem. In v 5 he mentions
Yahweh's eternal covenant of kingship with David. In vv 9-11
he condemns Jeroboam for driving out the Levites and describes
the true cultic site in Jerusalem as the place in which the Levites
serve.

P. *2 C 14:2-14.* These verses detail Asa's reforms, his fortifications, and his defeat of Zerah the Ethiopian. While it is true
that Chr has structured the material to fit his retribution dogma,
the material in vv 3-14 does not, for the most part, betray any
special interest or bias of Chr. The report of Asa's trust in Yahweh and the outcome of the battle in vv 11-13 fit with Chr's
belief that the righteous prosper, but this does not mean that

Chr invented the entire account. As will be seen later, there is reason to believe that Dtr 1 plays down the accounts of the prosperity of Asa and other good kings for his own purposes.

Q. *2 C 15:1–15.* A similar point may be made for the account of Asa's additional reforms in vv 8–15. Azariah's oracle in vv 1–7 accords well with Chr's schema of retribution and with his concern for the North. While the Northern cult is illegitimate (v 3), and the Northern inhabitants will suffer as a result (vv 5–7), they are still encouraged to seek the true God of Israel (v 4). The oracle, therefore, is likely Chr's composition, though Azariah may have been a genuine prophet referred to in Chr's sources.

R. *2 C 16:7–10.* These verses record Hanani's oracle against Asa and Asa's affliction of Hanani. Again, the events may be derived from a different source, but the oracle was probably composed by Chr. It explains the reason for Asa's impending punishment.

S. *2 C 17:2–19.* These verses describe the reforms and power of Jehoshaphat. There is little here that could be ascribed to Chr's interests. In vv 7–9 he gives a list of Levites who taught throughout Judah, but even there he may be dependent on a source outside of DH, as he probably is for the rest of this material.

T. *2 C 19:1–20:30.* This important passage about Jehoshaphat's reforms and wars has been treated in detail by a number of scholars. Albright argued for the historicity of the judicial reforms in chapter 19./10/ That some historical battle underlies C's account in chapter 20 has been acknowledged by several scholars./11/ Thus, Chr has made use of other sources to at least some degree in this account. Nonetheless, his hand is evident in the speeches and oracles in these two chapters. His dogma of retribution is clear from Yahweh's deliverance of the pious Jehoshaphat, and his interest in the Levites is apparent in both chapters. In fact, Petersen has argued that Chr revised the ancient holy war motif in chapter 20 in order to stress the role of the Levites as the agents of Yahweh's deliverance./12/

U. *2 C 21:2–4.* This is a list of Jehoram's brothers and an account of the treatment they received from their father and from Jehoram when he became king. There is nothing tendentious here, and the information is probably from a source outside of K.

V. *2 C 21:12–19.* Verses 12–15 contain a letter written by

Elijah to Jehoram condemning his unfaithfulness and describing
the punishment that he will incur as a result. Verses 16–19
record his punishment: the sacking of his city by the Philistines
and his death from a painful disease. Obviously the material has
been shaped by Chr into his schema of immediate punishment
for unfaithfulness. However, he may well be relying on other
sources for his information about the Philistines and Jehoram's
death. Even the prophetic letter may have its basis in another
source. K^M clearly presumes that Elijah is dead at the time of
Jehoram, and it is difficult to believe that Chr would commit
such an obvious chronological blunder vis-à-vis K without the
authority of another source. Furthermore, Shenkel has shown
that the original chronology preserved in the OG of K placed
Elijah in the time of Jehoram./13/

W. *2 C 23:1b–2*. C gives the names of the commanders of hundreds in v 1b. In this he probably reproduces a list from a different
source. In v 2 his pan-Israel interest is apparent in that the
commanders are to gather the Levites from all the cities of Judah.
The commanders are also to gather the heads of the families of
"Israel." Chr's pan-Israel interest surfaces in his use of this name
and in his desire to make the coronation of Joash an event in which
the entire nation participates./14/ This desire continues to be
strong throughout C's account of Joash's coronation.

X. *2 C 23:18–19*. These verses attest Chr's interest in the
Levites as they describe the role of the Levites in maintaining
the purity of the Temple area during Joash's coronation.

Y. *2 C 24:15–22*. The division between the first part of
Joash's reign in which he is rewarded for faithfulness and the
second part in which he is punished for unfaithfulness occurs in
C's account with the death of Jehoiada. Chr's doctrine of immediate retribution is obvious. It is still possible, though, that the
events narrated, Joash's idolatry and the murder of Zechariah,
were known by Chr from other sources, oral or written.

Z. *2 C 25:5–16*. The story of Amaziah's victory over the
Edomites with its rejection of the Ephraimites and the slaughter
of the Edomites (v 12) can hardly be an invention of Chr. He
probably composed the oracle in vv 15–16, and possibly the one
in vv 7–9. It is interesting that both oracles are delivered by
nameless prophets, which may indicate that Chr had no source
for them. His schema of immediate retribution is apparent here.
Because of his faithfulness, Amaziah is given victory over the

Edomites. His idolatry, however, brings about his defeat and death (vv 17–28). The present structure of this material clearly derives from Chr.

AA. *2 C 26:5–20.* Verses 5–15 recount Uzziah's military strength and building projects. Verses 16–20 describe Uzziah's sin of attempting to burn incense and the leprosy which he received as a punishment. Obviously, the material is organized according to Chr's scheme of retribution. However, much of this material probably derives from sources outside of DH that were available to Chr. While Chr may enlarge to an extent on Uzziah's sin (vv 16–21), the account in 2 K 15:5 certainly appears abbreviated with its simple statement that Yahweh smote Uzziah with leprosy without giving any reason for the smiting.

BB. *2 C 27:3b–6.* C details the building projects of Jotham and his suzerainty over Ammon. This material can hardly be considered tendentious and probably stems from sources other than K.

CC. *2 C 28:5–15.* These verses deal mainly with Israel's defeat of Judah and the harsh treatment of the Judean captives. While Chr is certainly responsible for the current shape of the narrative, especially the prophetic oracle of Oded (vv 9–11) and the speech in v 13, he may have acquired the story itself from his sources outside of DH.

The unparalleled material in 2 C 1–28 frequently betrays the interests of Chr that have been seen elsewhere such as his concern for the location of the Temple and its cult (3:1–2; 7:1b–3; 13:9–11), including its Levitical functionaries (5:11b–13; 7:6; 8:13–16; 11:13–17; 23:1b–2; 23:18–19). His hope in the Davidic covenant surfaces in 6:40–42 and 13:6, and his pan-Israel interest occurs in 11:5–12:1; 13:3–21; 15:1–15; and 23:1b–2. In addition, I have argued that his hand is apparent in the periodizing of several reigns. I have also argued that Chr's hand is evident in most of the speeches found in this material./15/

IV. *Parallel Material in 2 C and K*

The material not treated in sections II and III of this chapter falls into two classes: passages in 2 C and K that are closely parallel and passages that are not parallel in a strict sense but do deal with the same topic. I will discuss the parallel passages first.

Formulae, including accession formulae, death and burial notices, and source notices, will be discussed in Chapter 5.

A. *2 C 1:14–17 // 1 K 10:26–29*

These two passages are nearly verbatim the same, but they do not correspond in terms of their placement in the overall order of K and C. The similar passage in 2 C 9:25–28 holds the same place in C's order as 1 K 10:26–29 holds in K (see Excursus, pp. 152–53). However, the reading of 2 C 9:25–28 is not nearly as similar to 1 K 10:26–29 as is 2 C 1:14–17. This suggests that 2 C 1:14–17 is a secondary insertion of 1 K 10:26–29 into the text of C. In favor of this suggestion is the fact that 2 C 1:14–17 is isolated in its context. It is also the only passage in the first three chapters of 2 C which contains a close parallel in K. The other major witnesses also attest doublets to this passage (1 K 5:6 in M and 1 K 2:46i in the OG). It is clear, then, that we are dealing with a complex textual problem here. The original reading and its placement are quite uncertain. The motive for the insertion of 2 C 1:14–17 in its present place is also uncertain, but Chr can hardly be seen as responsible. In Chr's original account Solomon's first act upon ascending to the throne must have been to build the Temple. As it now stands, 2 C 1:14–17 puts off the account of beginning the Temple (2:1)

B. *2 C 4:1–5:1 // 1 K 7:23–51*

Except for 2 C 4:1, 7–9, and 1 K 7:27–37 which were discussed in II and III above, these two accounts are extremely close. Rudolph has argued that the majority of 2 C 4 has been secondarily copied into C from 1 K 7./16/ He apparently believes that the insertion occurred in at least two stages. He argues that 2 C 4:10–22 was inserted because the accounts in 4:1–9 and 5:1ff. closely followed the K account. But he then goes on to argue that only 2 C 4:2a, 3a, 6–9 are original, the rest of 4:1–9 having been added secondarily from 1 K 7. Rudolph's arguments are not convincing. There is no good literary basis for his conclusions. His view is due largely to his inability to understand why Chr would suddenly begin in chapter 4 to follow K closely. But this problem also exists elsewhere in Chr's use of K, and it is simply not always possible to determine why he has chosen to follow K. Rudolph's argument also presumes that Chr has made extensive, tendentious changes in his K source. Thus, in the preceding 2 C material,

Rudolph explains the differences from K as signs of Chr having rewritten his K source. But this is not the way in which Chr used his S *Vorlage* nor, as I hope to show, his K *Vorlage*. In addition, Rudolph's idea that only vv 2a, 3a, and 6–9 are original in 2 C 4 is also determined largely by his view of Chr's biases. This is particularly true in v 3a where Rudolph argues that Chr has added דמות before בקרים because the twelve בקרים were too similar to the bull-shaped idols of Jeroboam. However, this does not represent a consistent interest of Chr, and it is very slim evidence for taking only v 3a as originally from C. If the בקרים were so odious to Chr why did he include them in the first place? What is more, the addition of דמות "image" makes the reference to idolatry even more explicit and would directly contradict C's alleged aniconic tendency. דמות is better regarded as a simple explicating plus. בקרים has entered through graphic confusion with פקעים compounded no doubt by the fact that the latter was probably not understood. The word occurs only in this context in K and its meaning is uncertain.

C. *2 C 5:2–14//1 K 7:51–8:11*

Again the two accounts run nearly verbatim the same. 2 C 5:11–13 has been commented on in section III. Only 2 C 5:4//1 K 8:3 merits further comment. In this verse C has "Levites" where K has "priests." Chr has probably altered the reading of the verse to conform with the function of the Levites in his own day. He consistently distinguishes the priests from the Levites and views the transportation of the ark as a function of the latter group (1 C 15:2,13).

D. *2 C 6:1–42//1 K 8:12–53*

The two accounts are extremely close until the final few verses of each. In addition to the two haplographies in K which explain the lack of a parallel for 2 C 6:5b–6a, 13 (see III above), the text of C is haplographic in v 32//1 K 8:42. There, the phrase כי ישמעון את שמך was lost because of homoioteleuton (שמך). The only tendentious change in C occurs in vv 40–42 which have been discussed in section III above.

E. *2 C 7:4–22//1 K 8:62–9:9*

There is more variation between these two accounts than is found in other parallel sections, and this appears to be due largely to changes on the part of Chr. I have already discussed the additions in 2 C 7:6, 12b–15 (section III). There are several other verses in this section that deserve comment.

(1) 1 K 8:65–66a

M: ויעש שלמה בעת ההיא את החג וכל ישראל עמו קהל גדול מלבוא
חמת עד נחל מצרים לפני יהוה אלהינו שבעת ימים ושבעת ימים
ארבעה עשר יום (66) ביום השמיני

OG: και εποιησεν Σαλωμων την εορτην εν τη ημερα εκεινη και πας Ισραηλ μετ᾽ αυτου εκκλησια μεγαλη απο της εισοδου Ημαθ εως ποταμου Αιγυπτου ενωπιον Κυριου θεου ημων εν τω οικω ω ωκοδομησεν εσθιων και πινων και ευφραινομενος ενωπιον Κυ θεου ημων επτα ημερας (66) και εν τη ημερα τη ογδοη

2 C 7:8–9

M: ויעש שלמה את החג בעת ההיא שבעת ימים וכל ישראל עמו קהל
גדול מאד מלבוא חמת עד נחל מצרים (9) ויעשו ביום השמיני
עצרת כי חנכת המזבח עשו שבעת ימים והחג שבעת ימים

The variation here is difficult to interpret. However, the most primitive reading is probably that of the OG. K^M and the OG essentially agree in the plus at the end of 1 K 8:65. The OG indicates a haplography in K^M within this plus. The loss was triggered by homoioteleuton (לפני יהוה אלהינו . . . לפני יהוה אלהינו). The ending of the plus in K^M also appears corrupt. The repetition of שבעת ימים and the phrase ארבעה עשר יום probably reflect dittography and an expansionistic gloss. The plus in 2 C 7:9 is also an interpretation or elaboration of the duration of the celebration. It is likely the work of Chr in line with his interest in the cult. *Ant* VIII. 123 also mentions two seven-day periods (δις επτα ημερας). Thus, the reference to two seven-day periods probably existed in Chr's K *Vorlage*, but he has expanded that reference distinguishing between the altar dedication and the cultic festival.

(2) *2 C 7:11–12//1 K 9:1–3.* There are three major differences between the accounts here. The first two are the plus, בבית יהוה ובביתו הצליח in 2 C 7:11 and the minus in 2 C 7:12, כאשר נראה אליו בגבעון The latter phrase seems to be an expansion in K, and the first phrase may also be an expansion. In any case, it is

difficult to see any bias on the part of Chr in these differences. The final difference is the end of 7:12. The statement by Yahweh that he has chosen the Temple as a house of sacrifice corresponds to Chr's interests in the location of the Temple and in its cult. I have already argued that Chr composed 7:13–15. The end of 7:12 is probably his composition as well.

(3) *2 C 7:17–18//1 K 9:4–5.* The account in K has two phrases which are lacking in C: בתם לבב ובישר and על ישראל לעלם The first phrase describes David's walk before Yahweh, and Chr would obviously have no tendentious reason for omitting it. It is also difficult to believe that he would have omitted the second phrase, since virtually the same expression is used about Solomon in 1 C 17:12, 14. Indeed, the plus in K may well have been influenced by the language of the Nathan oracle (2 S 7:13//1 C 17:12). Thus, both phrases are probably expansions in K.

F. *2 C 8:6a–10//1 K 9:19–23*

The two passages are very close, and there is no significant difference between them. Only 8:8//9:21 merits special comment. Here, C states that the Israelites did not destroy (כלום) the inhabitants of the land, while K says that they were unable (יכלו) to destroy (להחרים)them. Several commentators have pointed to C's reading as a intentional weakening of the statement in K./17/ This is possible but not certain since the similarity in the verb forms כלום and יכלו is too great to dismiss the possibility of unintentional variation.

G. *2 C 8:11–12//1 K 9:24–25*

The plus in 2 C 8:11b makes the moving of Solomon's Egyptian wife out of the city of David an act of piety on the part of Solomon. The fact that it enhances Solomon's righteousness and mentions the ark indicates that it was added by Chr. In 8:12 Chr has abbreviated K by omitting the reference to the three yearly sacrifices. The precise reason for this is uncertain, but it may be related to Chr's addition in vv 13–16. Chr is more concerned to describe the daily maintenance of the Temple cult by the Levites than he is with Solomon's own cultic acts.

H. *2 C 9:1-12//1 K 10:1-13*

The two accounts of the visit of the queen of Sheba are
extremely close. Only in 9:8//10:9 is theological interest on the
part of Chr possible./18/ In that verse Chr states that Yahweh has
placed Solomon on his (Yahweh's) throne as his (Yahweh's) king,
while K merely states that Yahweh placed Solomon on the throne
of Israel. Thus, Chr seems to stress the notion that Yahweh is
Israel's true king. However, one must be cautious here. The differences are small and may easily have arisen in the evolving proto-
Rabbinic text. Similar minor variants occur in the next few verses.

I. *2 C 9:13-28//1 K 10:14-29*

The two accounts of Solomon's wealth and wisdom are very
close, but there are several passages that merit special comment.

(1) *2 C 9:14//1 K 10:15*. The additional phrase in C, מביאים
זהב וכסף לשלמה is probably an interpretive expansion. There is
no special bias here.

(2) *2 C 9:16//1 K 10:17*. The amount of gold in each
shield is increased beyond possibility in C. This is probably the
result of scribal error, influenced by the phrase, שלש מאות מגנים
זהב, earlier in the verse.

(3) *2 C 9:18//1 K 10:19*. K's reading in 10:19 is usually
emended from ראש עגול to ראש עגל on the basis of sense and the
reading of G (προτομαι μοσχων). C mentions a golden stool
(כבש) in place of the ראש עגול/עגל, and it has been suggested
that he omitted the reference to the calf because of its associa-
tions with the idol at Bethel./19/ There are two major problems
with this view. First, as mentioned in the case of 2 C 4:3, this is
not a consistent bias of Chr. There is no indication that he would
connect a bovine figure in Solomon's throne room with the idol
of Jeroboam, especially in the light of 2 C 4:3 when he refers to
בקרים in the Temple. Secondly, even if the emendation in K is
correct, as seems likely, it is not certain what was in C's *Vorlage*.
It is conceivable that the reading כבש represents an attempt to
explain the ראש עגול in K. The other possibility is that כבש and
ראש עגול/עגל were simply ancient variants in the proto-Rabbinic
text of K.

(4) *2 C 9:25-28//1 K 10:26-29*. These passages were
essentially discussed above (p. 94). 2 C 9:25-28 differs considera-
bly from 1 K 10:26-29 and 2 C 1:14-17. It lacks a parallel to 1 K

10:29//2 C 1:17. 2 C 9:26 is parallel to 1 K 5:1a, and 2 C 9:25a differs more in its language and numbers from its parallel in 1 K 10:26a than does 2 C 1:14a. I can offer no suitable reconstruction to explain the present variants. It seems clear, though, that none of the variants can be attributed to Chr's interests.

J. 2 C 10:1–11:4//1 K 12:1–24

Aside from Chr's omission of 1 K 12:20 (see section II) the two accounts are nearly verbatim the same. Still, several verses require comment.

(1) *2 C 10:2–3a//1 K 12:2–3a.* My reconstruction of this material is given in detail in the excursus. In short, the readings in 1 K 12:2–3a, 12 have been added secondarily into the proto-Rabbinic text of K. The OG reflects the original placement of this material in 11:43 and the original reading in 12:12. Its reading in 11:43 may reflect some expansion but is superior to the reading in K^M and C^M. This reconstruction explains the textual evidence and resolves the contradiction which currently exists between 1 K 12:3a and 12 on the one hand and 1 K 12:20 on the other. Jeroboam was not originally mentioned in 1 K 12:12, nor was the reference to him being summoned originally found in 1 K 12:3a (*sic*).

(2) *2 C 10:15//1 K 12:15.* This verse is an example of how closely Chr copied K. Here C refers to the prophecy of Ahijah as being fulfilled. Yet that prophecy has been omitted from C because it deals primarily with the North.

(3) *2 C 10:16–18//1 K 12:16–18.* Lemke argues that Chr's pan-Israel interest is apparent here./20/ He states that in C כל ישראל refers to both the Northern and Southern kingdoms, and בני ישראל refers only to the Northern kingdom, while in K, ישראל in this context refers to the North. Verse 17, according to Lemke, is a secondary intrusion from C into K because of its reference to Israelites in Judah. He may be correct that 1 K 12:17 is second-ary. As he points out, the fact that this verse is missing in G supports his suspicion. However, it is uncertain whether the verse was borrowed from C into K or vice-versa. 2 K 12:23 also indicates that there were non-Judahites living in Judah. Further-more, the evidence does not support Lemke's view about C's use of "Israel" here. In v 16 C reports that כל ישראל was displeased by Rehoboam's decision and returned "to their tents." This is

clearly a reference to the Northern inhabitants. Williamson is correct that Chr's pan-Israel interest is evident in this passage in the simple fact that he can still refer to the Northern tribes as part of "all Israel,"/21/ but Lemke's attempt to find here subtle changes by Chr in support of his interest must be rejected.

(4) *2 C 11:3//1 K 12:23*. The reference in C to "all Israel in Judah and Benjamin" undoubtedly represents a change by Chr. The precise motive for C's change here is not clear. It may reflect his desire to stress that true Israel consists of both North and South, as Williamson suggests./22/ One thing is clear; the language here does not mean that Chr believes true Israel to consist only in the South./23/ So much is clear from the next verse where those in the South are commanded not to fight against their "brethren."

K. *2 C 12:2a–b, 9b–11//1 K 14:25–28*

I have discussed in section III the additional material inserted by Chr into this context. It is clear that Chr has borrowed the K account as the framework for building his own account. That framework is found in the verses listed above which do not vary significantly from the account in K.

L. *2 C 14:1–2a; 15:16–16:6//1 K 15:11–22*

Again, Chr has used K's account as a framework into which he has inserted other information about Asa. In general, where C parallels K they are quite close. However, there are some important differences brought about through C's intentional change.

(1) *2 C 14:2a//1 K 15:12*. Most of the K verse is lacking in C. It is possible that this is simply the result of Chr's beginning to use other sources at this point. However, the use of יוסר את as in K seems to indicate that Chr is familiar with the K account. The verse in K refers to cult prostitutes and idols erected by Asa's fathers. Chr may have omitted this reference because in his account of Asa's predecessors, Abijah, Rehoboam, Solomon and David, only the latter half of Rehoboam's reign was wicked. The others were faithful. None of them is mentioned as an idolater in C.

(2) *2 C 15:16–18//1 K 15:13–15*. As Rudolph has argued, these verses are probably best viewed as a secondary insertion

into C from K because of the inconsistencies of 2 C 15:17 with other statements in C./24/ The statement that Asa did not remove the high places (v 17) contradicts earlier statements in vv 2 and 5, and the statement that Asa's heart was blameless does not accord with C's account in 16:7–12.

(3) *2 C 15:19//1 K 15:16.* The two accounts here are directly contradictory. C says that there was no war between Asa and Baasha until the thirty-fifth year of Asa. K says that Baasha died in Asa's twenty-sixth or twenty-seventh year. C's structure here fits with Chr's retribution dogma. Asa's troubles begin when he sins by trusting in Ben-Hadad instead of Yahweh (2 C 16). His wars are a punishment (16:9). Chr may have gathered Asa's wars with Baasha to the end of Asa's reign. At the same time, Chr is probably dependent on sources outside of K for his chronological information here. It is hard to believe that Chr would so obviously contradict K without a variant source. Moreover, Shenkel has shown that the chronology in K^M is secondary to that of the OG, and we have already seen that for the account of Elijah's letter (2 C 21:12–15) C probably used a source based on a different chronology from K^M.

M. *2 C 18:4–34//1 K 22:5–35*

The first three verses of 2 C 18 are an introduction to this story composed by Chr to replace the introduction in K which focuses on the North (see section V below). Otherwise these two accounts are extremely close.

(1) 2 C 18:31b
M: ויהוה עזרו ויסיתם אלהים ממנו
1 K 22:32
M,B: omit
L: Κς εσωσεν αυτον

L (K) reflects a line similar to C's ויהוה עזרו indicating that it is probably original. It was probably lost from the text reflected in K^{MG}, by haplography (homoioarchton: ויהוה ... ויהי). The additional line in C must then be an expansion or a gloss. It cannot be regarded as tendentious if ויהוה עזרו is original, since the two lines make basically the same point.

(2) *2 C 18:34//1 K 22:35.* C omits the reference to Ahab's blood. Besides being a part of the narrative about Ahab's death which Chr omits (vv 36–40), the phrase is of special

importance to K's prophecy—fulfillment schema (cf. 1 K 21:19).
C omits the prophecy since it concerns a Northern king.

N. 2 C 20:31–33//1 K 22:41–44

These two accounts are generally close. Only 2 C 20:33
requires special comment. This is an unusual verse. Verse 33a
stands in contradiction to 17:6. Verse 33b faults the people for
not having devoted themselves to God, and thus it stands in
tension to the account of the faithfulness of the people in 20:1–
30. Perhaps the best solution here is to see v 33 as a secondary
addition as Rudolph suggests./25/ The addition was based in
part on the text in 1 K 22:44.

O. 2 C 21:5–11//2 K 8:17–22

These two accounts are generally quite close with only two
significant variations.

(1) *2 C 21:7//2 K 8:19*. Most commentators are probably
correct in seeing Chr's hand in the change from "Judah" to "the
house of David" and in the addition of the phrase הברית אשר
כרת. Chr places his hope and a part of his program for restoration on the promise of Yahweh to the Davidic line.

(2) *2 C 21:10–11//2 K 8:22*. The interpretation in vv
10b–11, which is unparalleled in K, undoubtedly comes from the
hand of Chr. This material makes it explicit that the rebellions
of Judah's vassals occurred as a result of Jehoram's sin. The
notion of immediate retribution is strong in C.

P. 2 C 22:1–6//2 K 8:24b–29

The two accounts are very close, but there are two places
where they vary significantly.

(1) *2 C 22:1//2 K 8:24b–25*. As is usual in C, the synchronism with the North in 2 K 8:25 is omitted. However, 22:1 contains additional information about Ahaziah and his brothers not
found in K, and this information probably comes from sources
outside of K. The idea that Chr wishes to stress with this additional information the retribution of God (cf. 21:4) is dubious
since C is usually not so subtle in detailing that punishment is
the direct result of sin./26/

(2) *2 C 22:3–4//2 K 8:27*. C's account stresses that Ahaziah was evil because he was related to the Northern royal family and accepted them as advisors. Chr clearly considers the
Northern monarchy and cult apostate, though he does not

exclude the residents of the North from true Israel. Here he stresses that the Northern monarchy even caused (or at least contributed to) sin in the South.

Q. *2 C 22:10–12//2 K 11:1–3*

These accounts about the hiding of Joash are very close. The only significant variant occurs in 22:11 where Chr informs that Jehoshabat is the wife of Jehoiada./27/ While this detail may have its basis in another source, it certainly fits Chr's interest in priests and especially in the important figure, Jehoiada.

R. *2 C 23:1–21//2 K 11:4–20*

A good deal of the variation here is caused by Chr's interests. Since this story involves an intimate relationship between priest and king, with the former being dominant, Chr is especially interested in it.

(1) *2 C 23:1–6//2 K 11:4–6*. These verses attest Chr's interests to an extensive degree. There is particular concern about the Levites, and their role in these events is detailed (vv 2, 4b, 6). The statement in v 3b that Joash would reign as Yahweh had said to the sons of David is a clear allusion to the Davidic covenant which is so important to Chr. C also stresses that all the people joined in the coronation (vv 3a, 5, 6), while K refers only to the military leaders. Finally, there is a concern in C to assure that only qualified personnel enter the Temple area (v 6). The only variation in these verses that is not due to Chr's interests is the list of names in v 1 which probably stems from a different source available to Chr.

(2) *2 C 23:7//2 K 11:8*. The mention of the Levites again fits with Chr's interests. Otherwise, the two verses are very close.

(3) *2 C 23:8//2 K 11:9*. Chr replaces the reference to the captains of hundreds with a reference to the Levites and all Judah, according to his interests. The statement at the end of the verse about Jehoiada not dismissing the priestly divisions also accords with Chr's interest in cultic personnel.

(4) *2 C 23:10//2 K 11:11*. Chr's interest in having all the people participate in the coronation is evident from his substitution of כל העם for הרצים.

(5) *2 C 23:13//2 K 11:4*. C's reference to the singers and musicians leading in the praise is unparalleled in K and accords

with the interest shown elsewhere by Chr in cultic celebration and the roles of the different Levitical groups in that celebration.

(6) *2 C 23:18aβ–19//—.* Verse 18 clearly reflects Chr's interests in the cult and the functions of the Levitical divisions. The fact that David is here credited with the divisions of the Levites makes it certain that Chr is responsible for this plus. Verse 19 reflects Chr's concern that the Temple not be defiled by the entrance therein of any unclean or unqualified person.

S. *2 C 24:1–2//2 K 12:1–4*

Much of this passage consists of the accession formula for Joash. I will deal with such formulae in Chapter 5. The two passages here are generally very close. Chr omits the synchronism with the North in 2 K 12:2 as is customary for him. The reference to the high places in 2 K 12:4 is lacking in C. C frequently lacks these statements about the *bāmôt* where K has them, and there does not appear to be any reason in Chr's *Tendenz* for his having omitted them. Where C does have these statements (15:17//2 K 15:14 and 20:33// 2 K 22:44) there are good reasons for believing that they have been added secondarily (see pp. 100–102). This evidence suggests that the *bāmôt* references in K may be Dtr 2 additions. I will discuss this possibility more fully at the end of the comparison of C and K. Chr's periodization schema is obvious in his changing K's statement that Joash did right all his life because of Jehoiada's instruction to read that Joash did right only so long as Jehoiada lived.

T. *2 C 25:1–4//2 K 14:1–6*

Again this passage is largely an accession formula. The two accounts are very close except for the fact that most of 2 K 14:3–4 is lacking in C. First, Chr avoids the comparison with Joash because his account has pictured Joash in a less favorable light than did K. Secondly, the reference to the high places is again lacking in C.

U. *2 C 25:17–24//2 K 14:8–14*

The two accounts of the war between Amaziah and Jehoash are extremely close. The only significant difference occurs in the plus in 2 C 25:20 by means of which Chr interprets the story along the lines of his periodization schema. Yahweh brings about Amaziah's defeat as punishment for his idolatries.

V. 2 C 25:25–26:4, 21//2 K 14:17–15:5

Once again this material is largely formulaic. It contains formulae for Amaziah and Uzziah and provides a framework for C's additional information about the latter. The two accounts are very close where they are parallel. A significant difference occurs in the statement of 2 C 25:27, not paralleled in K, that the conspiracy against Amaziah began at the time of his unfaithfulness to Yahweh. It is clear that Chr's dogma of retribution is on view here. Other differences include the usual omissions of the synchronism with the North (2 K 15:1) and the statement about the high places (2 K 15:4). The periodization schema is articulated for Uzziah in 2 C 26:5.

W. 2 C 27:1–3a//2 K 15:32–35

Aside from the usual omissions of the synchronism with the North (2 K 15:32) and the reference to the high places (15:35) there are no significant differences between the two accounts here. In place of K's statement that Jotham did not remove the *bāmôt*, 2 C 27:2 states that Jotham did not enter the Temple as did Uzziah. Chr does state that the people are corrupt, but Jotham is without fault in his view.

X. 2 C 28:1–4//2 K 16:1–4

Besides the omission of the synchronism with the Northern monarchy (2 K 16:1), the only significant difference occurs in v 3 where C mentions making molten images and burning incense as sins of Ahaz in addition to sacrificing his son. K mentions only the last sin. It seems likely that C has expanded the list of Ahaz's sins, though he may have done so on the basis of some other source available to him.

In section IV I have compared twenty-four parallel passages in K and C. They are generally quite close throughout. There are a few cases of secondary borrowing from K into C (A, L2, N). As a rule, though, their similarity is due to Chr's close following of his *Vorlage*, a text of the same type as K^M. Many of the differences between the accounts are the results of the development and transmission of the texts of K and C (B, D, E1, 2, 3, F, I1, 2, 3, J3, M1). A few differences probably reflect other sources used by Chr (L3, P1, Q). Chr's interests are readily apparent in a number of passages: his pan-Israel interest (J4, R1, 3, 4), his interest in the cult and its personnel (C, E2, Q, R1, 2, 3, 5, 6), and his concern for the Davidic monarchy including his idealized view of Solomon (G, H, O1). 2 C 24 is particularly important for Chr's program because of its description of Joash's coronation by the priest Jehoiada in which all the people participate. Thus, this event affords Chr a forum for all three of these interests. In addition, Chr's dogma of immediate divine retribution has caused him to periodize the reigns of several kings (L3, S, U, V). These kings prosper during the first part of their reigns while they are faithful to Yahweh. But when they sin, punishment follows making the second part of their reigns disastrous and in some cases leading to the king's death.

V. *Passages Dealing with the Same Topics*

A. *2 C 1:7–13/1 K 3:5–15*

Both passages concern Solomon's vision at Gibeon. The nearly unanimous assumption of commentators with regard to these passages has been that Chr freely rewrote the account in 1 K 3. There are, however, two serious objections to this view. First, except for vv 7–8 the account in C scarcely shares a phrase with that of K. If Chr had used K at all, even as a basis for rewriting, one would expect more similarity between the two than currently exists. Such was the case in the speeches placed by Chr into David's mouth in 1 C 22, 29. It is obvious that those speeches have been composed from Deuteronomistic sources. Secondly, one must ask why Chr would rewrite his K *Vorlage* here when his usual practice is to cite K fairly closely where he uses it. There is nothing in C's account here vis-à-vis K that is a consistent interest of his or furnishes a motive for rewriting the K account. These considerations at least raise the possibility that Chr was using a different source from K in this passage.

B. *2 C 1:18–2:16/1 K 5:15–27*

Both passages deal with Solomon's communication with Hiram. They differ extensively, and Chr's hand is obvious in a number of places. However, the two accounts differ even where no *Tendenz* is apparent. An analogous example is 2 C 23//2 K 11 treated above. There also Chr introduced several tendentious changes, yet his account remains generally very similar to that of K. Such is not the case in 2 C 1:18–2:15. Thus, there is a possibility that Chr here used a source different from K.

(1) *2 C 1:18.* This verse is important in Chr's structuring of the material. As a result of omitting 1 K 4:1–5:14, Chr is able in v 18 to make Solomon's first thought upon ascending the throne the building of the Temple. This is particularly true if 2 C 1:14–17 is a secondary addition.

(2) *2 C 2:3–5.* The details of the worship to be conducted in the Temple and the doxology to Yahweh contained in these verses betray Chr's hand. Chr takes advantage of the opportunity of Hiram's letter to include some of his own theological interests. Verse 5 is very similar to a statement made in Solomon's dedication speech (2 C 6:18//1 K 8:27) and may be borrowed from there.

(3) *2 C 2:6, 13/1 K 7:14.* Some have argued that these verses in C reflect an attempt by Chr to make Hiram look like Bezelel (Exod 31:1–5; 35:30–35)./28/ The problem with this view is that the language of 1 K 7:14 is at least as close to that of the two Exodus passages as is the language of 2 C 2:6, 13. The phrase לעשות בזהב ובכסף (ו)בנחשת occurs in 2 C 2:6, 13; Exod 31:4; 35:32 and not in 1 K 7:14. However, the phrases וימלא את חכמה ואת תבונה and וידע את כל מלאכתו in 1 K 7:14 have parallels in the Exodus passages but not in 2 C 2:6, 13. Thus, C's description of Hiram is no more patterned after that of Bezalel than that of K. The fact that C lists Hiram's mother as coming from Dan while in K she is from Naphtali may be the result of Chr's following another source. The expansion of Hiram's capabilities in v 13 is reminiscent of the expansion of instruments in 1 C 15:28. It may stem from Chr's interest in the Temple building.

(4) *2 C 2:11/1 K 5:21.* Hiram's benediction of Yahweh and Solomon is more extensive in C than in K and has probably been expanded by Chr.

(5) *2 C 2:16/1 K 5:27.* C and K give different sources for Solomon's forced labor. K says here that Solomon took his *corvée* from all Israel. C states that it was taken from the aliens within Israel's borders. However, one cannot be certain that C is tendentious, since there is disagreement in K over this question (cf. 1 K 9:20–22).

C. 2 C 3:3–17/1 K 6:1–3, 21–28; 7:13–22

The major independent sections in 2 C 3:1–2; 1 K 6:4–20, 29–7:12 have been discussed in sections II and III. All of this material concerns the building of the Temple. The account of C differs extensively from that of K even where they describe the same thing, such as the cherubim (2 C 3:10–13; 1 K 6:23–27). They share few expressions in common, and it is difficult to find any evidence or motive for tendentious change in C. It is likely then, that the account in C is derived from a different source than K.

D. 2 C 8:1–6/1 K 9:10–18

Both accounts concern cities which Solomon built, but they differ extensively.

(1) *2 C 8:1–2/1 K 9:10–13*. Lemke argues against a number of commentators who hold that C here directly contradicts K./29/ Lemke's view is that C's account presumes K, i.e., that Hiram gave back the cities that Solomon had originally given him. Lemke may be correct. His argument is somewhat *ad hoc*, but his point that Chr would hardly make such a clumsy contradiction has some force. In either case, Chr has made a tendentious change, omitting the account of Hiram's displeasure at Solomon's cities which tends to reflect negatively on Solomon.

(2) *2 C 8:3–6a/1 K 9:17–18*. C and K share some names in common in their lists of cities here, but Chr clearly relies on another source. There is no evidence of any real bias on the part of Chr that has influenced his reading here./30/

E. 2 C 8:17–18/1 K 9:26–28

The two accounts of Solomon's acquiring gold from Ophir give different information. K says that Solomon had a fleet readied at Ezion Geber, while C says that he went to Ezion Geber. In K the fleet belongs to Solomon, and Hiram simply sends sailors to help man Solomon's fleet. In C the fleet is Hiram's and Solomon's sailors accompany Hiram's. Finally the number of talents of gold differs in the two accounts. Since there is no reason to suspect tendentious change in any of these differences, Chr has probably followed a different source for his account here.

F. 2 C 16:2–17:1/1 K 15:18bβ–24

Much of this material is formulaic. However, it is likely that Chr is using a source other than K for the narrative material in these verses. C portrays Asa's fatal illness as a punishment for sin. Thus, the judgment against Asa that he did not seek Yahweh even in his illness in v 12 comes from Chr. But the added details about his disease in that verse may come from another source. Similarly, the additional information about his burial in v 14 probably stems from a source outside of K.

G. 2 C 18:1–3/1 K 22:1–4

Chr has composed this introduction to the story of the battle in this chapter because of the fact that the introduction in K clearly focuses on the North. Chr changes that focus to Jehoshaphat in his introduction, explaining how Jehoshaphat came to visit Ahab because of their marriage alliance (vv 1–2). He depends more heavily on K for the conversation between Jehoshaphat and Ahab in v 3.

H. 2 C 20:35–37/1 K 22:49–50

The only real similarity of these two accounts is that they both mention a shipwreck of Jehoshaphat's boats. In K's narrative Jehoshaphat sends his fleet to Ophir to retrieve gold. They are destroyed on the way, and later when Ahaziah suggests a similar joint effort, Jehoshaphat declines. In C's account Jehoshaphat allies himself with Ahaziah, and the two undertake the venture of sending ships to Tarshish. The reason for the journey is not specified. A prophet, Eliezer, declares to Jehoshaphat Yahweh's displeasure at the alliance with the Omride and foretells the destruction of the fleet. Chr's tendentious concerns are evident. The destruction of the ships is, in his view, punishment for an alliance with the Northern royal house. The fact that a prophet foretells the shipwreck accords with the prophecy-fulfillment schema that is important to Chr. Still, not all of the differences between K and C here are attributable to Chr's interest, and it is possible that his account is based partly on sources outside of K.

I. *2 C 22:7–9/2 K 9:1–10:36*

The three verses in C are Chr's summary of the effect on Judah and its monarchy of Jehu's revolt which is narrated at length in 1 K 9:1–10:36. 2 C 22:7a in particular expresses Chr's judgment that Ahaziah's demise was brought about by Yahweh as punishment for his sins.

J. *2 C 24:3–14/2 K 12:5–16*

Both passages are concerned with the repairs done on the Temple under the leadership of Joash and Jehoiada. The accounts differ throughout, but Chr's interests are apparent in some of the differences./31/ His interest in the events narrated here is certainly understandable. After all, it is the story of a diarchy, rule by king and priest, in which the latter is dominant. It is also the story of work on the Temple involving cultic personnel. If any chapter in C would provide a forum for the expression of Chr's interests, this one certainly would. At the same time, there are several details throughout this chapter where no bias on Chr's part is visible and which may derive from other sources. This is a particularly good possibility in light of Chr's reference in 24:27 to a *midrash* of K as one of his sources for Joash's reign.

(1) *2 C 24:5–6, 11/2 K 12:5–8, 11*. Levites are mentioned by C as playing a major role in these events. In K the priests alone are mentioned. This accords with Chr's interest in the Levites. In addition, Chr may have omitted the narrative in vv 7–8 of K which tells of something akin to embezzlement by the priests of funds designated for the Temple repair. If he did omit that narrative, the omission was motivated by his interest in the priests and Levites.

(2) *2 C 24:5–6, 9–10/2 K 12:5–6*. Chr stresses the role of the entire people in donating to the repair of the Temple. Thus, in C the Levites are sent to the cities of Judah to collect money for the repairs "from all Israel" (vv 5–6), while in K the repairs are financed from donations received at the Temple (12:5).

(3) *2 C 24:14/2 K 12:14*. C and K directly contradict each other in this verse. K states that no Temple vessels were made from the donated silver, while C states that the surplus gold and silver were used to make vessels. It is difficult to see a motive for tendentious change at this point, and the discrepancy may be an indication that C's source here was not K as we know it.

K. *2 C 24:23–27/2 K 12:18–22*

Both accounts deal with Joash's defeat by Aram and the end of his reign, but they differ extensively in the details. Chr's interests are obvious throughout the account. However, some of the differences in details where no bias on Chr's part is apparent indicate that his source was not K.

(1) *2 C 24:23–25/2 K 12:18–20.* The accounts of the invasion of Aram differ. In K Hazael defeats Gath then besieges Jerusalem. He apparently does not fight against Jerusalem, for Joash sends him a large amount of tribute, and he withdraws. In C, however, Joash is severely wounded in the battle with Aram. The judgment given in C against Joash in vv 24–25 clearly comes from Chr's hand. In fact, C makes an explicit connection, not in K, both theologically and chronologically between Joash's defeat by Aram, the conspiracy against him, and his death. These events all occur at the end of Joash's reign as a punishment for his sin. This fits well with Chr's periodization of Joash's reign as a result of his belief in divine retribution.

(2) *2 C 24:25b/2 K 12:22b.* C and K disagree about Joash's place of burial. According to K he was buried with his fathers, in the city of David. According to C he was buried in the city of David but not with his fathers. It is doubtful that the difference is the result of Chr's bias./32/ It probably derives from a source other than K. In fact, it is the sort of expansion of the Deuteronomistic formula that one might expect to find in a *midrash* of K such as the one cited in 2 C 24:27.

(3) *2 C 24:26/2 K 12:22.* The additional information in C has been seen by some commentators as reflecting a polemic against mixed marriages which was a controversial issue in Chr's day./33/ Thus, the names of those who conspired against Joash are similar to names found in Ezra's list of those who renounced their foreign wives (Ezra 10:18–44), and their mothers are designated as "the Ammonitess" and "the Moabitess" (cf. Ezra 9:1), so that they are products of mixed marriages. This view cannot be accepted. C shows no tendency elsewhere to combat mixed marriage. Hiram, the temple artificer, was also the product of a mixed marriage, yet C says nothing against him (2 C 2:13). In fact, no judgment is given against the two conspirators here. Chr may view them as Yahweh's instruments for execution of judgment on Joash. The names of the conspirators do not indicate

any particular bias on Chr's part. The name (Jeho- or Jo-)Zabad was simply a popular one in the post-exilic period./34/ The fact that the conspirators' mothers are designated as foreign women in C can also hardly be tendentious. Again, this is the type of expansion one might encounter in a *midrash*./35/

L. 2 C 28:16–21/2 K 16:7–9

Both accounts deal in part with Judah's submission to Assyria. In K Ahaz' request is specifically motivated by the confederacy of Pekah and Rezin against him. In C the motivation appears to be the raids of the Edomites and Philistines (vv 17–18). Chr is probably relying here on a different source from K. The same is true for C's report of the tribute paid by Ahaz in v 21. Only v 19 is Chr's own composition. He interprets these events as the judgment of Yahweh upon Judah because of Ahaz' faithlessness.

M. 2 C 28:22–27/2 K 16:10–20

Both accounts deal with the same broad topic of Ahaz' unfaithfulness, but they are totally different in the details. Chr says nothing about the altar borrowed by Ahaz from Damascus. Rather, it describes the idolatrous practices of Ahaz. Also, C reports that the Temple was closed by Ahaz while K describes Ahaz' use of his new altar in the Temple. These differences are striking and difficult to explain. Has Chr suppressed K's information about the new altar? Was the Temple really closed?/36/ Myers suggests that Chr has interpreted the K account./37/ Ahaz' imported altar plan has come to be worship of the gods of Aram, and the removal of some Temple furniture (2 K 16:17–18) has been interpreted as a complete closing of the Temple. Myers's suggestion points out the interpretive nature of C's account. Since it is difficult to find a satisfactory motive for C's reading here as tendentious, Chr may again be following an interpretive source such as a *midrash*.

Section V has surveyed thirteen passages that deal with the same topic in K and C but are not strictly parallel. In one case (I) C abbreviates a lengthy narrative of Israelite history in order to focus on its importance for Judah. In another case (G) he composes a different introduction to a narrative borrowed from K again to focus on Judah. In the other eleven cases, I have argued that there is reason to believe that Chr was using a source other than K. Chr is probably still aware of K's narrative in these passages. He follows K's order throughout and may sometimes combine K with other sources. Also, most of the passages clearly attest Chr's interests. Yet even in 2 C 24:3–14, which displays Chr's interests throughout, he seems to be composing at least in part on the basis of sources other than K.

VI. *Conclusions*

The present study is concerned principally with two questions, the extent of Chr's use of DH and the technique(s) of his use. Since it is obvious that Chr used K through the reign of Ahaz, I have focused in this chapter on the way(s) in which he used K as a source. The study has been facilitated by the evidence that C's K *Vorlage*, unlike the text of S underlying 1 C, was proto-Rabbinic.

The conclusions for 2 C 1–28, are very similar to those reached for 1 C. Generally, where Chr follows K he cites it quite literally. Chr often uses K as a framework into which he inserts other material, but K is clearly his principal source. In passages where K and C treat the same topic but are not strictly parallel, C usually follows a source other than K at least in part. The amount of material freely composed by Chr is much smaller than most commentaries indicate. He does compose most of the speeches and oracles, but some of them may also be based on other sources.

Although Chr does not generally make extensive changes in his K *Vorlage* where he cites it, his interests are made clear from a variety of other techniques. One such technique is the omission of K material that lies outside of or conflicts with his interests. Thus, as with David in 1 C, he omits all negative information about Solomon. He also omits material about the Northern monarchy. His interests are also visible in his additions. I have mentioned the speeches and oracles placed by him into the mouths of his characters. At points, Chr supplements his citation of a K narrative with his own interpretation. He interprets a particular crisis or tragedy in the reign of a king as a judgment from Yahweh for the king's sin. There are three major interests which surface in Chr's omissions, additions, and changes in his K *Vorlage*: the Davidic monarchy, the cult and its personnel—especially the Levites, and pan-Israel. These are the same

themes encountered in 1 C, and they accord well with the view
of Chr's work as a program for the restoration movement shortly
after 520 B.C.

Chr also presents his belief in Yahweh's immediate retribution through his structuring of the narratives. He frequently
periodizes a king's reign. The first part of the reign prospers
because the king is faithful to Yahweh. But the king's reign ends
in tragedy as a result of his sin and Yahweh's subsequent punishment. This periodization also affords Chr the opportunity to
present a prophecy–fulfillment schema. Between the king's sins
and his punishment C often relates the oracle of a prophetic
figure who foretells the king's punishment. The punishment then
comes about precisely as forecast.

NOTES

/1/ J. D. Shenkel has provided a preliminary discussion of the history of
K's text, especially of the Greek recensions. See his *Chronology*, 4–21.

/2/ Fragments of K were found in caves 4, 5, and 6. The fragments
from caves 5 and 6 have been published by M. Baillet and J. T. Milik in
DJD III, 107–12 (6Q) and 171–72 (5Q). The material from cave 5 consists
of three fragments of 1 K 1:1, 16–17, 27–37 and agrees in all extant
readings with M. Cave 6 contained over ninety fragments, most of which
have yet to be identified. Eighteen of these fragments have been
identified and comprise parts of nine passages: 1 K 3:12–14; 12:28–31; 2 K
5:26; 6:32; 7:8–10; 7:20–8:5; 9:1–2; 10:19b–21. The only significant
readings among this group occur in 7:8–10 and 7:20–8:5 where, as Baillet
observed, the fragment attests a shorter text than M and shows occasional
agreement with G and the Vulgate. As Shenkel notes (*Chronology*, 3,
n. 14) the significant point is the agreement of the fragments with
Lucianic readings. The 4QKgs[a] material is unpublished. Professor Cross
has graciously allowed me access to these readings. Here there are
fragments of 1 K 7:20–21, 25–27, 29–31, 31–42; 8:1–9, 16–17. The extant
readings in these fragments agree for the most part with M. The one
major difference between the two is in 8:16 where 4QKgs[a] includes a part
of a reading found in 2 C 6:5–6 but lacking in K[M] and only partially
represented in G[B](K and C). This reading has been lost from K[M] by
haplography (see section III). The Greek readings also represent
haplographies caused in the Greek traditions by homoioarchton in the
words καὶ (οὐχ) ἐξελεξάμην. Thus, the agreement of 4QKgs[a] and C[M] at

this point is not particularly meaningful. In spite of its paucity, the 4QKgs[a] fragments offer significant evidence in their agreement with K[M] and C[M] against the OG. This evidence is explored in the excursus.

/3/ Barthélemy, *Les devanciers*, 89–143. See Shenkel, *Chronology*, 11–18.

/4/ Lemke, "Synoptic Problem," 362–63.

/5/ Compare the similar conclusion reached for C's report of the reigns of David, Hezekiah, and Josiah by M. Cogan, "Tendentious Chronology."

/6/ "Synoptic Studies," 93

/7/ *CMHE*, 274–85.

/8/ *Chronikbücher*, 207.

/9/ Lemke, "Synoptic Studies," 107. Cf. P. Joüon, *Grammaire de l'hébreu biblique* (revised edition; Rome: Pontifical Biblical Institute, 1965) para. 167 .

/10/ "Judicial Reform," 74–82. Cf. F. M. Cross and G. E. Wright, "The Boundary and Promise: Lists of the Kingdom of Judah," *JBL* 75 (1956): 202–6.

/11/ See Petersen's summaries in *Late Israelite Prophecy*, 70–71.

/12/ Ibid., 69–77.

/13/ Shenkel, *Chronology*, 102.

/14/ Thus, I am not convinced as is Williamson (*Israel*, 102) that "Israel" here refers to the Southern kingdom or that the title ראשי אבות ישראל is merely a holdover from the United Monarchy (ibid., 107). It is possible that Chr's use of "Israel" here reflects a belief that there were actually representatives of all the tribes living in Judah. Even if Williamson is correct about the meaning of "Israel" here, the entire passage displays Chr's desire to involve all the people. Obviously, he cannot explicitly include the Northern inhabitants in the coronation of a Southern king.

/15/ A note of caution is in order here. I have argued that Chr composed many of the speeches because of the parallel in ancient methods of historiography (Chap. 3, n. 13) and because the speeches often bear traces of Chr's interests. However, C frequently cites prophetic sources, and some of the speeches in C may well derive from them. It is also possible that he has composed some of the speeches on the basis of other sources as he composed the speeches in 1 C 22:6–16; 28:11–19; and 2 C 7:13–15 on the basis of material in S and K.

/16/ Rudolph, *Chronikbücher*, 205–7.

/17/ Rudolph, *Chronikbücher*, 218, and Curtis and Madsen, *Chronicles* 353.

/18/ See Lemke, "Synoptic Studies," 119.

/19/ So Ackroyd, *I & II Chronicles*, 122. Cf. Lemke ("Synoptic Studies," 120) who disagrees with Ackroyd.

/20/ Lemke, "Synoptic Studies," 137–38.

/21/ *Israel*, 108–9.

/22/ Ibid., 109.

/23/ Contra Rudolph, *Chronikbücher*, 227, and especially von Rad, *Geschichtsbild*, 30–31.

/24/ Rudolph, *Chronikbücher*, 241.

/25/ Rudolph, *Chronikbücher*, 263. However, Rudolph also argues that vv 31–32 are secondary, and in this I disagree. His main argument that similar information is found in 2 C 17:1–3 is insufficient to regard 20:31–32 as secondary.

/26/ Cf. Rudolph, *Chronikbücher*, 269, and Lemke, "Synoptic Studies," 175–76.

/27/ C's version of the name, יהושבעת, as over against K's, יהושבע, reflects a tendency to add ת to obviously feminine names. See M. Coogan, "The Use of Second Person Singular Verbal Forms in Northwest Semitic Personal Names," *Orientalia* 44 (1975): 194–95.

/28/ So Rudolph, *Chronikbücher*, 199 and Lemke, "Synoptic Studies," 88–89.

/29/ Lemke, "Synoptic Studies," 110. Lemke gives the reference to commentators who hold this view.

/30/ Kittel (*Chronik*, 120) and Rudolph (*Chronikbücher*, 219) hold that Chr has omitted the narrative about Pharaoh giving Gezer to Solomon (1 K 9:16) because it detracted from Solomon's power and prestige. This view is not convincing, since the story could have the opposite interpretation, i.e., Solomon's position in the world is enhanced by the fact that he has a marriage alliance with Pharaoh. The verse is also lacking in B (K). Cf. Lemke, "Synoptic Problem," 358–59. Rudolph also argues (219) that Chr has changed Tamar in the list of cities (1 K 9:18) to Tadmor (Palmyra) in order to enlarge Solomon's kingdom (2 C 8:4). Another view is that the association of Tadmor here with Hamath-Zobah is an anachronism which reflects the Assyrian-Babylonian-Persian system of provincial government. See Williamson, *Israel*, 84. The view goes back to Noth, as Williamson notes. The problem with both of these views is that there is no certainty that Chr made any change in his *Vorlage* here. The *Qere'* in 1 K 9:18 also has תדמר in place of תמר. Obviously, the two names were confused because of their graphic similarity. Even if C's reading is an anachronism, there is no guarantee that Chr is responsible. It probably existed already in the list used by him.

/31/ Cf. M. P. Graham, "The Composition of 2 Chronicles 24," *Christian Teaching* (Abilene, TX: Biblical Research Press) 138, 142.

/32/ Ibid., 148, n. 36, for different views that have been proposed in the commentaries. Commentators disagree as to exactly what Chr's *Tendenz* here might be. While it is true that C denies burial in the royal cemetery to some wicked kings (Jehoram, 2 C 21:20; Ahaz, 2 C 28:27), it allows Rehoboam to be buried with his fathers (2 C 12;16), and in the case of other wicked kings C mentions no judgment of them in their burial (Asa, 2 C 16:14; Ahaziah, 2 C 22:9; Manasseh, 2 C 33:20). Thus, the inconsistency is too great to establish any definite tendentious change on the part of Chr.

/33/ Ibid., 147, and the commentators cited there. Also, Torrey, *Ezra Studies*, 212f.

/34/ The element *zbd* derives from an Aramaic root meaning "to give." The name is especially popular in the post-exilic period. See M. Noth, *Die israelitischen Personnamen im Rahmen der gemeinsemitischen Namengebung* (Stuttgart: W. Kohlhammer, 1928) 46–47 and M. Coogan, *West Semitic Personal Names in the Murašu Documents* (HSM 7; Missoula, MT: Scholars Press, 1976) 71–72. The original K reading was probably ויוזכר as in a number of K manuscripts. However, the fact that other K manuscript have ויוזבד shows that C did not change his *Vorlage*.

/35/ Cf. Myers, *II Chronicles*, 139. The expansion may have occurred as a result of שמעת being construed as a feminine name. See J. Gray, *I and II Kings* (OTL; London: SCM, 1963) 534–35.

/36/ Curtis and Madsen (*Chronicles*, 461), and Lemke ("Synoptic Studies," 211–12), argue that Chr exaggerates in this datum.

/37/ *II Chronicles*, 163–64. Cf. also Hoffmann, *Reform*, 145.

Excursus

CHR'S K *VORLAGE*

The 4QSam[a] fragments have made it clear that Chr used a text of S that was different from S[M]. However, the situation in regard to Chr's *Vorlage* of K is not necessarily the same as it is for his *Vorlage* of S. Influenced by the striking evidence of 4QSam[a], Lemke and others assume that C's K *Vorlage* differed from K[M] without taking into account the different situation presented by the textual evidence of K./1/ The purpose of this excursus is to examine the textual evidence of 2 C//K in an effort to determine whether C's K *Vorlage* was of the same type as K[M]. I am not concerned here with establishing the affiliation of all the witnesses of the text of K to each other and to textual families. This is a complex problem, and the sparse evidence is difficult to interpret. Rather, my primary concern here is with K[M] and C[M] and their relationship to each other. Other witnesses are considered as they contribute to an understanding of this relationship.

I have limited the investigation to those passages in K where the OG is extant (1 K 2:12–21:29) and where C contains a parallel. Therefore, I will deal with thirteen passages in 1 K in the major textual witnesses (M, OG, L) in comparison with C[M]. Two classes of readings will be studied: K[M] = C[M] ≠ OG,L and C[M] = OG ≠ K[M]. The variants in each of the thirteen passages will be listed and discussed under these two categories. In each case an attempt will be made to form a judgment as to the original reading and how the variant readings have come about. The major concern in this process is not quantity but quality of variants. If two texts agree in an error, a relationship between them may be indicated. If such agreement is consistent one may conclude that the texts are affiliated. The comparison of the witnesses should reveal whether there is a pattern of affiliation between K[M] and C[M]. Those passages where the only difference between the witnesses concerns the conjunction or the article are omitted from consideration.

I. $K^M = C^M \neq OG, L$

A. 1 K 7:23–26 (OG = 7:10–12)//2 C 4:1–5/2/

(1) 1 K 7:23 M: הים מוצק

    7:10 OG,L: $\tau\eta\nu$ $\theta\alpha\lambda\alpha\sigma\sigma\alpha\nu$

2 C 4:2 M: הים מוצק

K^M and C^M agree in an expansion. The agreement is made more significant by the fact that the reading is ungrammatical. מוצק is a hophal participle used adjectivally and as such requires an article.

(2) 1 K 7:23 M: עגל סביב

    7:10 OG: $\sigma\tau\rho o\gamma\gamma\upsilon\lambda o\nu$ $\kappa\upsilon\kappa\lambda\omega$ τo $\alpha\upsilon\tau o$

        L: $\sigma\tau\rho o\gamma\gamma\upsilon\lambda\eta\nu$ $\kappa\upsilon\kappa\lambda\omega$ $\alpha\upsilon\tau\eta\varsigma$

2 C 4:2 M: עגול סביב

The OG and L apparently agree in reading a suffix (סביבו). This is probably the result of minor expansion.

(3) 1 K 7:23 M: שלשים

    7:10 OG,L: $\tau\rho\epsilon\iota\varsigma$ (L:$\tau\rho\iota\omega\nu$) $\kappa\alpha\iota$ $\tau\rho\iota\alpha\kappa o\nu\tau\alpha$

2 C 4:2 M: שלשים

The reading reflected in the OG and L is probably the result of dittography.

(4) 1 K 7:23 M: יסב אתו סביב

    7:10 OG: omit

        L: יסב אתו ($\epsilon\kappa\upsilon\kappa\lambda o\upsilon\nu$ $\alpha\upsilon\tau\eta\nu$)

2 C 4:2 M: יסב אתו סביב

The OG's reading makes little sense and is probably corrupt. The reading in L may be original. If so, K^M and C^M agree in an expansion.

(5) 1 K 7:24 M: מקפים את הים סביב שני טורים הפקעים יצקים ביצקתו

    7:11 OG: $\kappa\upsilon\kappa\lambda o\theta\epsilon\nu$

        L: $\alpha\nu\iota\sigma\tau\alpha\nu$ $\tau\eta\nu$ $\theta\alpha\lambda\alpha\sigma\sigma\alpha\nu$ $\delta\upsilon o$ $\sigma\tau\iota\chi o\iota$ $\tau\omega\nu$ $\upsilon\pi o\sigma\tau\eta\rho\iota\gamma$-$\mu\alpha\tau\omega\nu$ $\kappa\epsilon\chi\upsilon\mu\epsilon\nu o\iota$ $\epsilon\nu$ $\tau\eta$ $\chi\upsilon\sigma\epsilon\iota$ $\alpha\upsilon\tau\eta\varsigma$ $\epsilon\sigma\tau\omega\tau\epsilon\varsigma$

2 C 4:3 M: מקיפים את הים סביב שנים טורים הבקר יצוקים במצקתו

No mechanism for haplography is evident in the OG. However, the repetition of $\kappa\upsilon\kappa\lambda o\theta\epsilon\nu$ is superfluous and may indicate that the OG is corrupt. The only significant difference between K^M and C^M is the word בקר//פקעים. The meaning of

פקעים is obscure, and it occurs only in this context. It has been changed to בקר(ים) throughout this context in C because it was not understood. The graphic similarity between the two words probably contributed to the change.

(6) 1 K 7:25–26 (OG = 7:13, 12)//1 C 4:4–5

The order of these two verses in the OG and L is the reverse of that shared by K^M and C^M. It is impossible to determine which order is correct.

(7) 1 K 7:25 M: עמד על שני עשר בקר

7:13 OG,L: και δωδεκα βοες υποκατω της θαλασσης

2 C 4:4 M: עומד על שנים עשר בקר

The clauses are reversed, and it is unclear which reading is original.

(8) 1 K 7:25 M: והים עליהם מלמעלה לכל אחריהם ביתה

7:13 OG,L: וכל אחריהם ביתה והים עליהם מלמעלה = και παντα (L: παντων) τα οπισθια εις τον οικον (L: ενδον) και η θαλασσα επ' αυτων επανωθεν

2 C 4:4 M: והים עליהם מלמעלה וכל אחריהם ביתה

The clauses are reversed in the witnesses, and it is unclear which reading is original.

(9) 1 K 7:26 M: ועביו טפח ושפתו כמעשה שפת כום פרח שושן

4QKgs^a: [ועביו טפח ושפתו כמעש]ה שפת כום פרח שושן

7:12 OG,L: ושפתו כמעשה שפת כום פרח שושן(ה) ועביו טפח = και το χειλος αυτης ως (L: ωσει) εργον χειλους ποτηριου βλαστος (L: -τον) κρινου και το παχος αυτου (L: -της) παλαιστης

2 C 4:5 M: ועביו טפח ושפתו כמעשה שפת כום פרח שושנה

Again the clauses are reversed, and the original reading is uncertain. 4QKgs^a agrees with K^M and C^M.

B. 1 K 7:39b–8:11 (OG = 7:25b–37; 8:1–11)//2 C 4:10–5:11
(1) 1 K 7:39b M: נתן

7:25b OG: omit

L: εθετο

2 C 4:10 M: נתן

There is no mechanism for the loss of נתן in the OG. It is probably an expansion in the other witnesses.

(2) 1 K 7:41 M: אשר על ראש העמודים

7:27 OG,L: אשר על העמודים (τα οντα επι των στυλων)

2 C 4:12 M: אשר על ראש העמודים

Haplography in the Greek is possible: (των κεφαλον) των στυλων. However, the mechanism is not compelling, and ראש appears expansionistic. The shorter reading is probably original.

(3) 1 K 7:42 M: שתי גלות הכתרת אשר

7:28 OG: αμφοτερα τα οντα τα στρεπτα της μεχωνωθ

L: αμφοτερα τα στρεπτα της μεχωνωθ τα οντα

2 C 4:13 M: שתי גלות הכתרות אשר

The OG reflects a misplacement of אשר. Both the OG and L read המכנות where C^M and K^M have הכתרות. The reading of K^M, C^M, and L is probably original at this point, since the מכנות are not really introduced until the next verse.

(4) 1 K 7:45-47 M: ואת הסירות ואת היעים ואת המזרקות ואת כל הכלים
האהל אשר עשה חירם למלך שלמה בית יהוה נחשת ממרט (46) בככר
הירדן יצקם המלך במעבה האדמה בין סכות ובין צרתן (47) וינח
שלמה את כל הכלים מרב מאד מאד לא נחקר משקל הנחשת

7:31-33 OG: και τους λεβητας και τας θερμαστρεις και τας
φιαλας και παντα τα σκευη α εποιησεν χειραμ τω βασιλει
Σαλομων τω οικω Κυριου και οι στυλοι τεσσερακοντα και οκτω
του οικου του βασιλεως και του οικου Κυριου παντα τα εργα του
βασιλεως εποιησεν Χειραμ χαλκα αρδην (32) ουκ ην σταθμος
του χαλκου ου εποιησεν παντα τα εργα ταυτα εκ πληθους
σφοδρα ουκ ην τερμα των σταθμων του χαλκου (33) εν τω
περιοικω του Ιορδανου εχωνευσεν αυτα εν τω παχει της γης ανα
μεσον Σοκχωθ και ανα μεσον Σειρα

L: και τους λεβητας και τας θερμαστρεις και τας φιαλας και
παντα τα σκευη συνετελεσεν α εποιησεν Χειραμ τω βασιλει
Σολομωντι εν τω οικω Κυριου και οι στυλοι τεσσερακοντα και
οκτω του οικου του Κυριου και του οικου του βασιλεως παντα τα
εργα α εποιησεν Χειραμ χαλκα ην (32) ουκ ην σταθμος του
χαλκου ου εποιησεν αρδην παντα τα σκευη α εποιησε εκ του
πληθους σφοδρα ουκ ην τερμα τω σταθμω του χαλκου (33) εν τη
περιοικω του Ιορδανου εχωευσεν αυτα εν τω παχει της γης ανα
μεσον Σοκχωθ και ανα μεσον Σαρθαν

2 C 4:16-18 M: ואת הסירות ואת היעים ואת המזלגות ואת כל כליהם
עשה חורם אביו למלך שלמה לבית יהוה נחשת מרוק (17) בככר הירדן

יצקם המלך בעבי האדמה בין סכות ובין צרדתה (18) ויעש שלמה כל
הכלים האלה לרב מאד כי לא נחקר משקל הנחשת

The OG and L attest two lengthy plusses vis-à-vis K^M and
C^M, and there is reason to suspect haplography in K^M and C^M in
both cases. The first plus is in 1 K 7:31, καὶ οἱ
στυλοι . . . εποιησεν Χειραμ. I reconstruct the OG version of the
plus as follows:

והעמודים ארבעים ושמנה לבית המלך ולבית
יהוה. כל מלאכת המלך עשה חירם

The differences in the L version of the plus are minor except for
the reversal of the phrases לבית המלך and לבית יהוה. The plus
does not appear expansionistic. While no exact mechanism for
haplography is apparent, the phrases (אשר) עשה חירם and (ל)בית
יהוה occur just before the beginning of the plus and near the end
of it. If the order of the elements in the plus were transposed in
some version of it so that it ended with (ל)בית יהוה, haplography
could easily be occasioned by homoioteleuton. The transposition
of phrases in the versions of this plus in the OG and L shows
that such a possibility is not far-fetched.

The second plus is 1 K 7:32 in the OG and L. The real
difference here is actually one of order. In K^M and C^M the
reference to Solomon's making all the vessels and their weight
occurs in v 47//v 18 after the information about where he made
them (v 46//v 17). This latter verse seems intrusive, and the
order in the OG and L is probably better. The best reading at
the end of v 45 is probably simply נחשת. This reading is attested
by L and supported by what appear to be independent
expansions in K^M (ממרט) and C^M (מרוק). If נחשת alone is correct
it provides a good mechanism for the loss of the material in v 47
from its original position. In short, I regard the longer reading of
the OG and L as essentially primitive./3/ The agreement of K^M
and C^M is very significant. Not only do they agree in a
haplography but both reflect the reinsertion of the lost material
(v 47//v 18) in the wrong place.

(5) 1 K 7:48 M: ויעש שלמה

    7:34 OG: καὶ ελαβεν ο βασιλευς Σαλωμων

        L: καὶ εδωκεν Σολομων (+ ο βασιλευς b,o)

2 C 4:19 M: ויעש שלמה

המלך as reflected in the OG and L (b,o) is an expansion. The
difference in the initial verb is connected with the next variant.

(6) 1 K 7:48 M: אשר בית יהוה

    17:34 OG: אשר עשה בבית (α εποιησεν εν οικω)

    L: אשר עשה בבית יהוה (α εποιησεν τω οικω Κυριου)

2 C 4:19 M: אשר בית האלהים

K^M probably represents the original reading. The change of
יהוה to האלהים in C is common and probably comes from a pious
scribe. Thus, K^M and C^M have essentially the same reading. The
syntax of the phrase אשר בית in K^M and C^M is somewhat unusual
and may have motivated the addition of ב and the change of the
initial verb ויעש (see above).

(7) 1 K 7:50 M: לדלתי הבית להיכל

    17:36 OG, L: και τας θυρας του ναου (ודלתי ההיכל)

2 C 4:22 M: ודלתי הבית להיכל

The reading in K^M and C^M is probably due to conflation or
expansion.

(8) 1 K 7:51 M: כל המלאכה

    7:37 OG,L: המלאכה (το εργον)

2 C 5:1 M: כל המלאכה

כל is a minor expansion in K^M and C^M.

(9) 1 K 7:51 M: omit

    7:37 OG,L: ואת כל קדשי שלמה (και παντα τα αγια Σαλωμων
[L: Σολομωντας])

2 C 5:1 M: omit

This line is probably an expansion in the Greek witnesses.

(10) 1 K 7:51 M: ואת הכלים

    17:37 OG: omit

    L: και τα σκευη

2 C 5:1 M: ואת כל הכלים

The OG is probably original here. K^M and C^M agree in
expansion, though C^M further expands with the addition of כל.

(11) 1 K 8:1 M: omit

    OG,L: και εγενετο ως συνετελεσεν (L: εν τω συντελεσαι)
Σαλωμων (L: Σολομωντα) του οιχοδομησαι τον οικον Κυριου και
τον οικον εαυτου (L: αυτου) μετα εικοσι ετη

2 C 5:2 M: omit

The OG and L apparently expand on the basis of 1 K 9:10.

There is no mechanism that would explain the loss of this material from K^M and C^M.

(12) 1 K 8:1 M: שלמה

OG,L: ο βασιλευς Σαλωμων (L: Σολομων)

2 C 5:2M: שלמה

The OG and L reflect an expansion.

(13) 1 K 8:1 M: זקני ישראל ואת כל ראשי המטות נשיאי האבות לבני
                                    ישראל אל המלך שלמה ירושלם

4QKgs^a:/4/   [זקני ישראל ואת כל ר]אשי המטות נשי[אי האבות לבני
                                   ישראל אל המלך שלמה ירושלם]

OG,L: παντας τους πρεσβυτερους Ισραηλ εν Σειων
                             כל זקני ישראל בציון =

2 C 5:2 M: זקני ישראל ואת כל ראשי המטות נשיאי האבות לבני
                                    ישראל אל ירושלם

The כל and בציון reflected in the OG and L are probably expansions. Otherwise, the reading of the OG and L is original here. K^M, 4QKgs^a, and C^M are expansionistic. What is more striking, however, is the content of their plus. The three-fold reference to the elders of Israel, the heads of the tribes, and the leaders of the fathers' houses seems to fit with Chr's pan-Israel interest. The words נשיא and מטה are not common in DH or C. They are characteristically P words./5/ The plus was apparently introduced by a priestly redactor into a textual family of K represented by K^M and 4QKgs^a. The plus was later copied by Chr whose K *Vorlage* was of that same textual family.

(14) 1 K 8:2–3 M: ויקהלו אל המלך שלמה כל איש ישראל בירח האתנים
                               בחג הוא החדש השביעי (3) ויבאו כל זקני ישראל

4QKgs^a: [ויקהלו אל המלך (שלמה) כול איש ישראל בירח האתני]ם
                             בחג הוא חדש הש[ביעי ויבואו כל זקני ישראל]

OG,L: εν μηνι Αθαμειν

2 C 5:3–4 M: ויקהלו אל המלך כל איש ישראל בחג הוא החדש
                            השבעי (4) ויבאו כל זקני ישראל

The OG and L probably contain the original reading here. The plus in K^M and C^M again accords with Chr's pan-Israel interest. Also the reference to the festival (*Sukkōt*) in the seventh month seems to reflect Chr's concern for the cult (cf. pp. 96–97 on 2 C 7:8//1 K 8:65). But in this context the plus must be seen as the work of a priestly redactor.

(15) 1 K 8:4 M: ויעלו את ארון יהוה
    4QKgs[a]: [ויע]לו את ארון יהוה
      OG,L: omit
2 C 5:5 M: ויעלו את הארון

The reading of C[M] is primitive. The divine name in K[M] and 4QKgs[a] is an expansion. The OG and L reflect the loss of this phrase by haplography occasioned by the repetition of את הארון.

(16) 1 K 8:4 M: באהל
    OG,L: באהל מועד (εν τω σκηνωματι του μαρτυριου)
2 C 5:5 M: באהל

The OG and L expand slightly.

(17) 1 K 8:4 M: כל כלי
      L: παντα τα σκευη
    OG: τα σκευη
2 C 5:5 M: כל כלי

The reading of K[M], C[M], and L is a minor expansion.

(18) 1 K 8:4 M: ויעלו אתם הכהנים והלוים
    4QKgs[a]: [ויעלו אתם ה]כהנים והלוים
      OG,L: omit
2 C 5:5 M: העלו אתם הכהנים הלוים (24 MSS: והלוים)

K[M] and C[M] attest essentially the same reading. The difference between ויעלו and העלו is the result of graphic confusion of ה nd י./6/ The line seems to reflect Chr's interest in the cultic personnel. It is another priestly addition to the text of K reflected in K[M], 4QKgs[a], and Chr's *Vorlage*.

(19) 1 K 8:5 M: והמלך שלמה
    4QKgs[a]: והמלך שלמה
      OG,L: και ο βασιλευς
2 C 5:6 M: והמלך שלמה

K[M], C[M], and 4QKgs[a] agree in an expansion.

(20) 1 K 8:5 M: וכל עדת ישראל הנועדים עליו
    OG: και πας Ισραηλ
      L: και πας ο λαος
2 C 5:6 M: וכל עדת ישראל הנועדים עליו

The text represented by K[M] and C[M] attests an expansion.

The use of עדת is unusual in DH. It is P language. However, it is also uncommon in C./7/ This plus is another priestly addition to this textual tradition of K.

(21) 1 K 8:5 M: אשר לא יספרו ולא ימנו מרב

    4QKgs[a]: אשר לא יספרו ולא [ימנו מרב]

    OG,L: αναριθμητα

2 C 5:6 M: אשר לא יספרו ולא ימנו מרב

The reading in K[M], 4QKgs[a], and C[M] seems conflate. However, this expression may be something of a cliche, and the *Vorlage* of the Greek is uncertain (cf. 1 K 3:8 where the same phrase is encountered and the same Greek translation occurs). The original reading, then, remains uncertain.

(22) 1 K 8:6 M: ארון ברית יהוה

    OG,L: הארון (την κιβωτον)

2 C 5:7 M: ארון ברית יהוה

The two Hebrew witnesses agree in expansion.

(23) 1 K 8:8 M: ויהיו שם עד היום הזה

    OG,L: omit

2 C 5:9 M: ויהי שם עד היום הזה

The minus in the Greek witnesses is probably due to haplography triggered by homoioteleuton (החוצה . . . הזה).

C. 1 K 8:12–50//2 C 6:1–39

(1) 1 K 8:12–13 M: אז אמר שלמה יהוה אמר לשכן בערפל (13) בנה
    בניתי בית זבל לך מכון לשבתך עולמים

    8:53 OG: τοτε ελαλησεν Σαλωμων υπερ του οικου ως συνετελεσεν του οικοδομησαι αυτον Ηλιον εγνωρισεν εν ουρανω Κυριος ειπεν του κατοικειν εκ γνοφου οικοδομησον οικον μου οικον εκπρεπη σεαυτω του καοικειν επι καινοτητος.

2 C 6:1–2 M: אז אמר שלמה יהוה אמר לשכן בערפל (2) ואני
    בניתי בית זבל לך ומכון לשבתך עולמים

Gray has shown that the Greek version of this poem reflects a better text than that preserved in K[M] and C[M]./8/ The fact that K[M] and C[M] essentially agree in this fragmentary version of the poem and in its placement is significant.

(2) 1 K 8:14 M: ויברך
       OG: ויברך המלך (και ευλογησεν ο βασιλευς)
        L: και ευλογησεν
2 C 6:3 M: ויברך

The OG contains an independent expansion.

(3) 1 K 8:14 M: קהל ישראל
       OG,L: Ισραηλ
2 C 6:4 M: קהל ישראל

K^M and C^M agree in an expansion which has probably entered by attraction to the next phrase.

(4) 1 K 8:15 M: ישראל
       OG,L: ישראל היום (Ισραηλ σημερον)
2 C 6:4 M: ישראל

The OG and L again attest an independent expansion.

(5) 1 K 8:15 M: את דוד
       OG,L: על דוד (περι Δαυειδ)
2 C 6:4 M: את דויד

It is uncertain which variant is original.

(6) 1 K 8:16 M: מכל שבטי
       OG,L: בשבט אחד (εν ενι σκηπτρω)
2 C 6:5 M: מכל שבטי

Again it is difficult to determine which variant is original.

(7) 1 K 8:17–18 M: עם לבב
       OG,L: על לבב (επι της/την καρδιας/ν)
2 C 6:7–8 M: עם לבב

This variation in prepositions occurs three times in these two verses. In each case the Hebrew witnesses attest עם, and the Greek witnesses על (επι). It seems likely that the original text used different prepositions in different cases and that the witnesses have simply levelled through one of the prepositions in every case.

(8) 1 K 8:17 M: דוד אבי
       OG: אבי (του πατρος μου)
        L: Δαδ του πατρος μου
2 C 6:7 M: דויד אבי

K^M, L, and C^M agree in an expansion.

(9) 1 K 8:19 M: רק אתה

    OG: אתה (συ)

     L: רק אתה (πλην συ)

2 C 6:9 M: רק אתה

The OG is probably original. It is easy to see how רק could come in secondarily for the sake of sense.

(10) 1 K 8:20 M: דבר יהוה

    OG: דבר (ελαλησεν)

     L: ειπεν Κυριος

2 C 6:10 M: דבר יהוה

The addition of the divine name is an expansion.

(11) 1 K 8:23 M: לעבדיך ההלכים לפניך בכל לבם

    OG: τω δουλω σου τω πορευομενω ενωπιον σου εν ολη τη καρδια αυτου

     L: τω δουλω σου Δαδ τω πρι μου τω πεπορευμενω ενωπιον σου εν αληθεια και εν ολη τη καρδια αυτου

2 C 6:14 M: לעבדיך ההלכים לפניך בכל לבם

The Greek witnesses attest singular forms where the Hebrew have plurals. The reason for this consistent difference may be the desire to identify David or Solomon as Yahweh's servant (v 24). If so, the text with the plural forms is original. The other variants in L are expansions.

(12) 1 K 8:24 M: את אשר דברת לו ותדבר בפיך

    OG,L: דברת בפיך (και γαρ ελαλησας εν τω στοματι σου)

2 C 6:15 M: את אשר דברת לו ותדבר בפיך

The Greek witnesses attest a haplography apparently triggered by the similarity of דברת and ותדבר.

(13) 1 K 8:26 M: אשר דברת

    OG,L: omit

2 C 6:17 M: אשר דברת

Haplography in the Greek witnesses is possible here. A mechanism exists in the similarity of דבר(י)ך and דברת. However, expansion in the Hebrew witnesses is also possible.

(14) 1 K 8:27 M: אַף כִּי

       OG: πλην και

        L: πως

2 C 6:18 M: אַף כִּי

The *Vorlagen* of the OG and L are uncertain. The reading of K^M and C^M is probably original, and the OG and L may simply represent efforts to translate אַף כי.

(15) 1 K 8:27 M: omit

       OG,L: לִשְׁמֶךָ (τω ονοματι σου)

2 C 6:18 M: omit

The OG and L expand here.

(16) 1 K 8:28 M: אל תפלת עבדך ואל תחנתו

       OG,L: על תחנתי (επι την δεησιν μου)

2 C 6:19 M: אל תפלת עבדך ואל תחנתו

The OG and L attest a haplography, triggered by homoioarchton: אל ת . . . ואל ת. The other variants are insignificant.

(17) 1 K 8:28 M: אלהי

       OG,L: ο θεος Ισραηλ

2 C 6:19 M: אלהי

The text represented by the OG and L expands.

(18) 1 K 8:28 M: אל הרנה ואל התפלה

       OG: הרנה (της τερψεως)

        L: της δεησεως και της προσευχης = התחנה והתפלה

2 C 6:19 M: אל הרנה ואל התפלה

The original text was probably הרנה (אל). The OG apparently translates this. K^M and C^M expand it. L also expands, probably on the basis of the material earlier in the verse.

(19) 1 K 8:29 M: omit

       OG,L: ημερας και νυκτος (2)

2 C 6:20 M: omit

The expansion in the Greek witnesses is probably borrowed from earlier in the verse.

(20) 1 K 8:30 M: שמעת

       OG,L: ועשית (και ποιησεις)

2 C 6:21 M: שמעת

The Greek reading is probably original (cf. v 32). The verb שׁמעת occurs twice previously in this verse and probably influenced the change in K^M and C^M.

(21) 1 K 8:31 M: ונשׁא

      OG,L: και εαν λαβη (ואם נשׁא)

2 C 6:22 M: ונשׁא

The Greek reading is either an expansion or the result of the translation process.

(22) 1 K 8:32 M: עבדיך

      OG,L: עמך ישׁראל (τον λαον σου Ισραηλ)

2 C 6:23 M: עבדיך

"Israel" in the Greek is probably an expansion. עבדיך and ימך are simply variants, and it is hard to determine which is original (cf. on 8:36 below).

(23) 1 K 8:32 M: בראשׁו

      OG,L: לראשׁו (εις κεφαλην αυτου)

2 C 6:23 M: בראשׁו

The preposition ל may well be original here, since ב is the more common idiom.

(24) 1 K 8:33 M: לפני אויב

      OG: לפני אויבים (ενωπιον εχθρων)

      L: ενωπιον σου και πεσειν ενωπιον εχθρων αυτων

2 C 6:24 M: לפני אויב

L expands. The OG disagrees with the Hebrew witnesses only in reading the plural, אויבים. The singular is probably original.

(25) 1 K 8:36 M: ואתה תשׁמע

      OG,L: ותשׁמע (και εισακουση)

2 C 6:27 M: ואתה תשׁמע

The addition of the pronoun is probably an expansion.

(26) 1 K 8:36 M: עבדיך

      OG,L: עבדך (του δουλου σου)

2 C 6:27 M: עבדיך

The singular, identifying Solomon as Yahweh's servant, is probably original. The plural has likely come in under the influence of the plural forms in the previous verse.

(27) 1 K 8:36 M: אשר ילכו
      OG,L: ללכת (πορευεσθαι)
  2 C 6:27 M: אשר ילכו

The evidence does not indicate which variant is original.

(28) 1 K 8:36 M: על ארצך
        OG: על הארץ (επι την γην)
         L: επι την γην σου
  2 C 6:27 M: על ארצך

The suffix in K^M and C^M is an expansion.

(29) 1 K 8:36 M: לעמך
        OG: לעבדך (τω δουλω σου)
         L: τω λαω σου
  2 C 6:27 M: לעבדך

The variation here is probably due to graphic confusion between מ and כד./9/ Either reading could have produced the other, so the original reading is uncertain.

(30) 1 K 8:37 M: בארץ
      OG,L: omit
  2 C 6:28 M: בארץ

The Hebrew witnesses agree in expansion.

(31) 1 K 8:37 M: דבר כי יהיה
      OG,L: (L:και) θανατος εαν γενηται, οτι εσται
  2 C 6:28 דבר כי יהיה

The Greek witnesses attest an inner-Greek conflation. Both εαν γενηται and οτι εσται appear to translate כי יהיה.

(32) 1 K 8:37 M: שדפון ירקון ארבה חסיל
      OG,L: ευπυρισμος βρουχος ερυσιβη = שדפון ארבה ירקון
  2 C 6:28 M: שדפון ירקון ארבה חסיל

If the retroversions for the Greek words are correct, then חסיל in K^M and C^M is an expansion or conflation with ארבה. The order of ירקון and ארבה is reversed in the OG and L. The original order is uncertain.

(33) 1 K 8:37 M: בארץ שעריו
      OG,L: εν μια των πολεων αυτου = באחד שעריו
  2 C 6:28 M: בארץ שעריו

The reading in K^M and C^M is corrupt. בארץ has probably come about through graphic confusion with באחד./10/

(34) 1 K 8:38 M: לכל עמך ישראל
     OG,L: omit
  2 C 6:29 M: ולכל עמך ישראל

This line is an expansion in the Hebrew witnesses.

(35) 1 K 8:39 M: מכון
     OG,L: ממכון (ἐξ ἑτοιμου)
  2 C 6:30 M: מכון

If the retroversion is correct the additional *mem* in the OG and L is the result of dittography or expansion. However, the ἐξ could be the translator's addition since מכון stands in apposition to השמים (מן).

(36) 1 K 8:39 M: ככל דרכיו
      OG: כדרכיו (κατα τας οδους αυτου)
       L: κατα πασας τας οδους αυτου
  2 C 6:30 M: ככל דרכיו

כל in K^M, C^M, and L is probably an expansion.

(37) 1 K 8:40 M: על פני
     OG,L: על (ἐπι)
  2 C 6:31 M: על פני

K^M and C^M again expand slightly.

(38) 1 K 8:41 M: מעמך ישראל
     OG,L: מעמך (απο λαου σου)
  2 C 6:32 M: מעמך ישראל

"Israel" here is an expansion.

(39) 1 K 8:41b–42 M: (42) כי ישמעון את שמך ובא מארץ רחוקה למען שמך
הגדול ואת ידך החזקה וזרעך הנטויה ובא והתפלל אל הבית הזה
8:42 OG,L: και ηξουσιν (L: ηξει) και προσευξονται (L: -εται)
εις τον τοπον τουτον
  2 C 6:32 M: ובא מארץ רחוקה למען שמך הגדול וידך החזקה וזרוע
הנטויה ובאו והתפללו אל הבית הזה

The minus in the OG and L is due to haplography triggered by homoioarchton (ובא . . . ובא). C^M also attests a haplography occasioned by homoioteleuton (שמך . . . שמך).

(40) 1 K 8:42 M: הבית

OG,L: המקום (τον τοπον)

2 C 6:32 M: הבית

It is not certain which of these variants is original.

(41) 1 K 8:43 M: עמי הארץ

OG,L: העמים (οι λαοι)

2 C 6:33 M: עמי הארץ

The text in K^M and C^M expands.

(42) 1 K 8:45 M: ושמעת

OG,L: ואתה תשמע (και συ εισακουσει)

2 C 6:35 M: ושמעת

The Hebrew witnesses probably attest the original reading. The OG reading has come about by attraction to the phrase used in the apodosis of earlier conditions (vv 30, 32, 34, 36, 43).

(43) 1 K 8:45 M: את תפלתם ואת תחנתם

OG: της δεησεως αυτων και της προσευχης αυτων
= את תחנתם ואת תפלתם

L: της προσευχης αυτων και της δεησεως αυτων

2 C 6:35 M: את תפלתם ואת תחנתם

The order of the elements in the OG is likely original since the order of the two words תפלה and תחנה elsewhere in the chapter is that attested by K^M, C^M, and L here (cf. vv 28, 33, 38).

(44) 1 K 8:46 M: ואנפת בם

OG,L: και επαξεις (L:επ') αυτους

2 C 6:36 M: ואנפת בם

The Vorlage of the OG and L is uncertain, but they seem to reflect corruption./11/

(45) 1 K 8:47 M: והתחננו אליך בארץ שביהם

OG: εν γη μετοικιας αυτων και δεηθωσιν σου

L: και δεηθωσιν σου εν τη γη της μετοικεσιας αυτων

2 C 6:37 M: והתחננו אליך בארץ שביהם

The OG and L have understood שביהם as a reference to repentance, not captivity. The OG attests a different order of clauses from the other witnesses, and it is uncertain which is original.

(46) 1 K 8:49 M: את תפלתם ואת תחנתם ועשית משפטם

OG,L: omit

2 C 6:39 M: את תפלתם ואת תחנתיהם ועשית משפטם

There is no mechanism for haplography at this point. Thus, the plus in the Hebrew witnesses is best regarded as an expansion made on the basis of previous material (cf. v 45).

(47) 1 K 8:50 M: לעמך

OG,L: לעונותם (*ταις αδικιαις αυτων*)

2 C 6:39 M: לעמך

סלח is used twice previously (vv 34, 36) with ל plus the sin. It can also be used with ל plus the sinner./12/ Thus, neither reading has any special claim to originality. In fact, both may be expansions, the original line reading: וסלחת אשר חטאו לך.

D. 1 K 8:62–63//2 C 7:4–5

1 K 8:63 M: וצאן מאה ועשרים אלף

OG: omit

L: *και προβατων εκατον και εικοσι χιλιαδες*

2 C 7:5 M: וצאן מאה ועשרים אלף

The OG reflects a haplography triggered by homoioteleuton (אלף . . . אלף).

E. 1 K 8:64–9:3a//2 C 7:7–12a

(1) 1 K 8:66 M: וטובי לב

OG: *και αγαθη η καρδια*

L: *και αγαθη καρδια*

2 C 7:10 M: וטובי לב

It is impossible to tell which reading is original.

(2) 1 K 9:3a M: תפלתך

OG: קול תפלתך (*της φωνης της προσευχης σου*)

2 C 7:12 M: תפלתך

The reading in the OG is expansionistic.

F. 1 K 9:3b–9//2 C 7:16–22

(1) 1 K 9:3b M: והיו עיני ולבי שם כל הימים

OG: *και εσονται οι οφθαλμοι μου εκει εις τον αιωνα και η καρδια μου πασας τας ημερας*

L: *και εσονται οι οφθαλμοι μου και η καρδια μου εκει πασας τας ημερας*

2 C 7:12 M: והיו עיני ולבי שם כל הימים

The OG reading reflects expansion.

(2) 1 K 9:4 M: צויתיך

    OG,L: צויתיו (ενετειλαμην αυτω)

  2 C 7:17 M: צויתיך

It is impossible to determine which suffix is original.

(3) 1 K 9:6 M: נתתי

    OG,L: נתן משה (εδωκεν Μωυσης)

  2 C 7:19 M: נתתי

It is difficult to tell which reading is original. The OG and L may reflect an expansion. On the other hand, the first person sufixes on the previous two words could have influenced the change here.

(4) 1 K 9:9 M: מארץ מצרים

    OG: εξ Αιγυπτου εξ οικου δουλειας

    L: εξ οικου δουλειας εξ Αιγυπτου

  2 C 7:22 M: מארץ מצרים

All witnesses apparently expand. The original reading was probably simply ממצרים.

(5) 1 K 9:9 M: omit

    OG,L: τοτε ανηγαγεν Σαλωμων (L: Σολομων) την θυγατερα φαραω εκ πολεως Δαυειδ εις (L: τον) οικον αυτου ον ωκοδομησεν αυτω (L: εαυτω) εν ταις ημεραις εκειναις

  2 C 7:22 M: omit

There is no reason to suspect haplography in K[M] and C[M]. The plus in the OG and L appears to be out of place here. K[M] and C[M] have a parallel in 1 K 9:24//2 C 8:11 (see below). The OG also includes this information in 2:35–36.

G. 1 K 9:19–22 (OG = 10:23b–25)//2 C 8:6–9

(1) 1 K 9:19 M: ואת כל ערי המסכנות אשר היו לשלמה

  10:23 OG,L: omit

  2 C 8:6 M: ואת כל ערי המסכנות אשר היו לשלמה

The Greek witnesses attest a haplography here, which was triggered by homoioarchton (ואת כל ערי . . . ואת כל ערי).

(2) 1 K 9:19 M: ואת ערי פרשים

  10:23 OG,L: και πασας τας πολεις των ιππεων

  2 C 8:6 M: ואת ערי פרשים

The כל reflected in the OG and L is an expansion. כל occurs twice previously in this verse.

(3) 1 K 9:19 M: ובלבנון
    10:24 OG,L: omit
    2 C 8:6 M: ובלבנון

Since there is no mechanism for haplography in the OG and L, this plus in K^M and C^M is probably an expansion.

(4) 1 K 9:19 M: ארץ ממשלתו
    10:24 OG,L: τη γη του μη καταρξαι αυτου
    2 C 8:6 M: ארץ ממשלתו

The reading in K^M and C^M should be considered original, not only because it is shorter but also because the extent of Solomon's hegemony is increased by the Greek reading.

(5) 1 K 9:20 M: הנותר מן
    10:24 OG: του υποδεδειγμεννον υπο
       L: του υπολελειμμενον απο
    2 C 8:7 M: הנותר מן

The OG reading apparently stems from an inner-Greek, graphic confusion between λ and δ and perhaps γ and μ.

(6) 1 K 9:20 M: omit
    10:24 OG,L: και του χανavαιου
    2 C 8:7 M: omit

The OG and L probably reflect an expansion based on the elements found in this well known list in other places.

(7) 1 K 9:20 M: omit
    10:24 OG,L: και του γεργεσαιου
    2 C 8:7 M: omit

Again, the OG and L expand on the basis of previous lists.

H. 1 K 9:23–25 (OG = 2:35h, f, g)//2 C 8:10–12/13/
1 K 9:23 M: הרדים בעם
2:35h OG,L: επισταται του λαου
2 C 8:10 M: הרדים בעם

The *Vorlage* of the Greek reading is uncertain, but it probably reflects an attempt to translate the K^M reading.

I. 1 K 10:1–29//2 C 9:1–28
(1) 1 K 10:1 M: שמע
    OG,L: שם (το ονομα)
  2 C 9:1 M: שמע

The reading of the OG and L is probably original. ע came in under the influence of the verb שמעה.

(2) 1 K 10:6 M: המלך
    OG,L: τον βασιλεα Σαλωμων (L: Σολομωντα)
  2 C 9:5 M: המלך

The OG and L expand.

(3) 1 K 10:6 M: דבריך
  10:7 OG,L: דברך (του λογου)
  2 C 9:5 M: דבריך

It is impossible to tell whether the singular or plural is original here.

(4) 1 K 10:7 M: לא הגד לי החצי
      OG: ουκ εισιν το ημισυ καθως απηγγελαν μοι
       L: ουκ εστιν κατα το ημισυ καθως απηγγειλαν μοι
  2 C 9:6 M: לא הגד לי החצי

The *Vorlage* of the Greek readings is uncertain. They may be merely periphrastic renderings./14/

(5) 1 K 10:7 M: שמעתי
    OG,L: שמעתי בארצי (ηκουσα εν τη γη μου)
  2 C 9:6 M: שמעתי

The text in the Greek witnesses is expansionistic.

(6) 1 K 10:8 M: אנשיך
    OG,L: נשיך (αι γυναικες σου)
  2 C 9:7 M: אנשיך

K^M and C^M agree here in a clear error, making this reading very significant for our study.

(7) 1 K 10:8 M: חכמתך
    OG,L: כל חכמתך (πασαν την φρονησιν σου)
  2 C 9:7 M: חכמתך

The OG and L represent an expansion here.

(8) 1 K 10:9 M: ‏;לעשות משפט וצדקה

OG,L: τον ποιειν κριμα εν δικαιοσυνη και εν κριμασιν
αυτων (L: αυτου) = ‏ובמשפטם (L: ‏ובמשפטו) ‏לעשות משפט בצדקה
2 C 9:8 M: ‏לעשות משפט וצדקה

The Greek witnesses apparently represent a conflate reading.
K^M and C^M are probably original.

(9) 1 K 10:10 M: ‏למלך
OG,L: ‏לשלמה (OG: τω Σαλωμων) (L: Σολομωντι)
2 C 9:9 M: ‏למלך

It is not clear which of the variants is original.

(10) 1 K 10:12 M: ‏וכנרות ונבלים
OG,L: και ναβλας και κινυρας
2 C 9:11 M: ‏וכנרות ונבלים

The original order is uncertain.

(11) 1 K 10:13 M: ‏ועבדיה
OG,c^2,e^2: και παντες οι παιδες αυτης
b,o: και οι παιδες αυτης
2 C 9:12 M: ‏ועבדיה

The OG and the Lucianic MSS. b and o reflect expansion.

(12) 1 K 10:15 M: ‏מאנשי התרים
OG,L: των φορων των υποτεταγμενων
2 C 9:14 M: ‏מאנשי התרים

All witnesses show corruption. The reading in K^M and C^M
makes no sense in referring to men in a list of Solomon's
imports./15/ It is significant that K^M and C^M agree in this
bizarre reading.

(13) 1 K 10:16 M: ‏המלך שלמה
OG: Σαλωμων
L: ο βασιλευς Σολομων
2 C 9:15 M: ‏המלך שלמה

‏המלך is an expansion.

(14) 1 K 10:16 M: ‏מאתים
OG,L: τριακοσια
2 C 9:15 M: ‏מאתים

מאתים is probably original. "Three hundred" has probably entered the text under the influence of שלש twice in the next verse, once in the number 300.

(15) 1 K 10:16 M: שש מאות

      OG,L: שלש מאות (τριακοσια)

2 C 9:15 M: שש מאות

The reading of the Greek witnesses is probably original here, since it is the smaller figure. The loss of a ל led to the reading in K^M and C^M.

(16) 1 K 10:16 M: יעלה

      OG,L: יעלו (επησαν)

2 C 9:15 M: יעלה

The singular is probably original. The plural probably came in as the grammatically correct form.

(17) 1 K 10:19 M: וידת מזה ומזה

      OG,L: מזה ומזה (ενθεν και ενθεν)

2 C 9:18 M: וידת מזה ומזה

וידת should be regarded as original on the basis of sense. Its omission is probably due to haplography. It could be triggered by the similarity of יו in מאחריו to ת in וידת./16/

(18) 1 K 10:20 M: עמדים שם

      OG,L: עמדים (εστωτες)

2 C 9:19 M: עמדים שם

שם in the Hebrew witnesses is an expansion.

(19) 1 K 10:21 M: משקה המלך שלמה

      OG,L: τα υπο του Σαλωμων (L: Σολομωντος) γεγονοτα

2 C 9:20 M: משקה המלך שלמה

Montgomery is probably correct in regarding the Greek reading as a corruption of του ποτου του Σαλωμων γεγονοτα./17/

(20) 1 K 10:21 M: omit

      OG,L: και λουτηρες χρυσοι - וסירות זהב

2 C 9:20 M: omit

The reading in K^M and C^M appears to be haplographic due to homoioteleuton (זהב . . . זהב).

(21) 1 K 10:21 M: בית יער
     OG: δρυμου οικου
     L: οικου δρυμου
2 C 9:20 M: בית יער

The OG reading is clearly corrupt.

(22) 1 K 10:21 M: למאומה
     OG,L: omit
2 C 9:20 M: למאומה

This seems to be an expansion in the Hebrew witnesses.

(23) 1 K 10:22 M: שנהבים וקפים ותכיים
     OG,L: και λιθων τορευτων και πελεκτων
2 C 9:21 M: שנהבים וקפים ותכיים

The differences in the Greek reading are probably due largely to a misunderstanding of the Hebrew words./18/

(24) 1 K 10:23/19/ M: המלך שלמה
10:26 OG,L: Σαλωμων (L: Σολομων)
2 C 9:22 M: המלך שלמה

המלך in the Hebrew witnesses is an expansion.

(25) 1 K 10:23 M: מלכי הארץ
10:26 OG: המלכים (τους βασιλεις)
     L: τους βασιλεις της γης
2 C 9:22 M: מלכי הארץ

The reading of K^M, C^M, and L represents an expansion, perhaps influenced by the occurrence of ארץ in the next verse.

(26) 1 K 10:25 M: כלי כסף וכלי זהב
10:29 OG,L: כלי זהב (σκευη χρυσα)
2 C 9:24 M: כלי כסף וכלי זהב

The phrase כלי כסף has probably been lost by haplography.

(27) 1 K 10:27 M: הכסף
10:31 OG,L: הזהב והכסף (το χρυσιον και το αργυριον)
2 C 9:27 M: הכסף

The OG and L contain an expansion.

J. 1 K 11:43–12:24//2 C 9:31–11:4/20/
(1) 1 K 11:43–12:3a M: וישכב שלמה עם אבתיו ויקבר בעיר
                     דוד אביו וימלך רחבעם בנו

תחתיו (1) וילך רחבעם שכם כי שכם בא כל ישראל להמליך אתו (2)
ויהי כשמע רחבעם בן נבט והוא עודנו במצרים אשר ברח מפני שלמה
המלך וישב ירבעם במצרים (3) וישלחו ויקראו לו ויבאו ירבעם וכל קהל
ישראל

OG: και εκοιμηθη Σαλωμων μετα των πατερων αυτου
και εθαψαν αυτον εν πολει Δαυειδ του πατρος αυτου και
εγενηθη ως ηκουσεν Ιεροβοαμ υιος Ναβατ και αυτου ετι οντος εν
Αιγυπτω ως εφυγεν εκ προσωπου Σαλωμων και εκαθητο εν
Αιγυπτω κατευθυνειν και ερχεται εις την πολιν αυτου εις την
γην Σαρειρα την εν ορει Εφραιμ και ο βασιλευς Σαλωμων
εκοιμηθη μετα των πατερων αυτου και εβασιλευσεν Ροβοαμ υιος
αυτου αντ᾽ αυτου (1) και πορευεται βασιλευς Ροβοαμ εις Σικιμα
οτι εις Σικιμα ηρχοντο πας Ισραηλ βασιλευσαι αυτον.

2 C 9:31–10:3a M: וישכב שלמה עם אבתיו ויקברהו בעיר דויד
אביו וימלך רחבעם בנו תחתיו (1) וילך רחבעם שכמה כי שכם באו
כל ישראל להמליך אתו (2) ויהי כשמע ירבעם בן נבט והוא במצרים
אשר ברח מפני שלמה המלך וישב ירבעם ממצרים (3) וישלחו ויקראו
לו ויבא ירבעם וכל ישראל

The value of the Greek witnesses here has recently been
debated by R. Klein and D. W. Gooding./21/ In Gooding's view
the Greek reading is the result of timetabling in the LXX and an
effort to whitewash Jeroboam. K^{M} in his opinion contains the
best reading. Klein views the Greek witnesses as attesting an old
Hebrew tradition according to which Jeroboam did not return
from Egypt or participate in the Shechem assembly until after
the murder of Adoram. He argues that the mention of Jeroboam
in 1 K 12:12 is secondary. Also, according to Klein, the fact that
the OG omits the material at 1 K 12:2–3a indicates that it is
secondary. This is confirmed by evidence that 1 K 12:3a (M) has
been borrowed from C^{M}. That the LXX's inclusion of material
similar to 1 K 12:2–3a in 11:43 is secondary is evident in Klein's
view from the doubling of the regnal formula. My own
reconstruction is more similar to Klein's than to Gooding's, but I
disagree that the Greek reading at 11:43 is secondary. While all
witnesses may reflect some confusion, the order of the OG and L
is probably original. Although there is no exact mechanism for
the loss of this material from its original position in K^{M}, the
reference to Solomon sleeping with his fathers occurs in 1 K
11:43 both before the plus and at its end. אביו is the last word
before the plus and אבותיו the final word of the plus. This

suggests the possibility of haplography in v 43 (cf. the OG doublet in 1 K 12:24)./22/ A portion of the lost material has apparently been reinserted incorrectly in K^M and Chr's text of K after 12:1//10:1. This has produced a contradiction with 1 K 12:20. The contradiction does not occur in C because Chr omitted the latter verse along with other material dealing with Jeroboam and the North. If this reconstruction is correct, then the fuller reading of the OG is original, and the agreement of K^M and C^M is very significant for our study. In addition, the tension between 1 K 12:3a and 20 is removed. Jeroboam returns to his home town but is not involved in the revolt until he is crowned king.

(2) 1 K 12:3b M: וידברו
      OG,L: וידבר העם (και ελαλησεν ο λαος)
  2 C 10:3 M: וידברו

העם in the OG and L is an expansion, but it is not certain whether the original verb was singular or plural.

(3) 1 K 12:3b M: אל רחבעם
      OG,L: προς τον βασιλεα Ροβοαμ
  2 C 10:3 M: אל רחבעם

Again, the OG and L reflect an expansion.

(4) 1 K 12:6 M: ויועץ המלך רחבעם
      OG,L: και παρ(L: απ)ηγγειλεν ο βασιλευς = ויצו המלך
  2 C 10:6 M: ויועץ המלך רחבעם

The *Vorlage* of παρηγγειλεν is uncertain. If my retroversion is correct, ויצו is probably the result of graphic confusion. רחבעם in K^M and C^M is an expansion.

(5) 1 K 12:6 M: בהיתו חי
      OG,L: ετι ζωντος αυτου
  2 C 10:6 M: בהיתו חי

The *Vorlage* of the OG and L is again uncertain. בחיתו alone is possible here, and ετι may be an interpretation.

(6) 1 K 12:6 M: להשיב
      OG,L: και (L: + ινα) αποκριθω=ואשיב
  2 C 10:6 M: להשיב

The OG and L readings are probably interpretations of the

K^M reading.

(7) 1 K 12:9 M: ונשיב דבר

      OG,L: ומה אשיב (καὶ τι αποκριθω)

2 C 10:9 M: ונשיב דבר

The original reading is uncertain, but דבר in K^M and C^M is probably an expansion.

(8) 1 K 12:10 M: omit

      OG,L: העמדים לפניו (οι παρεστηκοτες [L: τα παρεστ-ηκοτα] προ προσωπου αυτου)

2 C 10:10 M: omit

The additional line in the Greek witnesses is an expansion motivated by its occurrence earlier in v 8.

(9) 1 K 12:10 M: ואתה

      OG,L: ואתה עתה (καὶ συ νυν)

2 C 10:10 M: ואתה

עתה in the OG and L is an expansion, influenced by its occurrence in the next verse.

(10) 1 K 12:11 M: העמיס עליכם על

      OG: επεσασσετο υμας κλοιω

      L: επετασσεν υμιν εν κλοιω

2 C 10:11 M: העמיס עליכם על

The *Vorlage(n)* of the Greek witnesses and the original reading are uncertain. The OG and L may simply reflect interpretations of K^M.

(11) 1 K 12:12 M: ויבו ירבעם וכל העם

      OG: ויבאו כל ישראל (καὶ παρεγενοντο πας Ισραηλ)

      L: ויבא כל ישראל (καὶ παρεγενετο πας Ισραηλ)

2 C 10:12 M: ויבא ירבעם וכל העם

K^M and C^M clearly expand here. Thus, Jeroboam was not originally mentioned here and does not become the leader of the "rebels" until after the murder of Adoram.

(12) 1 K 12:12 M: אל רחבעם

      OG,L: προς τον βασιλεα Ροβοαν = אל המלך רחבעם

2 C 10:12 M: אל רחבעם

המלך is an expansion.

(13) 1 K 12:16 M: ולא נחלה

    OG: και ουκ εστιν ημιν κληρονομια

    L: και ουκ εστιν ημιν ετι κληρονομια

2 C 10:16 M: ולא נחלה

The OG and L contain expansions here.

(14) 1 K 12:16 M: ראה ביתך

    OG,L: רעה ביתך (βοσκε τον οικον σου)

2 C 12:16 M: ראה ביתך

The imagery in the OG and L is perhaps more appropriate. David is told, in effect, that his leadership is to be limited to his own house.

(15) 1 K 12:17 M: ובני ישראל הישבים בערי יהודה וימלך עליהם רחבעם

    OG: omit

    L: και οι υιοι Ιουδα και οι υιοι Ιηλ οι κατοικουντες εν ταις πολεσιν Ιουδα εβασιλευσαν εφ εαυτοις τον Ροβοαμ

2 C 10:17 M: ובני ישראל הישבים בערי יהודה וימלך עליהם רחבעם

This verse is probably a secondary gloss in K^M and C^M. Lemke holds that it was introduced into C^M first in accord with Chr's pan-Israel interest, then was later assimilated into the text of K./23/ As argued earlier (pp. 99–100) the evidence regarding Chr's pan-Israel interest in this context is ambiguous. Thus, while the secondary nature of the verse is evident, the direction of borrowing between K^M and C^M is not certain.

(16) 1 K 12:18 M: (1) המלך רחבעם

    OG: ο βασιλευς

    L: ο βασιλευς Ροβοαμ

2 C 10:18 M: המלך רחבעם

רחבעם is probably an expansion.

(17) 1 K 12:18 M: אבן

    OG,L: εν λιθοις

2 C 10:18 M: אבן

אבן alone is somewhat elliptical, and the Greek witnesses probably interpret or reflect expansion.

(18) 1 K 12:18 M: לעלות במרכבה

    OG: לעלות (αναβησαι)

    L: לעלות על המרכבה (αναβησαι επι το αρμα)

2 C 10:18 M: לעלות במרכבה

The reading of the OG is likely original. The other witnesses appear to attest independent expansions.

(19) 1 K 12:21 M: ושמנים
      OG,L: ועשרים (εικοσι)
   2 C 11:1 M: ושמנים

The reading of the OG and L should probably be regarded as the more primitive since it is the lower number.

(20) 1 K 12:21 M: בחור עשה
      OG,L: νεανιων ποιουντων
   2 C 11:1 M: בחור עשה

The plural has probably entered because the number of warriors indicates a plural subject. The collective is original.

(21) 1 K 12:24 M: שובו איש
      OG,L: ישב איש (αποστρεφετω εκαστος)
   2 C 11:4 M: שובו איש

It is impossible to tell which reading is original.

(22) 1 K 12:24 M: וישובו
      OG,L: και κατεπαυσαν
   2 C 11:4 M: וישבו

The OG and L seem to presuppose וישבתו. This reading is probably original. יש(ו)בו has entered under the influence of the same root earlier in the verse.

K. 1 K 14:25–28//2 C 12:2, 9b–11
(1) 1 K 14:25 M: למלך
      OG,L: βασιλευοντος
   2 C 12:2 M: למלך

Since it is unlikely from the standpoint of Hebrew syntax that a participle is original here, the Greek reading is probably an interpretation.

(2) 1 K 14:26 M: אצרות
      OG,L: כל אצרות (παντας τους θησαυρους)
   2 C 12:9 M: אצרות

The OG and L reflect a minor expansion.

(3) 1 K 14:26 M: ואת הכל לקח ויקח את כל מגני הזהב אשר עשה שלמה

OG: και τα δορατα τα χρυσα α ελαβεν Δανειδ εκ χειρος των παιδων Αδρααζαρ βασιλεως Σουρα και εισηνεγκεν αυτα εις Ιερουσαλημ τα παντα α ελαβεν οπλα τα χρυσα

L: και τα δορατα τα χρυσα α ελαβεν Δανειδ εκ χειρος των παιδων Αδρααζαρ βασιλεως Σουρα και εισηνεγκεν αυτα εις Ιερουσαλημ τα παντα ελαβεν και τα οπλα τα χρυσα α εποιησεν Σολομων

2 C 12:9 M: את הכל לקח ויקח את מגני הזהב אשר עשה שלמה

The evidence here is difficult to interpret. The Greek plus refers to the account in 2 S 8:7 where G also contains a plus about Shishak taking the shields. K^M and C^M, in contrast, state that Solomon made these shields. The Greek phrase παντα α ελαβεν οπλα τα χρυσα presupposes a line very similar to ואת הכל לקח ויקח את מגני הזהב in K^M and C^M. The subsequent phrase אשר עשה שלמה is probably a later gloss based on 1 K 10:16//2 C 9:15. Finally, L's reference to both David and Solomon is probably the result of conflation.

L. 1 K 15:1–2//2 C 13:1–2

(1) 1 K 15:1 M: אבים
　　　　　OG: Αβιου υιος Ιεροβοαμ
　　　　　L: Αβια υιος Ροβοαμ
　　2 C 13:1 M: אביה

The OG expands, and L corrects the OG's obvious error.

(2) 1 K 15:2 M: שלש שנים
　　　　OG,L: שש שנים (εξ ετη)
　　2 C 13:2 M: שלש שנים

Shenkel has shown that the OG relies on a different chronology than the one in K^M. The variants here are apparently related to that problem and are therefore more than textual variants. C generally seems to follow the later chronology of K^M rather than the more original chronology of the OG. If this is correct, it is indeed a significant datum for our study.

(3) 1 K 15:2 M: מלך בירושלם
　　　　OG: מלך (εβασιλευσεν)
　　　　L: εβασιλευσεν εν Ιλημ
　　2 C 13:1 M: מלך בירושלם

בירושלם in K^M, C^M, and L is probably an expansion.

M. 1 K 15:11, 13–22//2 C 14:1; 15:16–16:6

(1) 1 K 15:13 M: וישרף

    OG,L: וישרף באש (και ενεπρησεν πυρι [L: εν πυρι])

2 C 15:16 M: וישרף

באש in the OG and L is an expansion.

(2) 1 K 15:15 M: קדשי אביו

    OG,L: τους κιονας του πατρου αυτου

2 C 15:18 M: קדשי אביו

The *Vorlage* of the Greek witnesses is uncertain. It is possible that κιονας translates קדשי./24/ In any case, the reading in K^M and C^M appears to be original.

(3) 1 K 15:15 M: בית

    OG,L: εισηνεγκεν εις τον οικον

2 C 15:18 M: בית

The plus in the OG and L is probably due to expansion in the Greek. εισηνεγκεν is used earlier in this verse.

(4) 1 K 15:17 M: לבלתי תת

    OG,L: του μη ειναι

2 C 16:1 M: לבלתי תת

ειναι in the Greek witnesses is probably an interpretation of תת.

(5) 1 K 15:19 M: ברית

    OG: διαθου διαθηκην

    L: διαθηκη εστω

2 C 16:2 M: ברית

The readings in the OG and L are expansions.

(6) 1 K 15:19 M: ביני ובינך בין אבי ובין אביך

    OG: ביני ואבי ואביך (ανα μεσον εμου και του πατρος μου και του πατρος σου)

    L: אביך (b,c$_2$: ובין) ביני ובינך ובין אבי = ανα μεσον εμου και ανα μεσον σου και ανα μεσον του πατρος μου και (b,c$_2$: ανα μεσον) του πατρος σου

2 C 16:3 M: ביני ובינך ובין אבי ובין אביך

The use of בין as in the Hebrew witnesses is so idiomatic that the shorter OG reading is probably not original here. The OG reading, then, is probably the result of haplography (בין occurs three times in a row in K^M and C^M where the OG reflects it only once) and interpretation.

(7) 1 K 15:19 M: בריתך את בעשא

    OG,L: την διαθηκην σου την προς Βαασα

2 C 16:3 M: בריתך את בעשא

The אשר reflected in the Greek witnesses (την 2) is an expansion.

II. $C^M = OG \neq K^M$

A. 1 K 7:23–26 (OG = 7:10–12)//2 C 4:1–4

No agreement of C^M and the OG against K^M.

B. 1 K 7:39b–8:11 (OG = 7:25b–37; 8:1–11)//2 C 4:10–5:11

(1) 1 K 7:40 M: בית יהוה

    7:26 OG,L: εν (L: τω) οικω Κυριου

2 C 4:11 M: בבית אלהים

The preposition in C^M is an expansion. The *Vorlage* of the Greek witnesses could have contained the preposition or they could be interpreting.

(2) 1 K 7:41 M: אשר על ראש

    7:27 OG: επι των κεφαλων

         L: τα οντα επι των κεφαλων

2 C 4:12 M: על ראש

K^M and L expand. Thus, C^M and the OG agree in an original reading, and it is not significant.

(3) 1 K 7:45 M: בית יהוה

    7:31 OG: τω οικω Κυριου

         L: εν τω οικω Κυριου

2 C 4:16 M: לבית יהוה

The agreement of the OG with C^M's reading here is uncertain, since the former could be an interpretation of בית.

(4) 1 K 7:47 M: מאד מאד

    7:32 OG,L: οφοδρα

2 C 4:18 M: מאד

The order of the verses here has been discussed (p. 123). K^M's repetition of מאד is a dittography.

(5) 1 K 7:51 M: המלך שלמה
    7:37 OG,L: Σαλωμων (L: Σολομων)
    2 C 5:1 M: שלמה

K^M contains a minor expansion.

C. 1 K 8:12–50//2 C 6:1–39
(1) 1 K 8:15 M: ובידו
        OG,L: και εν ταις χερσιν
        2 C 6:4 ובידיו

Since *yod* would not have been written in the old
orthography, this difference is insignificant, and it is impossible
to tell whether the singular or plural is original.

(2) 1 K 8:26 M: ועתה
      OG,L: και νυν Κυριε
    2 C 6:17 M: ועתה יהוה

The divine name could be an expansion, but it may also be
lacking in K^M as the result of haplography occasioned by
homoioteleuton (עתה . . . יהוה).

(3) 1 K 8:29 M: לילה ויום
      OG,L: ημερας και νυκτος
    2 C 6:20 M: יומם ולילה

The original order is uncertain.

(4) 1 K 8:32, 34, 43, 45 M: השמים
      OG,L: εκ του ουρανου
2 C 6:23, 25, 33, 35 M: מן השמים

The *Vorlage* of the OG and L is uncertain in this phrase. εκ
του ουρανου could be an interpretation of השמים.

(5) 1 K 8:39 M: ידעת לבדך
      OG,L: μονωτατος οιδας
    2 C 6:30 M: לבדך ידעת

The original order here is uncertain.

(6) 1 K 8:42 M: ובא והתפלל
        OG: και ηξουσιν και προσευξονται
         L: και ηξει και προσευξεται
    2 C 6:32 M: ובאו והתפללו

The plurals were probably introduced under the influence of שמעון earlier in the verse. This, plus the fact that they involve only the addition of *waw*, leaves open the possibility that the expansions were independent.

(7) 1 K 8:43 M: מכון שבתך
      OG,L: εξ ετοιμου κατοικητηριου σου
2 C 6:33 M: ממכון שבתך

(מ)מכון stands in apposition to השמים (מן). Thus, the variation here is related to that described above. The *Vorlage* of the OG and L is uncertain, and they may interpret מכון.

(8) 1 K 8:46 M: ארץ האויב
      OG,L: γην
2 C 6:36 M: ארץ

K^M expands here.

D. 1 K 8:62–63//2 C 7:4–5
(1) 1 K 8:63 M: שלמה
      OG,L: ο βασιλευς Σαλωμων (L: Σολομων)
2 C 7:5 M: המלך שלמה

המלך is an expansion in C^M, the OG, and L.

E. 1 K 8:64–9:3a//2 C 7:7–12a
  1 K 8:66 M: על כל הטובה
      OG,L: επι τοις αγαθοις
2 C 7:10 M: על הטובה

כל in K^M is an expansion.

F. 1 K 9:3b–9//2 C 7:16–22
(1) 1 K 9:5 M: איש מעל כסא ישראל
      OG,L: ανηρ ηγουμενος εν (L: επι) Ισραηλ
2 C 7:16 M: איש מושל בישראל

The reading of K^M is probably secondary and based on the similar phrase in 1 K 2:4.

(2) 1 K 9:7 M: הבית
      OG,L: τον οικον τουτον
2 C 7:20 M: הבית הזה

הזה is an expansion based on the frequent reference to "this house" in chaps. 8–9 (cf. especially 9:3, 8).

(3) 1 K 9:7 M: אשלח

    OG,L: αποριψω

2 C 7:20 M: אלשך

K^M's reading is obviously in error, since it makes no sense for Yahweh to say that he will send away the Temple.

(4) 1 K 9:9 M: הביא יהוה

    OG: επηγαγεν

    L: επηγαγεν Ks

2 C 7:22 M: הביא

The divine name here is an expansion.

G. 1 K 9:19–22 (OG = 10:23b–25)//2 C 8:6–9

(1) 1 K 9:19 M: ערי הרכב

    OG,L: πασας τας πολεις των αρματων

2 C 8:6 M: כל ערי הרכב

כל is an expansion brought on by its use elsewhere in the verse.

(2) 1 K 9:20 M: האמרי החתי

    OG,L: του Χετταιου και του Αμορραιου

2 C 8:7 M: החתי והאמרי

It is impossible to tell which order is original. Both are found in other lists of these peoples in the OT.

H. 1 K 9:23–25 (G = 2:35 h, f, g)//2 C 8:10–12

No agreement of C^M and the OG against K^M.

I. 1 K 10:1–29//2 C 9:1–28

(1) 1 K 10:24 M: הארץ

10:27 OG,L: (L: οι) βασιλευς της γης

2 C 9:23 M: מלכי הארץ

מלכי may be an expansion. However, the participle in K^M is plural (מבקשים), and the similarity of מלכי with כל may have been enough to bring about the loss of מלכי from K^M.

(2) 1 K 10:26 M: ויאסף שלמה רכב ופרשים ויהי לו אלף וארבע
                                     מאות רכב

10:29 OG,L: και ησαν τω Σαλωμων τεσσαρες (L: Σολομωντι τεσσερακοντα) χιλιαδες θηλειαι ιπποι (L: ιππων θηλειων) εις αρματα

2 C 9:25 M: ויהי לשלמה ארבעת אלפים אריות סוסים ומרכבות

1 K 5:6 M: ויהי לשלמה ארבעים אלף אריות סוסים למרכבו

I have suggested that 2 C 1:14 lies within a passage that was secondarily borrowed from 1 K 10:26–29 (p. 94). We are apparently dealing in this series of variants with an original reading that has been fragmented and misplaced. The evidence is insufficient to reconstruct the original reading or its placement.

(3) 1 K 5:1 (OG = 10:30)//2 C 9:26

Here again C^M agrees with OG and L against K^M in the placement of a verse. The original placement is again uncertain. There is an additional parallel to this verse in the OG doublet in 1 K 2:46k. The OG and C^M also contain the following agreements against 1 K 5:1.

(4)1 K 5:1 M: ושלמה היה
10:30 OG,L: και ην
2 C 9:26 M: ויהי

Solomon's name is probably an expansion.

(5) 1 K 5:1 M: ארץ פלשתים
10:30 OG,L: και εως (L: της) γης (L: των) αλλοφυλων
2 C 9:26 M: ועד ארץ פלשתים

The phrase ארץ פלשתים is usually regarded as a gloss on the next phrase גבול מצרים. If this is correct, then ועד is probably a secondary addition in an effort to interpret the text.

J. 1 K 12:1–24//2 C 10:1–11:4
(1) 1 K 12:1 M: שכם
        OG,L: εις Σικιμα
2 C 10:1 M: שכמה

The *Vorlage* of the OG and L is uncertain. It could be שכם. This is clear from the use of εις Σικιμα later in this verse where both K^M and C^M have שכם.

(2) 1 K 12:1 M: בא כל ישראל
        OG,L: ηρχοντο πας Ισραηλ
2 C 10:1 M: באו כל ישראל

It is difficult to tell whether the singular or plural is original. The singular is grammatically correct, but ישראל is a collective and could easily take a plural verb.

(3)1 K 12:6 M: את העם הזה

        OG,L: τω λαω τουτω

2 C 10:6 M: לעם הזה

The OG and L appear to agree with C^M in reading ל and not את before עם. However, the *Vorlage* of the OG and L is not certain. τω λαω could translate את העם or לעם here.

(4) 1 K 12:15 M: אשר דבר יהוה

        OG,L: ο ελαλησεν

2 C 10:15 M: אשר דבר

K^M contains an expansion in the divine name.

K. 1 K 14:25–28//2 C 12:2a–b, 9b–11

1 K 14:26 M: כל מגני הזהב

        OG,L: τα δορατα τα χρυσα

2 C 12:9 M: מגני הזהב

כל in K^M is an expansion.

L.1 K 15:1–2//2 C 13:1–2

No agreements of C^M and OG against K^M.

M. 1 K 15:11, 13–22//2 C 14:1; 15:16–16:6

1 K 15:20 M: ויך את עיון

        OG,L: και επαταξαν την Αιν

2 C 16: 4 M: ויכו את עיון

Either reading could be original here. If singular, it would refer to Ben-Hadad, if plural, to his captains.

The preceding study demonstrates the textual affiliation of C^M and K^M. Obviously, there are fewer agreements of C^M and the OG against K^M than there are agreements of K^M and C^M against the OG. What is more significant, however, is the quality of those agreements. Most of the places where the OG and C^M agree against K^M are due to expansion or other error in K^M or can easily be viewed as independent expansion in C^M and the OG. The only real exception is 1 K 10:26; 5:1 (OG 10:29–30)//2 C 9:26 where the C^M and OG agree against K^M in the placement and content of two verses. However, in these two verses the evidence is quite uncertain. Each verse has doublets in the various witnesses and their original placement and content are unclear. K^M and C^M, on the other hand, show striking agreement against the OG throughout. With the exception of

1 K 10:26–29//2 C 9:25–28, they agree against the OG in the placement of several of the passages treated above. More importantly, they are consistently in agreement in erroneous readings including expansions (e.g., 1 K 7:23//2 C 4:2; 7:50//4:22; 14:26//12:9) and minuses due to haplography (1 K 7:45–47//2 C 4:16–18; 7:51//5:1; 10:21//9:20)./25/ Even more significant is their agreement in a variety of other passages. In 1 K 10:8//2 C 9:7 they agree in reading a clear error. In 10:15//9:14 they agree in an obvious corruption. In 8:1–5//6:2–6 they agree in a series of glosses which attest priestly interests. In 8:12–13//6:1–2 they agree in an inferior text of the poem. In 12:2–3a//10:2–3a I have argued that they agree in haplography and secondary insertion. Finally, in 15:2//13:2 they appear to follow the same chronology. 1 K 8:1–5 is particularly significant because of the 4QKgs^a fragment of that passage, which shows agreement with K^M and C^M. The fact that the pluses are also attested in 4QKgs^a indicates that we are dealing with recension within a text type and not just assimilation between K^M and C^M. Indeed, I have found no evidence for secondary borrowing from C^M into K^M in any of the thirteen passages considered.

There can be little doubt that K^M and C^M reflect a single text type of K, i.e., Chr's *Vorlage* of K was proto-Rabbinic. It is important to recognize that the evidence for each biblical book must be taken on its own merits. Conclusions reached for the witnesses in other books do not necessarily apply. The evidence gathered here demonstrates that the conclusions reached for Chr's *Vorlage* of S do not hold for his *Vorlage* of K.

NOTES

/1/   Cf. Lemke, "Synoptic Problem," 362–63, where he describes the evidence from 4QSam^a as applying to the text of S–K.

/2/   One of the most obvious differences between K^M and the OG in this passage and others is their respective placement of the pericopes. Usually the original order of verses within a passage or the placement of a passage cannot be established. In some passages I have attempted to suggest how the difference in order arose. In every case where there is a difference of order or placement, C^M agrees with K^M against the OG. The one exception is 1 K 10:26; 5:1 = the OG's 10:29–30//2 C 9:25–26.

/3/   All witnesses attest some disruption in these verses. The double
reference in the OG and L in v 32 to the weight of the bronze probably
represents a conflation. The mechanism for haplography in K^M and C^M
remains valid, however.

/4/   The reconstruction of 4Qgs[a] here simply follows K^M. It is
uncertain whether המלך שלמה, המלך, or שלמה should be reconstructed.
Line length requires that one of these three readings was present
(contra C), but it is not certain which one.

/5/   See *BDB*, 641, 672. נשיא is used in C almost exclusively in the
genealogical material in 1 C 1–11. The only exceptions are this verse
and 2 C 1:2. Similarly, מטה occurs outside of 1 C 1–11 only here (2 C
5:2) and in 1 C 12:31. In DH, the use of both words is confined largely
to sections in Joshua that are frequently assigned to P.

/6/   In the Hasmonean script *yod* and *waw* written close together
could easily be mistaken for *he*. See the charts provided by Cross, "The
Development of the Jewish Scripts," *BANE* (ed. by G. E. Wright,
Winona Lake, Eisenbrauns, 1979), 133–202.

/7/   It is used only here in C (see *BDB*, 417).

/8/   Gray, *I and II Kings*, 195–96.

/9/   Again see Cross, "Jewish Scripts," especially figure 1 (p. 137),
lines 2, 3, and 7, and figure 4 (p. 149), line 1. It is easy to see how *bet*
and *dalet* written close together could be mistaken for *mem*,
particularly in a period when *mem* was written with a pronounced tick
in the upper left corner. The same could be true in reverse, i.e., a
poorly written *mem* might be confused with *bet dalet*.

/10/   The first two letters of each word are the same: *bet alef*. The
horizontal and right vertical strokes of the *ḥet* could easily be taken for
resh. It is more difficult to see how *ṣade* could be derived from the
remaining stroke of *ḥet* and the *dalet*, but this may have been possible
with poorly written letters or a poorly preserved manuscript.

/11/   επαξεις in the OG and L may be a corruption of επαταξεις which
would seem to presuppose הכית. However, this is only conjectural. Only
a_2 reads a form of πατασσω here.

/12/   See *BDB*, 699. Both uses are found in K.

/13/   Again, the witnesses disagree about the placement of these verses,
and their original context, is uncertain. The information here is included
in the collection of material in 1 K 2:35 of the OG. It may be out of order
in all versions. It is significant that C^M and K^M follow the same order. The

real motive for the collection of material in the Greek witnesses at 2:35 is uncertain. Most of the verses there are doublets of material found elsewhere in both the Hebrew and the Greek text. However, the material in 2:35f, g, and h is not found elsewhere in the Greek text. The references to Pharaoh's daughter and Solomon's sacrifices in 9:24–25 of K^M seem out of place. Thus, neither the Hebrew nor the Greek witnesses give the original location of this material.

/14/ C. F. Burney, *Notes on the Hebrew Text of the Books of Kings* (Oxford: Clarendon Press, 1903) 144.

/15/ See Burney, *Notes*, 146 and the commentaries for proposed emendations. Even if מאנשי is emended to some word with the connotation of "revenue" or "that which is brought," the problem of the meaning of התרים remains. תור does not have the sense of "trading" but refers to spying.

/16/ Admittedly this is not a strong mechanism. The left leg of *taw* usually extends below the line of writing. However, confusion of *taw* with *yod waw* is possible in Herodian and Post-Herodian cursive scripts. See Cross, "Jewish Scripts," especially figure 5 (p. 162).

/17/ J. A. Montgomery, *The Books of Kings* (ICC; Edinburgh: T. & T. Clark, 1951), 230.

/18/ For a discussion of the words in the Hebrew and Greek texts see Burney, *Notes*, 149–50.

/19/ Vv 23–25 in the OG and L are parallel to 9:19–22 in K^M (see note 7 above). C^M follows the order of K^M.

/20/ There is a lengthy supplement in the Greek text in 1 K 12:24a–z concerning the history of Jeroboam. Its value is debated among scholars. Montgomery (*Kings*, 251–54) gives the different views. It is true, as Shenkel points out (*Chronology*, 32), that this supplement belongs to an early stage in the development of the Greek text. However, it is also clear, as Olmstead observes, that the supplement is composite in nature. See A. T. Olmstead, "Source Study and the Biblical Text," *AJSL* (1913) 20. It is also obviously selective in the passages it repeats. Because it does belong to the early stages of the Greek text it is valuable for Shenkel's study of the OG's chronology. However, because of its composite and selective nature it is not particularly helpful in a detailed analysis such as ours. Hence, I have omitted it from consideration here.

/21/ The publications in order of their appearance are as follows: Gooding, "The Septuagint's Rival Versions of Jeroboam's Rise to

Power," *VT* 17 (1967): 173–89; Klein, "Jeroboam's Rise to Power," *JBL*
89 (1970): 217–18; Gooding, "Jeroboam's Rise to Power: A Rejoinder,"
JBL 91 (1972): 529–33; Klein, "Once More: 'Jeroboam's Rise to
Power,'" *JBL* 92 (1973): 528–84.

/22/ The problem with Klein's view is that 1 K 11:43 (G) contains
information not found in M, particularly the reference to his return to
his home town in Ephraim. Where does this material come from? It is
true that the double mention of Solomon's sleeping with his fathers
appears clumsy. However, to refer to this as a doubling of the regnal
formula is not quite accurate. In fact, it is striking that Jeroboam is
discussed after the first reference to Solomon's death and Rehoboam
after the second such reference. Could it be that the writer here brings
together materials from the Israelite and Judean annals, hence the
double reference to Solomon?

/23/ Lemke, "Synoptic Studies," 137–38.

/24/ קרשי means "boards." This is a suggestion cited by Montgomery
in *Kings*, 280.

/25/ It should be noted that the received text of K does not show the
same tendency to haplography attested by the MT of S.

Chapter 5

2 C 29:1–35:19//2 K 18:1–23:22

The reigns of the Judean kings from Hezekiah to Josiah inclusive present special problems in the study of the accounts of the history of Israel in C and DH. I shall begin with a survey of this material as in the previous two chapters.

I. *K Material Unparalleled in C*

A. *2 K 18:9–12*

These verses review the capture and exile of the Northern kingdom by Assyria. They have been omitted by Chr because, like 2 K 17, they deal with the North and hence lie outside of Chr's interests.

B. *2 K 18:14–16*

K describes Sennacherib's invasion in two stages. In the first stage (2 K 18:14–16), Hezekiah and Jerusalem submit to Sennacherib through the forfeit of tribute. In the second stage Yahweh delivers Jerusalem from the Assyrians. Both C and K relate this second stage, but C says nothing about Hezekiah's payment of tribute./1/ C clearly had the K account with its two stages in front of him, and it seems clear that his concern is to present the divinely wrought victory of Hezekiah over the Assyrians. This fits well with his retribution dogma and with his view of Hezekiah. Hezekiah is a faithful king, and Yahweh rewards him with victory.

C. *2 K 19:1–14, 15b–34//Isa 37:1–14, 16–35*

2 K 19 details Yahweh's deliverance of Jerusalem from the Assyrians. This account includes two oracles of Isaiah assuring Hezekiah that Yahweh will deliver him, the Rabshakeh's threatening letter to Hezekiah, and Hezekiah's prayer for deliverance

in the Temple./2/ C refers briefly to Hezekiah's prayer (32:20; cf. 2 K 19:15a; Isa 37:15) and recounts Yahweh's deliverance itself (32:21-23; cf. 2 K 19:35-37; Isa 37:36-38). Precisely why Chr chooses to abbreviate the account in this way is not certain./3/ It is hard to imagine that the omitted material, particularly Isaiah's oracle, lay outside of Chr's interests. However, Chr's omission of this material does fit with the picture he paints of Hezekiah in this entire episode as calmly confident in Yahweh (see on 2 C 32:2-8 below).

D. *2 K 21:10b-16*

These verses detail the wickedness of Manasseh and place the blame for Judah's fall upon him. C's view of Manasseh is very different from K's. This passage describes Manasseh's reign as thoroughly evil. Manasseh caused Judah to sin and eventually brought about its downfall. In C Manasseh repents and the second half of his reign is good (see on 2 C 33:11-17 below). Chr would hardly invent such a striking difference. He could be following a different source. Another possibility is that the differences here are due to changes made by Dtr 2. I shall explore this possibility in more detail in Chapter 7.

E. *2 K 23:24-27*

This passage consists of two parts. Verses 24-25 praise Josiah for his faithfulness to Yahweh. Verses 26-27 explain that Yahweh was still angry against Judah because of Manasseh's great sins and predict that Yahweh will remove Judah as he removed Israel. There is no parallel for this passage in C^M. However, 2 Par 35:19a-d does contain a parallel, and its origin has been debated among scholars./4/ Nevertheless, there is substantial agreement that it represents a secondary borrowing of K material, whether this borrowing originally took place from a Hebrew text or a Greek text. It is hard to imagine Chr blaming Manasseh for Judah's fall as in 2 K 23:26-27 not only because he describes Manasseh's repentance and reforms but also because he gives his own reason for Judah's demise in 36:13-14. The fact that 2 K 23:24-27 blames Manasseh for Judah's fall makes it a good candidate, at least in part, for Dtr 2 material.

II. *C Material Unparalleled in K*

A. *2 C 29:3–31:21*

Chapters 29–31 of 2 C deal basically with Hezekiah's reforms. The same general topic is covered in 2 K 18:4–8 so that the two passages could be treated under section IV, passages that deal with similar subject matter but are not strictly parallel. However, such a comparison between the two passages would be completely artificial. There is no real similarity between them. K concentrates on Hezekiah's reforms against idolatrous cults. C is much broader and clearly displays some of Chr's interests, especially his interest in the Levites./5/ C's account begins with a speech by Hezekiah to the priests and Levites (29:3–11). A list of Levites follows (29:12–14), similar to other lists of Levitical personnel employed in C. Then the work of the priests and Levites in cleansing the Temple is detailed (29:15–19). This is followed by a description of Hezekiah's cultic celebration at the rededication of the Temple (29:20–36). Included in this last description is an account of Hezekiah's reestablishment of the Levitical divisions for the music of the cult along the lines set up by David (29:25–30). There is also an interesting statement here that the Levites were more righteous in purifying themselves (29:34). The statement seems to betray Chr's sentiments favoring the Levites.

2 C 30 describes the celebration of the Passover under Hezekiah, an event not even mentioned in K. Chr's pan-Israel interest is apparent throughout the chapter. Hezekiah sends invitations to the Passover not only throughout all of Judah but also into the North (vv 1, 5–9, 10–12, 18, 25). In addition, Chr's interest in the Levites continues in this chapter (vv 15–17, 21–22, 25, 27). Finally, the chapter as a whole, particularly vv 13–27, accords well with Chr's interest in the cult.

The same three concerns of Chr, pan-Israel, the Levites, and the cult, are also visible in chapter 31. The cultic reforms in v 1 are carried out by "all Israel" not only in Judah and Benjamin but also in Ephraim and Manasseh in the North. Hezekiah's appointment of the Levites for various tasks in v 2 is reminiscent of David's establishment of Levitical divisions. The account about the contributions brought for the cult in vv 3–10 involves people from both Israel and Judah (vv 5–6). Verses 11–19 describe further Levitical divisions for the maintenance of the cult and the Temple grounds as well as the enrollment of the priests and Levites for receiving provisions from the offerings. These verses include the names of those Levites in charge of the contribution and distribution among the cultic personnel.

The fact that these three chapters are replete with topics of interest to Chr does not necessarily mean that he has composed freely without some basis in other sources. In fact, there is strong evidence to indicate that he has followed other sources for at least the basic story of Hezekiah's reform and celebration of the Passover (see pp. 171–73 below).

B. 2 C 32:2–8

In roughly the same place as K's account of the first stage of Sennacherib's invasion (2 K 18:14–16), C describes Hezekiah's preparations for the Assyrian attack on Jerusalem. The information about these preparations in vv 3–6 probably derives from other sources. However, the speech of Hezekiah in vv 7–8 is probably a composition of Chr. C's portrayal of Hezekiah's reaction to Sennacherib's invasion is very different from K's. In K Hezekiah panics. He is frightened, as his prayer in 2 K 19 shows. C omits most of 2 K 19 and presents Hezekiah as a calm individual who is certain that Yahweh will deliver him. Such is the message of his speech in 32:7–8.

C. 2 C 32:22–23

These two verses represent, for the most part, Chr's interpretation of the episode of Sennacherib's invasion. The reference in v 23a to gifts may be based on information such as that in 2 K 20:12. However, the rest of these two verses expresses Chr's view that Yahweh delivered Hezekiah and that, as a result, Hezekiah was exalted in the opinion of his subjects.

D. 2 C 32:25–30

Verses 27–30 tell of Hezekiah's prosperity and probably derive from sources outside of K. The only exception may be the statement in v 30 that Hezekiah prospered in all his works, which could be an addition by Chr. The reference in vv 25–26 to Hezekiah's pride and his failure to return to Yahweh as he had received is obscure. It could be an allusion to the episode with the

Babylonian envoys (2 K 20:12–19//Isa 39:1–8). The same episode is mentioned in 2 C 32:31 with another obscure reference to Yahweh's leaving Hezekiah alone in order to test him. In both cases (vv 25–26 and v 31) Chr's hand seems evident.

E. *2 C 33:11–17*

This account of Manasseh's repentance in Babylon is strikingly different from K's account of Manasseh. It is quite likely, in view of the Assyrian vassal treaties, that Manasseh was indeed taken to the Assyrian court for a time./6/ Manasseh's return to Judah has been interpreted by Chr as Yahweh's doing, brought about by Manasseh's repentance. Commentators have argued that the story of Manasseh's repentance and subsequent reforms has arisen in an effort to account for his long reign./7/ However, the story cannot be ascribed with any certainty to Chr. If Dtr 2 blames Manasseh for Judah's fall, it is likely that he would have omitted this story from his edition. Thus, Chr's source for the story may have been Dtr 1.

F. *1 Esdr 1:21–22*

Torrey argued that this passage was the translation of the original passage in C that had experienced corruption./8/ He perceived a gap between 2 C 35:19 and 20. 1 Esdr 1:21–22 fills that gap by summarizing Josiah's reign as good and preparing for the disaster to come by referring to those who sinned more than the nations so that Yahweh's words against Israel were confirmed. Verse 21 offers a positive judgment on Josiah which agrees with Chr's previous assessment (35:2) and uses expressions not unfamiliar to C (cf. 25:2). I have already discussed why I regard v 22 as corrupt (pp. 20–21). The allusion here to those who sinned against Yahweh is obscure./9/ Rudolph has criticized Torrey's reconstruction of the Vorlage of 1 Esdr 1:21–22 and has argued that there is no mechanism for haplography to explain the lack of a similar reading in C^M./10/ I agree that Torrey's reconstruction is not convincing. It is impossible to reconstruct these verses correctly without further information. However, the evidence does suggest a mechanism that could have led to haplography in C^M. 1 Esdr 1:21 begins καὶ ὠρθώθη τα εργα Ιωσειου. Torrey retroverted this line as follows: וַיִּשְׁרוּ מעשי יאשיהו. The first line after the plus, 1 Esdr 1:23, begins καὶ μετα πασαν την πραξιν ταυτην Ιωσειου. Omitting *and* πασαν and ταυτην, which are probably expansions, one may reconstruct ואחרי מעשי יאשיהו. The similarity between this line and the beginning of the plus in 1:21 is obvious and is clearly enough to trigger a haplography./11/

III. *Parallel Passages in C and K*

A. *2 C 29:1-2//2 K 18:2-3*

The two accession notices for Hezekiah are nearly *verbatim* the same. The only real difference is C's customary omission of the synchronism with the Northern monarchy in 2 K 18:1. I shall deal in more detail with the formulae momentarily. This formula is included here in order to point out the change that occurs in Chr's use of his K source with regard to the reign of Hezekiah. In contrast to previous accounts where it is common for C to follow K closely for at least part of each king's reign, these two verses represent the only truly parallel portion of the accounts in C and K about Hezekiah.

B. *2 C 33:1-10a//2 K 21:1-10a*

The two accounts of Manasseh's wicked deeds as king are very close. The only significant difference is the lack of his mother's name in the accession formula (v 1). I shall say more about this in my treatment of the formulae later in this chapter.

C. *2 C 33:21-25//2 K 21:19-26*

These two accounts are generally close, but there are several differences worthy of comment.

(1) *2 C 33:21//2 K 21:19*. The queen mother's name is again lacking in the accession formula in C as is the case in every occurrence of the formula after Hezekiah. The reason for this phenomenon will be discussed below.

(2) *2 C 33:22//2 K 21:21*. Both accounts refer to the idols that Amon served. C lacks the phrase, "He walked in all the way in which his father walked." The omission is probably due to haplography in C^M triggered by homoioteleuton (אביו . . . אביו).

(3) *33:23//—*. This verse alludes to Manasseh's repentance. If Dtr 2 omitted the story of Manasseh's repentance from his edition, he may also have omitted this verse.

(4)—//*21:25-26*. The concluding formula for Amon has been lost from C by haplography occasioned by homoioteleuton (יאשיהו בנו תחתיו at the end of vv 24 and 26).

D. *2 C 34:1-2, 8–21//2 K 22:1-13*

These two accounts about the restoration of the Temple and the finding of the book of the law are very close, but again there are several important differences.

(1) *2 C 34:1//2 K 22:1*. The name of the queen mother is again missing from C's version of the accession formula.

(2) *2 C 34:8//2 K 22:3*. There are two major differences in the two accounts here. First the phrase לטהר את הארץ והבית occurs in C but not in K. C places the finding of the law after Josiah had already executed some cultic reforms as detailed in vv 3–7. No bias on the part of Chr is apparent in this change, and it probably derives from other sources available to him. The second difference is the additional names in v 8 beside that of Shaphan. Again, the names probably stem from a source other than K.

(3) *2 C 34:9//2 K 22:4*. C contains two significant additions here vis-à-vis K. First, the Levites are specified as "the guardians of the threshhold," and this may be due to Chr's interest in the Levites. Secondly, while the donors in K are designated simply as "the people," the description in C is expanded and detailed to include not only Judah and Benjamin but also Ephraim and Manasseh and the remnant of Israel. Chr's pan-Israel interest is apparent.

(4) *2 C 34:12-14//*—. This additional material clearly stresses the role of the Levites in supervising the work of restoration in the Temple. As such, it accords with Chr's interest in the Levites even though some of the information it includes, especially the additional names, may stem from other sources.

(5) *2 C 34:21//2 K 22:13*. Chr's pan-Israel interest is again apparent in his version of those for whom the king asks his servants to intercede. In K they are told to inquire "on behalf of me, the people, and all Judah." In C they are to inquire for the king and for "the remnant in Israel and in Judah." Chr obviously still regards the members of the Northern tribes as part of Israel.

E. *2 C 34:22–28//2 K 22:14–20*

These two accounts of Huldah's oracle are extremely close.
There are only two differences of any importance, and neither
can be viewed as tendentious on the part of Chr.

(1) *2 C 34:22//2 K 22:14.* The names of the other members of the envoy beside Hilkiah are lacking in C. C^M appears
corrupt at this point. As the text stands ואשר המלך makes little
sense. Some of the names of those sent by Josiah may have fallen
out or C may have originally contained a statement such as וכל
אשר שלח המלך that has become corrupt through textual transmission. In any case, the difference here cannot be ascribed to
Chr's bias.

(2) *2 C 34:24//2 K 22:16.* The view that Chr has changed
כל דברי to כל האלות הכתובות because of the lists of curses in
Deut 28–29 and Lev 26 cannot be accepted./12/ These curses
were undoubtedly well known, and Huldah's oracle in K is
clearly reminiscent of them. Thus, the change in C's wording
could have existed in his *Vorlage* or have been made by a later
scribe. There is no reason to hold Chr responsible for the change,
since he has not shown any particular tendency to change K in
order to bring it into agreement with the Pentateuchal narratives, and the difference in readings here betrays no other special interest.

F. *2 C 34:29–31//2 K 23:1–3*

Both accounts detail some of Josiah's reforms. They are very
close. The only difference worthy of note is in 24:30//23:2
where C has הלוים instead of הנביאים as in K. Although the reading corresponds to Chr's interest in the Levites, it is dubious that
he actually altered his *Vorlage* here, since several K manuscripts
also have הלוים at this point.

G. *2 C 35:18–19//1 Esdr 1:18–20//2 K 23:22–23*

It seems clear that Chr used K in these verses to conclude his
account of the Passover. Chr probably inserted the statement in
35:18b (1 Esdr 1:19b) that the kings of Israel did not keep a
Passover like that kept by Josiah, the priests, Levites, and people.
This statement fits with Chr's interests in the Levites and in pan-
Israel. The other main difference is the reading "from the days

of Samuel the prophet" in C where K has "from the days of the judges." It is difficult to find a motive for change on the part of Chr here. The time period referred to is roughly the same. It is likely that the two readings are merely variants in the proto-Rabbinic text.

IV. *Passages that Concern the Same Topics*

A. *2 C 32:1/2 K 18:13*

These two verses introduce the respective accounts of Sennacherib's invasion with roughly the same information. There are two main differences between them. First, C lacks the dating of the invasion to the fourteenth year of Hezekiah as in K. Secondly, K says that Sennacherib took the cities of Judah while C says simply that he camped against them. It is difficult to find any tendentious reason for the lack of a date in C. The different information about the cities of Judah might be ascribed to Chr's bias, but how else could Sennacherib have arrived at Jerusalem if not by defeating other Judean cities? Indeed, in 2 C 32:9 Chr mentions that Sennacherib was besieging Lachish. Moreover, since vv 2–8 probably derive, at least in part, from another source available to Chr, the same is likely true for v 1.

B. *2 C 32:9–19/2 K 18:17–37*

These are two versions of Sennacherib's speech through his messenger to the citizens of Jerusalem. C's account is much shorter than K's, but both employ similar expressions. In view of Chr's tendency to place speeches in the mouths of his characters, it seems likely that he has here composed his version of the speech on the basis of the K material. In fact, his composition appears to be a summary of the K version. His summary is particularly obvious in vv 16–19. He focuses his version of the speech on the religious aspect of the conflict, especially the Assyrian's blasphemy of Yahweh in speaking of him on the same level with the gods of the nations. Other aspects of the speech in K lie outside of his interests.

C. *2 C 32:20/1 K 19:15a//Isa 37:15*

Both accounts refer to Hezekiah's prayer for deliverance. Since Chr omits the detailed version of the prayer that follows in

K, he has apparently altered his reference to that prayer in this verse. He states that Isaiah joined Hezekiah in the prayer and that they cried out to the heavens "about this," i.e., about Sennacherib's invasion and his threats. Chr's alterations in this verse are motivated by his omission of Hezekiah's prayer (2 K 19:15b–19) and Isaiah's oracle (2 K 19:20–34).

D. 2 C 32:21/2 K 19:35–37//Isa 37:36–38

C's account of Yahweh's deliverance of Jerusalem is again shorter than K's version. As in the previous two examples there is no really new or different information given in C's version. Hence, it is doubtful that C's variant account here is due to his following other sources. It seems more likely that he has again composed an abbreviated version of the K account. He focuses on Yahweh's mighty act, omitting such details as the number of slain Assyrian soldiers and the escape of Sennacherib's murderers.

E. 2 C 32:24/2 K 20:1–11

The verse in C is clearly a brief summary of the account in K of Hezekiah's request for an extended life and of Yahweh's confirmation of the request by means of a sign./13/

F. 2 C 32:31/2 K 20:12–19

This verse in C appears to be another composition by Chr summarizing the K material. Chr clearly assumes that his readers know the story of the Babylonian envoys at least in some form. However, the interpretation given by Chr is somewhat obscure. He understands the visit of the Babylonian emissaries to represent a testing of Hezekiah by Yahweh. He does not indicate how Hezekiah fared in the test, and it is not certain whether he is attempting to connect this "testing" with the allusion to Hezekiah's pride in vv 25–26.

G. 2 C 34:3–7, 32–33/2 K 23:4–20

Both accounts deal with Josiah's cultic reforms. K's account is longer and more detailed. However, it is doubtful in this case that C's account is due to abbreviation of K. C's account contains additional information to that of K as well as information that is completely different. C states that Josiah turned toward Yahweh

in his eighth year and then began his reform in his twelfth year
(34:3). K lacks this information and does not mention any
reforms of Josiah before the finding of the law in Josiah's eighteenth year (2 K 22:3). C agrees in dating the finding of the law
to Josiah's eighteenth year and describes further reforms following its discovery. The very fact that K agrees in relating that the
law was found while the Temple was being restored indicates that
Josiah's reforms began before the law was found. Furthermore,
there is evidence to indicate that these religious reforms were
connected with a renewed nationalism and a movement toward
political independence. Cross and Freedman have argued that
Chr's information correctly reflects a sequence of movements
toward religious nationalism and political freedom corresponding
to events in the decline of the Neo-Assyrian empire./14/ They also
point out that there is good evidence to believe the report in C that
Josiah's reforms extended into the North (34:6)./15/ This evidence, therefore, indicates that Chr here relies on sources outside
of K. It is striking, nonetheless, that Chr has again omitted the
polemic against Jeroboam and Bethel in 2 K 23:4, 15–19. This
polemic is an important element in Dtr 1's edition of DH. As I
have pointed out, the complete lack of this polemic in C is an
indication of Chr's desire to attract the Northerners to return to
the legitimate Israelite monarchy and cult in the South.

H. *2 C 35:1–17//1 Esdr 1:1–17/2 K 23:21*

Chr's account of the Passover is much more detailed than is
K's. However, Chr's account clearly betrays his own interest in
the cult. Verses 3–6 contain a speech of Josiah to the Levites
instructing them in the preparation of the Passover. It is probably a composition of Chr. Some of the other material in this
passage such as the figures and names in vv 7–9 may also derive
from other sources.

This survey of the material from Hezekiah to Josiah may
now be summarized. First of all, with regard to the extent of
Chr's use of K, it is clear that Chr is familiar with K's account of
this period. Chr has not cited K as frequently nor as literally
here as in 1 C and 2 C 1–28. However, he has clearly cited K
sporadically as seen from the passages in section III. There are
also several passages treated in section IV in which Chr has composed an abbreviated account of the K narrative.

The accounts of C and K for Hezekiah through Josiah diverge more than for any previous historical period. Chr begins with a lengthy section on Hezekiah's reforms and Passover celebration (2 C 29–31) which is hardly paralleled at all in K (cf. 2 K 18:4–18). Their accounts of Sennacherib's invasion vary substantially. C lacks K's "first stage" of the invasion (2 K 18:14–16) as well as Sennacherib's letter, Hezekiah's prayer, and Isaiah's oracle (2 K 19). Chr also abbreviates the account in 2 K 20 about Hezekiah's sickness and the visit of the Babylonian emissaries. The major difference for Hezekiah's reign, therefore, is C's lengthy account of Hezekiah's reforms about which K reports almost nothing. The other narratives in C, though much shorter, are counterparts to longer K narratives.

For Manasseh's reign there are two major differences. First, C includes an account relating Manasseh's repentance in Babylon and his subsequent reforms in Judah after his return (33:11–17). This account is not in K. Secondly, C lacks the judgment against Manasseh, found in 2 K 21:10b–16, that blames him for the impending judgment on Judah. Aside from a few minor changes by Chr there is no significant difference between the accounts of Amon's reign in C and K.

In Josiah's reign the major differences between the two accounts have to do with Josiah's reforms, some of which C dates before the finding of the law in his eighteenth year, and Josiah's Passover, which is larger and more detailed in C than in K.

Most of the differences in the two accounts for this period accord with Chr's use of DH material as we have seen in the two previous chapters. Two cases stand out, however. One of them is the strikingly different perspective of K and C on Masasseh. For K in its present form Manasseh is the worst king of all, while for C Manasseh ends his reign as an essentially good king. I have already suggested that the difference here is due to changes made by Dtr 2, and I shall discuss this proposal in greater detail in the final chapter.

The other striking difference in this material is C's lengthy account of Hezekiah's reforms, including his Passover celebration, where K has but a brief reference to Hezekiah's reforms. Certainly, as has been observed, Chr's interests permeate these accounts, but this alone is not sufficient to account for all of C's extra material here where K has hardly any. Moreover, it is not in line with Chr's use of DH material that he should fabricate the story of Hezekiah's reforms out of whole cloth.

Fortunately, this question has been discussed in detail in a recent article by J. Rosenbaum./16/ Rosenbaum's argument takes place in three levels. He provides strong evidence against the position, which goes back to Wellhausen, that C's account of Hezekiah's reform is an invention by later writers for the purpose of imitating Josiah's reform./17/ Here he points out that there are few similarities in details between C's account of Hezekiah's Passover celebration and K's account of Josiah's Passover celebration. Thus, the evidence for Chr's having read Josiah's Passover back into Hezekiah's time is slim. On another level, Rosenbaum gathers the archaeological evidence indicating that Hezekiah's administration may have been superior to that of Josiah in terms of political and geographic control. Building projects which were previously dated to Josiah's time must now be attributed to Hezekiah. In terms of the literary evidence this means that C's account of Hezekiah's reform certainly has its basis in sources outside of K and that it is not simply Chr's fabrication on the basis of K's account of Josiah. The third aspect in Rosenbaum's article is a disscussion of the literary evidence of DH and C. He discusses the purpose of each and adopts a position very close to the one I have adopted. He finds in their respective purposes a solution for the large difference in their reports about Hezekiah's reform. Chr included the material about Hezekiah's reform because it was reported in his other sources, and it fit well with his concern for the practice of the cult and the continuation of the Davidic line. Dtr 1, in contrast, suppressed the information about Hezekiah in favor of the hero of his work, Josiah. Indeed, the fact that the two kings were similar in many ways and that Hezekiah's attempt at reform had failed caused Dtr 1 to give only slight consideration to Hezekiah.

Rosenbaum's argument is basically sound./18/ He shows that the difference between the accounts of C and K in Hezekiah's reign is not a matter of one being tendentious and the other historical but is caused by the fact that their interests diverge at Hezekiah's reign. Rosenbaum does not, perhaps, stress fully the interests of Chr that are obvious here, but we have seen that the account of Hezekiah's reforms in C is replete with his own concerns. Nonetheless, Rosenbaum has gathered convincing evidence indicating that C's account is based on historical sources. Rosenbaum's conclusions can be extended farther than

he has done. He points out that Dtr l's omissions in the case of
Hezekiah's reforms have in common that they are complimentary to Hezekiah./19/ Dtr 1 did not wish to detract from the
main focus of his work, Josiah./20/ However, Hezekiah is not
the only king of Judah for whom C has complimentary information that is lacking in K. A cursory examination of section III in
the previous chapter reveals a number of passages that have no
parallel in K in which C describes a Judean king's cultic reforms
and/or political strength. A list of those passages and the kings
involved follows.

2 C 11:5–12	*Rehoboam's* fortifications in Judah
2 C 13:3–21	*Abijah* defeats Jeroboam by the will of Yahweh
2 C 14:2–14	*Asa's* cultic reforms, fortifications, and victory over Zerah the Ethiopian
2 C 15:8–15	*Asa's* additional reforms and purification of the Temple
2 C 17:2–19	*Jehoshaphat's* dedication to Yahweh and the strength of his kingdom
2 C 19:1–20:30	*Jehoshaphat* encourages the people to turn to Yahweh, and Yahweh gives him victory over his enemies
2 C 26:5–15	*Uzziah's* military prowess and building projects
2 C 27:3b–6	*Jotham's* building projects and victory over Ammon

The very fact that for so many kings C provides positive,
detailed information where K has little or no such information is
striking in itself. The evidence reveals even more upon closer
examination. In some of these cases K gives only a brief statement
of the king's piety and reform (cf. Asa, 1 K 15:9–15). In the cases of
Uzziah (2 K 15: 1–7) and Jotham (2 K 15:32–36) K's positive statement is entirely formulaic, "he did what was right in the eyes of
Yahweh, according to all that his father PN had done." The positive information regarding Jehoshaphat in K is similarly brief and
formulaic. K gives no positive information for Rehoboam or Abijah. Abijah's case is especially interesting, because K's reference to
him is almost completely formulaic (1 K 15:1–3). This suggests
that Dtr 1 merely employed the same negative, stereotyped judgment for him as he did for most of the Judean kings.

In my treatment of the passages about these kings I have suggested two possible reasons for the differences in K and C. One was Chr's tendency to periodize. While this tendency may explain the arrangement of the material in C's account, it does not explain the content of the positive reports about these kings. The second reason was simply that Chr had sources available to him that differed from K. However, this possibility does not account fully for the consistency with which the positive details about these kings in C are lacking in K and for the extensive differences in several cases between C's detailed positive remarks and K's brief, stereotyped summaries.

On the basis of Rosenbaum's conclusions for the accounts of Hezekiah and Josiah I suggest that Dtr 1's own interests may explain why K has virtually nothing good to say about some kings, at least not in any detail, while C gives a detailed account of their piety and power. Since Dtr 1's work points toward and eventually focuses on Josiah, it may be that he sometimes ignored positive information about other kings, as he did with Hezekiah, in order to stress Josiah's uniqueness or to remove any potential rivals of his religious and political prowess. This bias of Dtr 1 may not have been active for all of the six kings cited above. It is difficult, for example, to imagine that Dtr 1 could have perceived in Rehoboam's reforms as they are detailed in C a rival to Josiah. However, in most of the other cases it is possible that Dtr 1's focus on Josiah led him to play down the reform attempts of previous kings. The extensive reforms of Jehoshaphat, especially, could easily be perceived as rivaling Josiah's reforms.

The important point raised by Rosenbaum's work is that both Dtr 1 and Chr produced tendentious works. This must be recognized in any comparative treatment of their accounts, and it applies to the accounts about kings before Hezekiah as well as Hezekiah and Josiah. The fact that DH was written with certain interests and biases has not always received sufficient recognition in scholarly comparisons with C./21/ There is no tendentious motive for Chr's invention of the additional complimentary information about the six kings listed above. However, there is a bias on the part of Dtr 1 which surfaces clearly in his treatment of Hezekiah that could account for the omission from his history of the details of some of these kings' reforms.

V. *Formulae*

In his study of Chr's sources, H. R. Macy offers an analysis of the three types of formulae that typically enclose the narratives about kings in C and K: the accession formulae, death-burial notices, and source notices./22/ A summary of his arguments and conclusions for each of the three types follows.

The only similarity of any kind between the source notices in C and those in K is the initial expression *yeter dibrê* PN. Every other element of the notices in the two versions, both in terms of content and form, is consistently different. Even in the initial expression the similarity breaks down. While K always has *yeter dibrê* PN,/23/ C shows more variation and sometimes has only *dibrê* PN. Once it has *šĕ'ar dibrê* (2 C 9:29) and once the entire expression is lacking (2 C 24:27). Macy concludes that the consistent differences in this formula are too great to believe that Chr borrowed the formula from K. There is, therefore, no evidence for the position that C's source citations represent literary embellishments patterned after K./24/ This does not rule out the possibility that Chr invented the names that he cites as sources, but what possible motive would he have for doing so? The evidence, then, suggests that Chr relied on a different formula from that of K for his source notices and that the contents of those notices were also drawn from sources other than K.

The similarity in form and certain details of content make it clear that Chr knew the death-burial notices found in K, at least in some form. It is also clear that he frequently changes or supplements K's notices on the basis of other sources available to him./25/ Macy points out some interesting facts regarding the death-burial notices in C and K. First, C does not report the death of any king after Josiah. I shall have more to say about this in the next chapter. Secondly, two expressions, "with his fathers" and "in the city of David," which are commonly used in K to describe the place of burial for kings before Hezekiah, are no longer used in K or C in the burial notices for any king after Hezekiah. Macy ascribed this difference to a change in the scribal convention of the Deuteronomistic school./26/

The accession formulae for Judean kings normally consist of three parts: (1) the king's age at accession, (2) the name of the queen mother, and (3) an evaluation of the king in religious terms. K has accession formulae for all Judean kings except Solomon and

Athaliah. C has them for all but David, Solomon, Asa, and Athaliah. Macy comments on the last two elements of the formula. He
notices that after Hezekiah's accession the name of the queen
mother no longer appears in C's accession formulae, though it does
continue in K. This change cannot be the result of any bias on the
part of C, since the formulae in C consistently include the queen
mother's name up to and including Hezekiah's accession. Nor is
there any indication that the change is due to textual corruption.
Therefore, the difference must be due to a change in C's source for
the accession formulae. Next, Macy deals with the third element of
the accession formulae, the religious evaluation. It is clear from the
regularity of vocabulary and phraseology of these brief evaluations, in contrast to the other information that both K and C sometimes give about the religious practices of various kings, that the
evaluations are indeed a part of the accession formula. It is also
clear that this part of the accession formula is Deuteronomistic.
Macy, however, postulates that the formulae do not stem from Dtr
1 but from an earlier Deuteronomistic source. He concludes,
therefore, that Dtr 1 and Chr each used an earlier Deuteronomistic source for their accession formulae and that C does not depend
on K in its present form for those formulae./27/

Macy's observations are significant for two periods of our
present study. First, his work indicates that none of the three
formulae are borrowed by C from K after the time of Josiah.
The implications of this observation will be explored in the next
chapter. Secondly, Macy's observations about the name of the
queen mother in the accession formulae and the phrases "with
his fathers" and "in the city of David" in the death-burial notices
point to a definite change in C's source(s) for these formulae at
the time of Hezekiah. All three of these changes have apparently
taken place within the Deuteronomistic school. The accumula-
tion of these changes for the time of Hezekiah is striking in light
of the hypothesis that the *Grundschrift* of DH (DtrG) was issued
shortly after the fall of the North in 721 B.C./28/ The evidence
is still too vague to support any definite conclusions, but it is
possible that the changes perceived by Macy in the Deuteronomistic school at Hezekiah's reign are to be attributed to the conclusion of DtrG with Hezekiah./29/

I have sought to extend the conclusions of two recent contributions to the study of C in order to explain the changes that
occur in C's use of K at the reign of Hezekiah and to explore the

implications of those conclusions for C's use of DH. I have suggested that Rosenbaum's conclusion, which points to Dtr 1's bias as the main reason for the large difference between the accounts of Hezekiah's reform in C and K may also be extended to the reigns of previous kings of Judah for whom K says little positive while C details their reforms. This is not to deny C's interests and biases in the accounts of these kings. The point is that both histories were written as programs. More exactly, both are theological interpretations of the past written in support of contemporary political and cultic reforms. Macy's observations about the formulae in K and C indicate that Chr sometimes follows a source other than K for his formulae and that several changes in Deuteronomistic scribal practice surface at the time of Hezekiah. I have suggested the possibility that the scribal change is related to the appearance of a preliminary edition of DH or DtrG during Hezekiah's reign. I have argued that the conclusions reached in this chapter have implications for earlier material in C and K. They are also important for the investigation of the reports about Josiah's heirs which is taken up in the next chapter.

NOTES

/1/   This is, of course, a complex historical problem. K may conflate two accounts of Sennacherib's campaign. See the discussions of B. Oded, "Judah and the Exile," *Israelite and Judean History* (ed. J. H. Hayes and J. M. Miller; OTL; Philadelphia: Westminster, 1977) 449–51, and B. S. Childs, *Isaiah and the Assyrian Crisis* (SBT 2/3; London: SCM, 1967).

/2/   The literary relationship between these accounts of Isaiah and K is also a complex problem and does not concern us here. See Childs, *Assyrian Crisis*, 69–103, 137–40.

/3/   Pratt's paper, "Incomparability of Hezekiah," argues convincingly that Hezekiah's prayer in this passage is a composition of Dtr 1, thus effectively removing the possibility that this material is missing from C because it is a later addition to K by Dtr 2.

/4/   The debate began with Torrey ("Revised View," 405–10) who argued that the gap between vv 19 and 20 of 2 C 35 was filled by the insertion of 2 K 23:24–28 in the Hebrew text. The gap was caused by the deletion of the original reading which had become corrupt. It is the original reading that underlies 1 Esdr 1:21–22 (see B below). Klein ("New Evidence for an Old Recension of Reigns," *HTR* 60 [1967]: 93–105) has challenged Torrey's views by arguing that the addition in vv 19a–d was borrowed from a pre-*kaige* (probably proto-Lucianic) recension of K. L. C. Allen, in a response to Klein's article entitled "Further Thoughts on an Old Recension of Reigns in Paralipomena" (*HTR* 61 [1968]: 483–91), argued that vv 19a–d are a translation of a Hebrew text by the same person who translated the rest of Paralipomena. Klein defended his original position in "Supplements in the Paralipomena: A Rejoinder," *HTR* 61 (1968): 492–95. Finally, a second response by Allen is found in his *Greek Chronicles*, I, 214–16. Klein's arguments appear to be the strongest. Allen's view that the text of Paralipomena reflects a continual "drifting back" to K on the part of its *Vorlage* is difficult to accept. Certainly there is a degree of assimilation between texts, but Allen's examples are not convincing because he does not take into account the possibility of different text types and the natural results of textual evolution.

/5/   For a detailed treatment of Chr's interest in the Levites in this chapter see Petersen, *Late Israelite Prophecy*, 78–85. In addition to Chr's interests which pervade this material, there is reason to believe that Chr has moved up the beginning of Hezekiah's reform to the first month of his first year (29:3) as evidence of his piety. This is the argument of Cogan, "Tendentious Chronology," 165–72.

/6/   See the discussion of Myers, *II Chronicles*, 198–99.

/7/   See Rudolph, *Chronikbücher*, 318. Cf. Myers, *II Chronicles*, 199.

/8/   Torrey, "Revised View," 405–10.

/9/   The language is somewhat similar to what is said of Manasseh in 2 C 33:9//2 K 21:9, but in the light of Chr's account of Manasseh's repentance it is questionable that he had Manasseh in mind here. Torrey and others have seen v 22 as a reference to 1 K 13:2.

/10/ Rudolph, *Chronikbücher*, 330–31.

/11/ The parallel to 1 Esdr 1:23 in C^M (35:20) begins אחרי כל זאת אשר הכין יאשיהו את הבית. This phrase clearly appears expansionistic. However, its reading אחרי is preferable to the ואחרי reflected in 1 Esdr 1:23. The graphic similarity between אחרי and וישרו (the *mater lectionis* would not have been written) increases the homoioarchton. The final letters (*yod/waw*) could easily be confused and יו written close together could also be mistaken for א by a careless eye. See Cross, "Jewish Scripts."

/12/ Contra Rudolph, *Chronikbücher*, 324.

/13/ The latter half of the verse in C is probably corrupt, since ויאמר לו without a quotation following it makes no sense. It is possible that ויעתר לו should be read (cf. G^B: και επηκουσεν αυτω), but the graphic similarity is not strong. Rudolph (*Chronikbücher*, 320) has conjectured that a quotation beginning with מרפא (מרפה) originally followed לו and has been lost by haplography occassioned by homoiarchton.

/14/ F. M. Cross and D. N. Freedman, "Josiah's Revolt Against Assyria," *JNES* (1953) 56–58. The article requires some revision because of the apparent assumption of its authors that the Assyrians imposed their religion upon their vassals so that any religious reform would automatically constitute a political rebellion against the suzerain. This position has been disproved by M. Cogan, *Imperialism and Religion: Assyria, Judah and Israel in the Eighth and Seventh Centuries B.C.E.* (Missoula: Scholars Press, 1974), and by J. W. McKay (*Religion in Judah Under the Assyrians 732–609 B.C.*). However, it is still likely that Josiah's reforms were a part of a new nationalistic thrust in Judah or that the nationalism was a part of his religious reform. It is striking that while Chr moves Hezekiah's reforms up to the beginning of his reign as proof of his piety (see n. 5), Josiah's reform does not begin until his eighth year. This is another indication that Chr is drawing on historical sources outside of K for his dates and information on Josiah's reign. Thus, while the chronology employed by Cross and Freedman may stand in need of some revision, their basic point is still valid.

/15/ Cross and Freedman "Josiah's Revolt," 57.

/16/ J. Rosenbaum, "Hezekiah's Reform and the Deuteronomistic Tradition," *HTR* 72 (1979) 23–43.

/17/ On the history of scholarly opinion regarding the historicity of Hezekiah's reform see Rosenbaum, "Hezekiah's Reform," 23–24.

/18/ There is one major error in the article. He states that the submission to Assyria meant forced acceptance of their deities (37). Again, this notion has been shown incorrect by Cogan, *Imperialism and Religion*, and McKay, *Religion in Judah.*

/19/ "Hezekiah's Reform," 41.

/20/ Dtr 1's bias on behalf of Josiah and his apparent suppression of information about Hezekiah leads one to suspect that Hezekiah's reform in fact served as a model for Josiah's reform and perhaps for part of Dtr 1's report of Josiah's reform. The general similarity of the two reforms is obvious, and their occurrence within one hundred years of each other makes it difficult to believe that Josiah's actions were not influenced by what his predecessor had done. This would be particularly true if, as C's accounts indicate, Hezekiah's reform was actually the more illustrious of the two. I owe this suggestion to Prof. Michael Coogan of Harvard University. It is certainly a possibility that merits investigation.

/21/ Cf. von Rad, *Geschichtsbild*, 121.

/22/ Macy, "Sources of the Books of Chronicles" (unpublished Ph.D. Thesis, Harvard University, 1975) 115–65.

/23/ In 1 K 15:23 M varies slightly, but the usual expression is preserved in the OG.

/24/ See Macy ("Sources," 151) for some who hold this position.

/25/ I have already had occasion to refer to Chr's use of other sources in his account of Joash's burial (p. 111). Other kings for whom C has different or additional death-burial information include Asa (2 C 16:14; 1 K 15:24), Jehoram (2 C 21:18–20; 2 K 8:24), Uzziah (2 C 26:23; 2 K 15:7), Ahaz (2 C 28:27; 2 K 16:20), and Hezekiah (2 C 32:33; 2 K 20:21).

/26/ Macy, "Sources," 141–42. His position here contrasts with that of S. Bin-Nun ("Formulas from Royal Records of Israel and of Judah," *VT* 18 [1968]: 430–31) who argues that the variation in reporting the burials of kings from Hezekiah on represents a change in the actual burial practice.

/27/ Macy suggests that his hypothesis that C follows an earlier Deuteronomistic source for its accession formulae helps to explain the cases where C's formula differs slightly from K's (e.g., 2 C 22:3–4//2 K 8:27 and 2 C 25:2//2 K 14:3) as well as the fact that for Rehoboam C has an accession formula where K has none (2 C 12:14). Macy's example from 2 C 25:2 must be rejected since the difference here is due to intentional change on the part of Chr (cf. p. 104). Also, although K has no accession formula for Rehoboam, 1 K 14:21–28 parallels C's formula. The only difference is that the evaluation is given for Judah not for Rehoboam. Still, the point made by Macy may be valid. The only remaining case of differing formulae is 2 C 22:3–4//2 K 8:27. Here Macy's suggestion that the differences are due to C's following an earlier Deuteronomistic source may well be correct.

/28/ The most thorough presentation of this hypothesis is Nicholson's *Deuteronomy and Tradition*.

/29/ Nicholson actually dated DtrG to Manasseh's reign (ibid., 101–2), but he had very little evidence for this assertion. Hezekiah's reign is a much better setting a priori for a work which could have served as a program for nationalistic and Yahwistic revival. Such a work might also include an explanation of why Israel had fallen but not Judah. This may be a part of the reason for the stress on Yahweh's eternal pact with David. Macy's observations also point to a Hezekian date. The idea of an eighth century *Grundschrift* might help explain statements such as "There was none like him (Hezekiah) among all the kings of Judah after him" (2 K 18:5). It is difficult to believe that Dtr 1, whose hero was Josiah, could have written such a statement. One may also point out that the late eighth century was a time of significant literary activity in Israel. The Northern prophetic stories in K were probably brought to Judah at this time along with the Northern royal annals used as a source by Dtr 1. Furthermore, there are important prophetic works from this period, especially Hosea and Amos. Nicholson argues that Deuteronomy and DtrG stem from the same prophetic circles as Hosea and Amos (ibid., 58–82). Whether or not this conclusion is correct, his arguments do show that the end of the eighth century was probably an important literary period within the Deuteromistic school.

Chapter 6

JOSIAH'S DEATH TO THE EXILE
2 C 35:20–36:23 (1 Esdr 1:23–2:5)/2 K 23:29–25:30

I. *Material in K Unparalleled in C*

A. *2 K 24:3–4*

These two verses place the blame for Judah's fall on Manasseh. I have already observed that C presents a different view of
Manasseh and attributes the demise of Judah to causes other
than Manasseh's evil. It is striking that according to 2 K 24:4
Manasseh's greatest sin was shedding blood in Jerusalem. Yet in
the initial report about Manasseh (2 K 21:1–9//2 C 32:1–9)
nothing is mentioned about Manasseh's blood shedding. There
his sin is cultic. This difference within K itself may signal a
change in editorial levels within DH that is concentrated in the
reports about Manasseh. This possibility will be explored more
fully in the next chapter.

B. *2 K 25:22–26*

The K account of the appointment of Gedaliah as governor
over Judah and his murder at the hands of Ishmael appears to be
a shortened form of the similar narrative in Jer 40:7–41:18. C
has no reference at all to Gedaliah but goes from the account of
the exile directly to the story of Cyrus' edict.

C. *2 K 25:27–30//Jer 52:31–34*

The well known reference to the improvement of Jehoiachin's status has a close parallel in Jeremiah. Again, however, C
reports nothing about the period between the fall of Judah and
Cyrus' edict.

II. *C Material Unparalleled in K*

A. *2 C 36:13b–17 (1 Esdr 1:46b–50)*

It is usually argued that because of his dogma of immediate retribution Chr blames Zedekiah and his contemporaries for the exile./1/ Certainly the focus of vv 13b–14 is Zedekiah's reign. However, vv 15–16 appear broader in their perspective. They describe an extended period of time in which Yahweh's compassion (*ḥml*) is stretched to its limit "until there was no remedy" because the people continuously spurn his prophets. To be sure, the notion of immediate retribution is important to Chr. However, in most of the earlier cases where Chr's retribution dogma is apparent, the focus is on the sins of a single king and his resulting destruction. The exile, in contrast, is a major national calamity that is brought about over a period of time by more than the sins of an individual king or reign. It is unclear how extensive a period Chr has in mind. He may be thinking about the entire history of Israel. Another possibility is that he thinks only about the reigns of kings following Josiah. His account of each of these kings is brief, and his dogma of divine retribution does not surface in the case of any one of these kings, though all of them are sinful.

B. *2 C 36:22–23 (1 Esdr 2:1–5; Ezra 1:1–3)*

As discussed in Chapter 2, Chr's work continues with a description of the foundation of the Temple, completing the real focus of his program for the restoration of the Davidic monarchy and the Temple cult. These two verses are the final verses of C in its canonical form, but they are actually the beginning of the final episode of Chr's history. Since DH does not extend beyond the exile, there can be no question of Chr's use of DH from this point on.

III. *Parallel Material in K and C*

2 C 36:2, 5, 9, 11–12a (1 Esdr 1:32b–33a, 37, 41b–42, 44b–45a)//2 K 23:31–32, 36–37; 24:8–9, 18–19

The only verses in this entire section that can be considered in any way parallel are the accession formulae. Even so, it is clear from Macy's conclusions that C has not borrowed these formulae from K. None of the four formulae in C includes the name of the queen mother in contrast to their K counterparts./2/ Different sources may also be indicated in 2 C 36:9//2 K 24:8–9 where C states that Jehoiachin began to reign at eight years old and reigned three months and ten days, while K gives his age at accession as eighteen and his length of reign as three months. The difference in regard to his accession age may be due to textual corruption, but the difference in regard to his length of reign is probably due to Chr's different source.

The formulae in C also differ from from those in K in the evaluation of the kings. Once, C lacks the evaluation altogether (36:2). In the other three cases, C lacks the modifying phrase, "according to all that his father(s)/PN did," which consistently occurs as a part of these four formulae in K. One might argue that this phrase has been deleted from 2 C 36:5 because K has "according to all that his fathers did" at this point (23:37), and C did not view Josiah as an evildoer. This argument is not valid for the other two formulae, however, and is nullified by the fact that in the other two formulae C's lack of a similar phrase cannot be explained as Chr's bias.

These four formulae are strikingly different in K and C from the formulae encountered earlier in both works. K uses similar formulae for Uzziah (2 K 15:3), Jotham (15:34), Hezekiah (18:3), and Amon (21:20), though in each case there are minor differences. K tends to vary the formulae for kings before Josiah. Sometimes the formula *wy'ś hyšr/hr' b'yny yhwh* occurs. Other times K uses *wylk (bkl) drk* PN. When K does have the former type a comparison often follows: *k'šr 'śh* PN, *kkl 'šr 'śh* PN *('byw)*, or simply *k*PN./3/ There is a good deal of variation within the formulae in K, even those of the same type. It is striking, therefore, that suddenly for the final four kings of Judah one finds what is essentially the same formula with very little variation. Furthermore, the evaluative supplements, which occur fairly regularly in K for the previous kings suddenly disappear from Josiah on./4/ These changes reflect the difference in the Dtr 1 and Dtr 2 editions of DH. Dtr 2 has adopted one type of accession formula which he repeats almost slavishly for the last four kings.

The situation for C is no less striking. While C previously uses the formula *wy'ś hr' b'yny yhwh*, it never stands alone. There is always an additional phrase of comparison (2 C 25:2;

26:4; 27:2; 28:1; 29:2; 33:2, 22) or specification of some kind
(12:14; 24:2; 25:2) following the formula. The only exception is
2 C 14:1, and there the formula differs slightly by reading *ḥṭwb
wḥyšr.* . . . It is striking, therefore, that C uses precisely the
same, brief formula for the last three kings./5/ There is another,
related question here. As Macy pointed out, the evaluation
marks the accession formulae as Deuteronomistic. Since C did
not borrow his accession formula from K, at least after Hezekiah, how can one explain the Deuteronomistic formulae in C?
Must one postulate a Deuteronomistic source after Dtr 1, but not
identical to Dtr 2, from which C has borrowed the final three
accession formulae? While this is not impossible, it is perhaps
more likely that the formula used for the last three kings in C
derives from Chr himself. The formula is very stereotyped, and
Chr was certainly familiar enough with the Deuteronomistic
formulae to employ this brief evaluation for the final three
kings. Chr did not use K as a source for his accession formulae
after Hezekiah, and as I will argue, he did not use DH as a
source after Josiah. The information in his accession formulae
about the king's age at accession and length of reign could easily
have been borrowed from the Judean annals or other sources
based on them. This possibility may help to explain the different
information in 2 C 36:9//2 K 24:8 about Jehoiachin's accession.
In order to complete the formula as he had learned it from his
Deuteronomistic source, Chr could have composed the very
short evaluation used for the final three kings.

IV. *Passages About the Same Topic that are not Parallel*

A. *2 C 35:20–27 (1 Esdr 1:23–31)/ 2 K 23:29–30a*

The account in C is much longer than the one in K, and C
presents a good deal of information that is not found in K including the place of battle, Carchemish (35:20), Neco's letter (v 21),
Josiah's death by archers (v 23), the changing of chariots (v 24),
and the mourning for Josiah (v 25). These additional details make
it obvious that C's account is based on a source other than K./6/ In
Chr's view, Josiah's failure to heed Yahweh's warning through
Neco led to his death. Admittedly, this explanation is unusual for
Chr, but Josiah's death was not an ordinary circumstance. The
event posed a theological crisis. Josiah's faithfulness made his vio-
lent death difficult to comprehend.

B. *2 C 36:1–4 (1 Esdr 1:32–36)/2 K 23:30b–35*

While the two accounts of Jehoahaz' reign are more similar than the other material about this period, there are still good reasons for believing that Chr follows a source other than K. The accession formula in 36:2/23:31–32 has already been discussed. In 23:35 K alone refers to Jehoiakim's collecting taxes for Pharaoh Neco. C's omission of this information can hardly be due to bias and is more likely due to his different source. Also in 2 C 36:3a/2 K 23:33a K relates that Neco bound Jehoahaz and exiled him in Riblah while C states merely that the king of Egypt deposed him in Jerusalem. Again the difference is probably due to Chr's using a different source from K for his account. In the rest of this material C and K contain the same basic information. This does not necessarily mean that Chr's source for this information was K. It could be derived from an independent source, written or oral, especially since the content of the material is purely factual. Moreover, it is important to recall here that Chr used a proto-Rabbinic text of K as his source. This means that if Chr used K for the account of Jehoahaz one expects to find that the two accounts are nearly verbatim the same, as in 2 C 1–28 and its K parallels. In 2 C 36: 1–4//2 K 23:30b–34 K and C deal with the same basic subject matter, but they vary in the expressions they employ. There is enough variation in language to indicate that C's source was not K. This fits well with the situation in the surrounding material where C's source is clearly not K.

C. *2 C 36:6–8 (1 Esdr 1:38–40)/2 K 24:1–2, 5–6*

The only real similarity between the two reports about Jehoiakim's reign is the statement in 36:6/24:1 that Nebuchadrezzar came up against Jehoiakim. I have already argued that the accession formulae (36:5/23:36–37) and the source notices (36:8/24:5) reflect different sources in C from those reflected in K. I have also discussed the judgment of K in 24:3–4. The rest of the material in this section is totally different in the two accounts. There can be no question of Chr's giving an abbreviation of the K account, since the two accounts give altogether different information. C refers to Jehoiakim's being fettered and sent to Babylonian and to Nebuchadnezzar's taking some of the Temple utensils. K says nothing about either of these matters and refers instead to the raiding bands from the surrounding nations that attacked Judah.

D. *2 C 36:10 (1 Esdr 1:43–44a)/2 K 24:10–17*

C's account of Jehoiachin's reign is extremely brief compared to that of K. Again it is clear that Chr is following a
source other than K because of the different information contained in C. For example, C alone dates Jehoiachin's exile to the
spring of the year. Also C says only that Nebuchadrezzar sent
and had Jehoiachin brought, while K states that Nebuchadrezzar
himself came to Jerusalem. C has no parallel to K's lengthy list
of persons and things taken by Nebuchadrezzar into exile to
Babylon. C states simply that he took the precious vessels of the
Temple. Nor does C record Zedekiah's name change from the
original Mattaniah as found in K (24:17). Since C does record a
similar name change for Jehoiakim (36:4), there can be no bias
that would prevent him from relating Zedekiah's name change.
The reason for this difference must be sought in Chr's different
source.

E. *2 C 36:12b–13a (1 Esdr 1:45b–46a)/2 K 24:20//Jer 52:3*

The references to Zedekiah's rebellion against Nebuchadrezzar are quite different in K and C. C ascribes Zedekiah's problems
to the fact that he did not humble himself before Jeremiah, Yahweh's messenger. C also implies that Zedekiah's rebellion against
Nebuchadrezzar was sinful because he had sworn allegiance to
him by Yahweh. K, in contrast, states only that Yahweh was angry
with Jerusalem and Judah and that Zedekiah rebelled against the
king of Babylon. It is clear that Chr's source here is not K.

F. 2 C 36:18–21 (1 Esdr 1:51–55)/2 K 25:1–21//Jer 52:4–27

The accounts of the destruction of Jerusalem in K and C are
very different. K is longer and more detailed. They hardly share a
phrase in common. Also, the order of the information they present
varies. C describes the sacking of the Temple (v 18) before the
burning of the city and the exile (vv 19–20). In K the destruction of
the city and the exile (vv 8–12) are described before the plunder-
ing of the Temple (vv 13–17). There is much in K here that really
has no counterpart in C, including the report of the siege of Jerusalem and its fall in 2 K 25:1–7 and the capture and death of certain
noteworthy citizens of Jerusalem (vv 18–21). C also contains some
non-paralleled information in its brief account. In v 18 C refers to

the treasures of the king's princes (*śārāyw*) which K does not mention. Also in vv 20–21 C refers to the establishment of the Persian kingdom and the length of the Judean exile. The seventy-year exile fulfills a prophecy of Jeremiah. C's reference to this fulfillment along with the different endings of the canonical books reflects a very different perspective of the respective writers. Dtr 2 writes from the middle of the exile. He describes events leading up to his time. Whatever hope he holds for the future is an uncertain one. Chr, on the other hand, describes the exile as an event that is past. It is an unpleasant memory that may serve as a warning for the future but does not require elaboration. Chr holds a great deal of hope for the future.

In this survey of the material from the death of Josiah to the exile we have found that in every passage Chr relies on sources other than K for his account. This phenomenon stands in striking contrast to the situation for the material surveyed earlier. There it is clear that DH is C's main source for every king. Even for the reign of Hezekiah where Chr uses other sources extensively, it is still obvious that he knows K and has abbreviated some of its accounts. In the earlier material I suggested that where Chr uses DH he generally follows it closely. Again, this is especially evident in 2 C where Chr's K *Vorlage* was proto-Rabbinic. It is, therefore, very striking to find no truly parallel passages beginning with Josiah's death. This evidence, then, provides the answer to the question of the extent of Chr's use of DH, which has been born in mind throughout this survey. Chr uses DH up to the account of Josiah's death, but not thereafter.

Why would Chr cease to use DH from the time of Josiah's death on? This change obviously cannot be attributed to his bias nor to textual corruption or text type. It must, therefore, have to do with a change in Chr's sources, specifically his Deuteronomistic source. I have already expressed agreement with the theory that the Dtr 1 edition of DH was a program for the Josianic reform and that DH was subsequently extended by an exilic editor. The fact that Chr's use of K ceases with the death of Josiah fits well with this theory of two editions of DH. I suggest, therefore, that Chr uses the work of Dtr 1 as a source but not the work of Dtr 2. If this suggestion is correct, then C may furnish something of an objective criterion for distinguishing between Dtr 1 material and Dtr 2 material. This possibility and its implications will be investigated in the following chapter.

NOTES

/1/   Cf. Williamson, *Israel*, 19.

/2/   The name of the queen mother is found in B (C) in the formulae of Jehoahaz (36:2) and Jehoiakim (36:5). However, it is obvious that most of 36:1–8 has been secondarily borrowed into C^G from K. This is particularly clear from 36:2a–c, 4a, 5a–d, all of which parallel K material not found in C^M. In these eight verses C^G conflates the accounts of K and C.

/3/   See Macy's chart in "Sources," pp. 128–30.

/4/   Ibid., 126–27, and the chart on p. 134.

/5/   2 C 36:5 and 12 have *b'yny yhwh 'lhyw*, while 2 C 36:9 has only *b'yny yhwh*. However, the reading in 1 Esdras reflects only *yhwh* in all three cases. Therefore, *'lhyw* in 2 C 36:5, 12 is probably an expansion.

/6/   Williamson's recent attempt to connect C's report here with an extension of DH used by Chr is not convincing ("The Death of Josiah and the Continuing Development of the Deuteronomic History," *VT* 32 [1982]: 242–47). His view does not account for all of these differences, some of which show no tie with the K material. He argues that 2 C 35:21–22 cannot be Chr's composition, because elsewhere he places such warnings in the mouths of prophets or Levites. However, Williamson himself points out that 1 Esdr 1:28 ascribes words of warning to Jeremiah not Neco as in 2 C 35:22. Contrary to Williamson, the Esdras reading here must be regarded as original. Not only does 1 Esdras frequently preserve a better text of Chr's work, as has already been argued, but in this reading, it is easy to see how "Jeremiah" would be changed to "Neco" in order to accord with 2 C 35:21//1 Esdr 1:25. Thus, 2 C 35:21–22 probably comes from Chr's hand. Williamson also argues that the similarity of Josiah's death with that of Ahab in 1 K 22:34–37 supports his contention about an extension of DH. He is correct that C's report of Josiah's death shares several characteristics with K's report of Ahab's death. C does not report Ahab's death because he was a Northern king. However, Chr was surely familiar with the account in K, and he could have composed his report of Josiah's death on the basis of that account. Chr clearly composed on the basis of his DH source in some of the earlier material. In short, Chr's account of Josiah's death is a mixture of his own composition and information from other sources probably including oral tradition.

Chapter 7

THE USE OF C IN SEPARATING
REDACTIONAL LEVELS IN DH

The purpose of this chapter is to investigate the implications of the suggestion that Chr used only Dtr 1's edition of DH. Of particular interest is the question as to whether C can be used as an objective criterion for separating material of the Dtr 2 edition from that of the Dtr 1 edition. Those passages in K that have been attributed by different scholars to Dtr 2 will be considered here in the light of C's parallels./1/ C contains a close parallel to four of these passages: 1 K 8:23–61; 9:4–9; 2 K 21:2–15; 22:15–20. If C indeed reflects only Dtr 1's edition, then these passages must all be ascribed to Dtr 1. However, I have taken the position that the original work of Chr was extended and revised by later editors (Chr 2 and Chr 3), and a few passages which contain secondary additions to C have already been found (2 C 1:14–17; 15:16–18; 20:33). Thus, one must consider the possibility that the C parallels to these four alleged Dtr 2 passages are secondary revisions of C by a later editor. Hence, the present investigation entails an evaluation of the arguments, primarily literary and thematic, from the side of DH for deriving each of the passages below from Dtr 2. Where C contains a close parallel one must also consider whether there is literary or thematic evidence from the side of C for viewing the C parallel as a secondary addition.

The chart on the next page displays the passages in K which four scholars, whose works are discussed in chapter one, ascribe to Dtr 2./2/ Cross initially suggested that Dtr 2's work consisted of bringing the Dtr 1 edition up to date with the addition of 2 K 23:25b–25:30 and blaming Manasseh for the fall of Judah (2 K 21: 2–15; cf. 24:3–4)./3/ In addition, he discerned Dtr 2 passages under three categories: passages that make the promise to David conditional (1 K 2:4; 6:11–13; 8:25b; 9:4–5); passages that seem to presuppose the exile (2 K 17:19; 20:17–18; 22:15–20); and passages

that appear addressed to the exiles or call for their repentance
(1 K 8:46–53; 9:6–9)./4/ Since the studies of Friedman and Nelson
have resulted in lists of Dtr 2 passages that are generally quite
similar to that of Cross, I will discuss the various alleged Dtr 2
passages within the rubric of these five categories.

Cross	Friedman	Nelson	Levenson
1 K 2:4			
6:11–13	(6:11–13)		
8:25b, 46–53		8:44–51	8:23–61
9:4–9	9:6–9	9:6–9	
2 K 17:19	(17:19,35–40a)	17:7–20, 23b, 24–40	
20:17–18			
21:2–15	21:8–15	21:3c–15	
(22:15–20)	(22:16–20)	22:15–20	
		23:4b–5, 19–20, (24), 25b	
23:25b–25:30	23:26–25:26 (27–30)	23:26–25:30	

I. *The End of Dtr 1's Work*

Cross, Friedman, and Nelson all agree that the narrative of the
period following Josiah's death is Dtr 2 material. As noted in the
previous chapter, the evidence of the parallel in Chr, which ceases
with Josiah's death, accords well with their view. However, there is
disagreement over the point at which Dtr 2's work begins. Cross
sees 2 K 23:25b as the beginning of the Dtr 2 addition. Friedman
holds that the Dtr 2 material begins with v 26./5/ He argues that
there are two expressions in v 25 connected elsewhere in DH only
with Moses: the precise expression "none arose like him" (Deut
34:10) and the three-fold reference to all of one's "heart, soul, and
strength" (Deut 6:5). This connection between Moses and Josiah is
a clear sign for Friedman of Dtr 1 material. Nelson's view is that v
25b was composed after Josiah's death./6/ He also thinks that v 24
is an exilic addition, and he gives the following reasons for his
judgment: (1) it sound like an afterthought attached with *wĕgām*;
(2) its generalizing nature characterizes it as the work of an
editor/compiler not a historical source; (3) the rites and objects
mentioned in v 24 are not among Dtr 1's special interests nor are
they mentioned in the part of 2 K 23 considered by Nelson to stem
from Dtr 1; (4) v 24 is reminiscent of Manasseh's sins in 2 K 21:6
which Nelson regards as exilic.

I have argued that Chr ceases to use DH as a source after 2 K 23:23. Verses 26–27 clearly stem from Dtr 2 since they blame Manasseh for Judah's fall. The question, then, focuses on the origin of vv 24–25. Verses 24–27 as a whole provide a transition from Josiah's reign to the account of his death and the events leading up to the exile. Verses 24–25 summarize Josiah's reign, and vv 26–27 explain the reason for the coming disaster. This same function is provided by 1 Esdr 1:21–22 which I have argued is original to Chr's work. Verse 21 summarizes Josiah's reign; v 22 in essence gives the reason for the imminent disaster. These two passages indicate a significant change after 2 K 23:23. There is a sudden shift in the histories from optimism to disaster, and a need is felt to provide a transition. This is essentially the same caesura noticed by Torrey when he argued that there was a lacuna between 2 C 35:19 and 20. 2 K 23:23 would be an abrupt ending to Dtr 1's edition. It has no summary of Josiah's reign. However, one expects just such an ending for a programmatic work whose hero has suddenly and inexplicably been killed. Thus, I regard 2 K 23:23 as the end of Dtr 1's edition. Friedman's argument that 25b must stem from Dtr 1 because of the similar statement about Moses overlooks the reference to Hezekiah (2 K 18:5) as a king without future equal. The language of 18:5 is at least as similar to that of 23:25 as is the language of Deut 34:10, and Hezekiah and Josiah were both kings. Also the statement that none arose like Josiah after him is most easily explained as the work of a post-Josianic writer. At the same time, I am not comfortable with the assignment of 2 K 23:24–25 to Dtr 2. The strong praise of Josiah in these verses is unusual for Dtr 2. Also the connections which Nelson notices between Manasseh's sin in 21:6 and Josiah's reform in 23:24 are an indication that v 24 is not from the hand of Dtr 2. Why would Dtr 2, who blames Manasseh for Judah's fall, take special pains to show that Manasseh's sins were corrected by Josiah's reforms? I suggest, therefore, that vv 24–25 are an addition to Dtr 1's edition by a hand other than Dtr 2. The abruptness of the ending at v 23 was felt and the two subsequent verses were added to provide a summary for Josiah's reign. Dtr 2's addition, then, begins with v 26.

II. *Manasseh Blamed for Judah's Fall*

Cross, Friedman, and Nelson all agree that Dtr 2 blames Manasseh for Judah's fall. So much is clear from 2 K 24:3–4, which is included within Dtr 2's ending to DH. They agree, therefore, that 2 K 21:10–15, which also blames Manasseh for Judah's demise, is Dtr 2 material. C actually lacks a parallel to 2 K 21:10–16. Thus, if the theory that Chr used only Dtr 1 is correct 21:16 may also stem from Dtr 2. This possibility is supported by the fact that the only other reference to Manasseh's shedding much blood is found in the Dtr 2 material at 24:3–4. Verse 16 is unlike the other treatments of Manasseh's sins, because it does not concern cultic offenses. Also, unlike Manasseh's other offenses, his shedding blood receives no counterpart in Josiah's reforms. Thus, there is good reason for believing that v 16 is secondary to the work of Dtr 1 and that it comes from Dtr 2's hand. In regard to 2 K 21:1–9, opinions vary about the extent of Dtr 2's work. Cross assigns vv 2–9 to Dtr 2. Similarly, Nelson sees vv 3c–9 as Dtr 2's work, though he finds Dtr 1 material incorporated within this section in vv 4a, 6a, and 7a./7/ Friedman gives two arguments for seeing vv 1–7 as the work of Dtr 1./8/ First, these verses describe the sins of Manasseh in terms relating to Josiah's reforms (23:4–14)—*bāmôt*, Asherah, altars to the "host of heaven" in the Temple precincts, and the '*wb*(*wt*) and *ydʿnym*. Secondly, v 7, which employs Deuteronomistic name theology stating that Yahweh will place his name in the Temple forever, is hardly possible for an exilic writer. Friedman concludes that vv 8–9 represent an addition by Dtr 2 making the promise in v 7 conditional.

2 C 33:1–9 is closely parallel to 2 K 21:1–9, and there is nothing in 2 C 33:1–9 that leads one to suspect that it has been added secondarily to the text of C. Thus, if the suggestion about Chr's use of Dtr 1 alone is correct, 2 K 21:1–9 must derive from Dtr 1. Friedman's observation about the connection of Manasseh's sins with Josiah's reforms is a convincing reason for assigning both passages to Dtr 1. The question, therefore, focuses on vv 8–9. These two verses do not explicitly blame Manasseh for the destruction of Jerusalem as do vv 10–16, but as they stand, vv 8–9 clearly imply that Manasseh's sins brought about the exile. Yahweh had promised that Israel's feet would never again wander from the land if they would follow the law. Manasseh disobeyed the law, hence the exile. It is peculiar to find this conditional promise here. Manasseh was not the first to break the law. Why is exile specified in his case? One possibility is that Dtr 2 introduced the conditional statement. Another possibility is offered by C's account. As observed in Chapter 5, C's account goes on to describe Manasseh's exile to Babylon and his subsequent repentance there. I

suggested that Dtr 2 may have omitted a similar story from his edition because it did not accord with his blaming Manasseh for Judah's demise. With the attachment of the story in 2 C 33:10–13, the allusion to exile in 2 K 21:8–9//2 C 33:8–9 is most easily understood as a reference to the exile of Manasseh and probably some of his subjects. Thus, 2 K 21:1–9 stems from Dtr 1. Dtr 1's edition also probably contained the story of Manasseh's exile and repentance. By replacing that story with the addition in 2 K 21:10–16 Dtr 2 has effectively made 2 K 21:8–9 refer to the exile of 586 B.C. and has placed the blame for that exile on Manasseh.

III. *Passages that Make the Promise to David Conditional*

As mentioned in Chapter 1, Friedman and Nelson have argued independently and convincingly that most of the verses under this category are better ascribed to Dtr 1 because they address Solomon and refer to the loss of the Northern kingdom, "Israel," from the kingdom of Solomon's son./9/ Friedman is less certain about 1 K 6:11–13 because the promise contained in the apodosis of this condition concerns not the throne of Israel but Yahweh's continuing presence with the people./10/ Thus, he concludes that 1 K 6:11–13 may stem from Dtr 2.

The conclusion of Friedman and Nelson corresponds to the theory that Chr used only the Dtr 1 edition of DH. 1 K 8:25b and 9:4–5 have close parallels in C indicating, according to this theory, that they are from Dtr 1's edition. 1 K 2:4 and 6:11–13 stand within sections of K omitted by Chr for other reasons. Based on the conclusions of Friedman and Nelson, 2:4 is best regarded as a part of Dtr 1's edition. 6:11–13 is clearly an insertion. It interrupts the context which deals with Solomon's work on the Temple. Verse 14 seems to have been borrowed from v 9 and should probably be considered part of the insertion. The OG and L lack these four verses, and this may indicate that 6:11–14 is not an insertion of Dtr 2 at all but a secondary gloss by a later scribe after the separation of the textual families.

IV. *Passages that Seem to Presuppose the Exile*

A. *2 K 17:1–23*

Opinions vary widely as to the extent of Dtr 2 material in this chapter. In the first part of the chapter, Cross assigns only v 19 to

Dtr 2. Friedman regards v 19 as a possible addition of Dtr 2./11/
He cites the awkwardness of the verse with its mention of Judah in
the context of the peroration on Israel as the major reason for this
suggestion. However, he also raises the possibility that the verse is
used by Dtr 1 to develop the theme of wrongdoing in Judah as a
background to Hezekiah's reforms. Nelson, in contrast, sees most
of 17:1–23 as the work of Dtr 2./12/ He argues that vv 7–20 are a
unit, since v 7 represents the protasis of a long sentence whose
apodosis is in v 18. Verses 19–20 are a comment on v 18 but are not
from another hand. The major aspect of Nelson's argument is his
comparison of certain phrases within vv 7–20 to language used in
other passages which he assigns to Dtr 2. He further argues that 2
K 18:12, which also explains the reason for Israel's demise, is the
original explanation by Dtr 1. The longer discussion of Israel's sin
in 17:7–20 must be assigned, in Nelson's opinion, to Dtr 2, who
would have been more concerned theologically about the reason
for Israel's exile than Dtr 1. Verses 21–23a are an even later
insertion which interrupts the original end of 17:7–20 in v 23a.

    C has no parallel to 2 K 17 because the latter deals with the
Northern kingdom. However, some of the conclusions reached for
other passages may be helpful here. Nelson's position that all of vv
7–20 is Dtr 2 material can hardly be accepted. I reject his
comparison of phrases in 17:7–20 with other passages that he
assigns to Dtr 2, because I regard most of the latter passages as Dtr
1 material. One example is the reference to divination and augury
in v 17. Similar references occur in 2 K 21:6 and 23:24, both of
which Nelson assigns to Dtr 2. I have argued that 21:6 is Dtr 1
material and that 23:24, though not Dtr 1's work, does not appear
to be Dtr 2's work either.

    Nelson also believes that 17:7–20 would be of less interest
theologically to Dtr 1 than Dtr 2. However, it is easy to see how
Dtr 1 would be strongly interested in Israel's demise. What
happened to Israel would serve as a strong warning to the people
of Josiah's day who had been led into idolatry under Manasseh./13/ Along with this warning there may be an implicit
contrast between the Northern monarchy and Josiah (cf. vv 21–
23). Indeed, one may turn Nelson's argument around. Why
would an exilic editor insert such a long peroration on Israel's
exile at this point but include no such explanation about Judah's
demise? One would expect the opposite, a lengthy peroration on
Judah's fall and a briefer word on Israel's demise.

The reference to Judah in v 19 may be a part of the warning for Judah that Dtr 1 perceives in Israel's fall. But the expression "all the seed of Israel" in v 20 may refer to both Israel and Judah, as Nelson suggests. In that case, both vv 19 and 20 would be the work of Dtr 2. Still, this use of "Israel" to include Judah seems overly subtle in the context of a chapter that clearly explains the fall of the Northern tribes and uses "Israel" throughout to refer to the North. Both Dtr 1 and Dtr 2 are possible here and without further evidence one is hard pressed to decide between them.

B. *2 K 17:24–41*

Opinions about the amount of Dtr 2 material in the second part of the chapter also vary widely. Cross does not include any of these verses in his list of probable Dtr 2 additions. Friedman regards vv 35–40a as Dtr 2 material at least in part./14/ He states that vv 34 and 40b refer to the Samaritans while the intervening material deals with the exiled Israelites. However, he admits that thematic and stylistic evidence of Dtr 2's hand is lacking, and he concludes that material from both editors is present. Nelson finds more Dtr 2 work here than does Friedman./15/ He holds that the story in vv 24–28 was preserved by Dtr 2, because it is prepared for by v 23b, which Nelson assigns to Dtr 2, and because Dtr 1 could not have left the non-centralized worship described in the story uncriticized. He further holds that vv 29–34a are an exilic expansion on vv 24–28, though not from Dtr 2's hand. A new hand begins in v 34b. Verses 34b–40 return to the theme of vv 7–20, the sins of the Israelites. Verse 34b attempts to correct v 33 and indicates an awareness of the dangers of the Samaritan heresy. Hence, it is Dtr 2's work in Nelson's view.

Once again there is no parallel in C for the second half of chapter 17. Therefore, only the literary and thematic arguments presented by Friedman and Nelson can be discussed. There is good reason to believe that vv 34b–40 are an insertion. Verse 34b seems to directly contradict v 33a, but the two verses deal with different groups of people, as Friedman points out. The change from the discussion about the foreigners who were settled in Israel in vv 24–33 to the reference to the exiled Israelites in vv 34b–40 is so abrupt and obvious that one wonders whether a transitional verse may have fallen out from between vv 34a and 34b. In addition, the expression, "they did/do according to their former custom," in vv

34a and 40b provides an *inclusio* for the insertion. There is, however, no compelling reason for assigning the insertion to Dtr 2 not Dtr 1. Nelson's major argument for assigning it to Dtr 2 is related to his belief that the story in vv 24–28 was preserved by Dtr 2 because Dtr 1 would have criticized the non-centralized cult. This argument is weak. In the first place, it is likely that vv 24–33 form a unit explaining the origin of the syncretistic cult in the North. If vv 29–33 are indeed a part of the unit, then the syncretistic Northern cult is not condoned at all but is implicitly condemned. Secondly, it is no less difficult to imagine that Dtr 2 would condone the Northern cult and Bethel priesthood than to imagine that Dtr 1 did so. Finally, it is quite possible to find in Josiah's reign an appropriate setting for vv 34b–40. M. Cogan has recently argued for such a setting, stressing Josiah's claim to be the legitimate heir of the Northern territory which the Israelites have forfeited because of their sin./16/ One may also point to the warning function of these verses for Dtr 1's Judean audience. The Northern tribes lost their inheritance because of their idolatry and their failure to listen. The same fate is possible for the inhabitants of Judah unless they follow the lead of their king in returning to Yahweh.

C. *2 K 20:17–18*

Cross includes Isaiah's oracle in these verses in his list of probable Dtr 2 passages apparently because he regards its reference to the Babylonian captivity of Hezekiah's sons as *vaticinium ex eventu*. Friedman does not treat this passage and therefore apparently regards it as Dtr 1's work. Nelson discusses the passage at length./17/ He states that there is no literary evidence to suggest that the story or the oracle have been either inserted or retouched by the exilic editor. As it stands it fits well into the context and is of the same character as the other prophetic stories in K. Nelson goes on to argue that the story is not *vaticinium ex eventu* at all The obvious point of the story is to show the dangers of an alliance with Babylon, and this is a subject in which Isaiah is interested (Isa 7; 13; 20; 30:1–7; 31). Moreover, there is not enough detail in this oracle to qualify it as *vaticinium ex eventu*. There is only general mention of the national treasures and of Hezekiah's sons being in the Babylonian court. There is no mention of defeat by Babylon or of a change in Judah's relationship

with Yahweh. The oracle merely warns against the dangers of
vassalhood. Such an oracle would have been appropriate not only
in Hezekiah's time with the revolt of Marduk-apaliddina, but also
in 651–648 B.C. at the revolt of Shamash-shum-ukin and especially
in Josiah's time with the Babylonian resurgence under Nabopolas-
sar. The exilic editor may have referred to the fulfillment of this
oracle in 2 K 24:13, but Nelson regards this as the work of a post-
redactional glossator. Thus, he finds no reason for regarding
2 K 20:17–18 as exilic.

The obscure reference to the Babylonian envoys in 2 C
32:31 indicates that this story in some form derives from Dtr 1,
if the theory that Chr used only Dtr 1 is correct. Thus, I agree
with Nelson's point that the story cannot be viewed simply as a
case of *vaticinium ex eventu*. However, the exact contents of
Chr's *Vorlage* for the story are uncertain. One cannot know, for
example, whether it contained Isaiah's oracle, which Cross
assigns to Dtr 2. Indeed, Chr's obscure reference to the event
may reflect his suppression of a negative oracle against his hero,
Hezekiah. On the other hand, the story with its mention of
Babylon would furnish an excellent opportunity for retouching
by Dtr 2. In short, our hypothesis does not help to draw any
certain conclusion about redactional levels in 2 K 20:17–18.
Retouching by Dtr 2 is likely, but not absolutely certain.

D. *2 K 22:15–20*

Cross and Friedman believe that Huldah's oracle as it now
stands is the work of Dtr 2, but that there is an "old nucleus
which predates Josiah's unpeaceful end."/18/ Nelson finds two
original oracles here: vv 15–17 and 18–20./19/ He argues that v
18 is broken off, indicating a literary seam at that point. As the
oracle stands it is incompatible with the zeal for reform in the
rest of the narrative, since disaster is inevitable in Huldah's
oracle (vv 16–17, 20a). Josiah's death is also incompatible with
the prophecy here that he would die in peace. Nelson gives two
possible solutions which scholars have suggested to explain these
inconsistencies. The first possibility is that the oracle was
originally positive and directed toward Josiah. Verses 18–20a
would represent an earlier layer with some of the content
missing in the lacuna between vv 18 and 19. Then vv 16–17, 20b
were added secondarily. The second possibility is that the oracle
was originally a judgment against the nation (vv 16–17, 20b,

with part of v 18 having been lost). The positive oracle to Josiah was added later to explain the delay of that judgment./20/ Nelson accepts the first explanation, because the second, in his opinion, disregards the meaning of dying in peace and fails to explain how a pessimistic oracle could serve as a motive for Josiah's reform. He takes vv 16–17, 20b as the work of Dtr 2 because of the phrase "all the works of their hands" in v 17, which refers to idols but is used by Dtr 1 to mean simply "deeds."

As it stands, this oracle consists of two parts, the first dealing with the people (vv 16–17), the second with Josiah (vv 18–20). However, contra Nelson, there are no good literary criteria for distinguishing two different oracles or levels here. Verse 18b may reflect literary activity, as Nelson argues. However, it could simply be an example of *casus pendens*, "as for the words which you have heard." It is most uncertain that this line is broken off or indicates a lacuna. Cross, Friedman, and Nelson agree that the reference to Josiah's peaceful death is pre-exilic, the work of Dtr 1. This is certainly correct. The view that vv 18–20 merely give an explanation for the delay of judgment does not take seriously enough the fact that Josiah's death in battle can hardly be referred to as a peaceful one. The question focuses, therefore, on the first part of the oracle in vv 16–17 and perhaps on v 20b.

The reference to exile in these verses does not automatically signal Dtr 2 material. This is obvious from the frequent references to exile as a curse in Ancient Near Eastern treaty texts, including passages such as Lev 26 and Deut 28./21/ The exile of the Northern tribes would have been well known to Dtr 1. Moreover, Dtr 1 had precedent and even company in the prophetic movement for his threats. One need only point to the book of Jeremiah as a work replete with threats of impending doom and exile from a man whose career began in Josiah's thirteeth year (1:1). Nelson objects that a pessimistic oracle such as this one could not serve as a motive for Josiah's reform and is inconsistent with the zeal for Josiah's reform in the rest of the narrative. However, one could argue the reverse, i.e., that Dtr 1 uses such a pessimistic oracle to motivate the people to repent in order that Yahweh would repent of the destruction threatened against Judah. As for the argument that the phrase "the works of their hands" here refers to idols, Nelson himself admits that this is merely an assumption from context that is not assured. The interpretation "deeds" would be quite appropriate.

Thus, contra Nelson, nothing in the Huldah oracle compels one to ascribe it to Dtr 2. On the other hand, the oracle and its setting provide an excellent opportunity for retouching, and it is hard to believe that Dtr 2 would pass it up. Unfortunately, the theory that Chr used only Dtr 1's edition may not be much help in solving this dilemma. 2 C 34:22–27 contains a close parallel to the story of Huldah's oracle in 2 K 22:15–20. However, C's account as it now stands may not be the work of Chr 1. It is difficult to believe that Chr, whose work was designed as a program for the restoration of the monarchy and the Temple cult in Jerusalem, would have included the statement in 2 C 34:25// 2 K 22:17 that Yahweh's wrath against "this place" would not cease (*wĕlō tikbeh*). Such a statement would run counter to his hopes and objectives, and its presence may indicate that C's account here has been revised toward the version in K. If this is the case, then one cannot determine the original contents of the Huldah's oracle in either Chr 1's version or his DH *Vorlage*. I conclude, therefore, with Cross, Friedman, and Nelson that both Dtr 1 and Dtr 2 material are possible in 2 K 22:15–20.

V. *Passages that Appear Addressed to the Exiles and Call for Repentance*

A. *1 K 8:23–61*

The criteria for this category are clearly somewhat subjective. Two passages in 1 K 8 and 9 are at issue. In 1 K 8 there is wide variation among the scholars being surveyed about the amount of Dtr 2 material. Cross attributes 1 K 8:46–53 to Dtr 2. Friedman does not treat the passage in any detail, but he does give his reason for rejecting vv 46–53 as Dtr 2's work: the context of chapter 8 refers to the Temple as a channel to Yahweh and an exilic writer could hardly have written such a thing./22/ To the objection that the Temple had to be mentioned in order to avoid anachronism Friedman responds that "it would have been better to write nothing at all than to inform exiles that their channel to salvation is the building which no longer exists."/23/

Nelson's view is closer to that of Cross./24/ He sees vv 44–51 as the work of the exilic editor. He argues that 8:14–43 fit well with Dtr 1's work in the pre-exilic period. The petitions in vv 30–43 deal with issues of concern to the people who were still in the land such as military defeat, drought, and famine. Verses 33–34, which mention exile, probably refer to the writer's hope for the restoration of the Northern captives to Northern territory redeemed by Josiah. Verses 41–43 refer not to proselytes but to foreigners on diplomatic missions such as Naaman. They come, therefore, from a time when the kingdom of Judah was still viable enough to attract foreigners who were not just conquerors. However, Nelson holds that there are literary grounds for regarding vv 44–51 as a separate unit. First, there is a shift in these verses to *wĕšāma'tā* from the earlier *wĕ'attâ tišma'*. Secondly, there is also a shift here to praying in the direction (*derek*) of the Temple or Jerusalem. Thirdly, vv 46–50 take up the same topic as vv 33–34, indicating two distinct authors. Fourthly, vv 44–51 avoid the designation "Israel" which is common in the earlier verses. Fifthly, v 50 alone uses the word *peša'* for the people's sin. Finally, the hope offered in v 50 is much more sombre than that of v 34. Nelson goes on to argue that vv 52–53, 59–60 are even later additions.

J. Levenson takes up the question of redactional levels in an article on 1 K 8./25/ There are four stages to his argument. First, he argues for the unity of 8:23–53. Here, he cites several differences noticed by Jepsen between vv 44–53 and the rest of the chapter. The first two of these are the first two given by Nelson above. Levenson's major critique of these differences is that they are insignificant compared to the similarities of vv 44–53 with the material that precedes. For example, the shift to *wĕšāma'tā* represents no difference in meaning whatsoever, and the change to praying toward the Temple is meaningless, since the passage concerns exiles who by definition cannot pray in the Temple. Levenson then shifts to the positive arguments for unity. He points out that the exact expression, *lihyôt 'ênêkā pĕtūḥôt*, which occurs in 8:29 and 52, occurs elsewhere only in the parallel to v 52 in 2 C 6:40. He also refers to the tendency of 8:23–53 to reflect Lev 26:14–45 and especially Deut 28:15–68. 1 K 8:23–53 follows the same pattern as Deut 28:15–68 in moving from topic to topic and ending with a discussion of exile. In the second stage of his article Levenson argues for an exilic date for 8:23–53. He states that prayers for return from exile in the Bible usually derive from the Judean exile. Thus, Second Isaiah, Ezekiel, and Lamentations all demonstrate a fervent hope for restoration. "What stamps vv 44–53 as Exilic is not that is speaks of exile, but that it strives to awaken in its audience the hope for restoration, secured through repentance. This unambiguous hope of return makes sense only within a community already in exile."/26/ This position is supported in Levenson's view by the reference in vv 41–43 to the conversion of the foreigner who makes a pilgrimage to the Temple. He states that the closest parallels to such a hope are exilic or post-exilic. The exilic date is further supported for Levenson by the passage's focus on the Temple as a place of prayer, not sacrifice. Again, he states that the closest parallels are exilic.

In the third stage of the article Levenson compares various phrases in 1 K 8:23–53 with similar phrases from Deut 4 and 30 (once from Deut 29) which he considers to be Dtr 2 material. He also finds affinities between 1 K 8:23–53 and Dtr 2 material in terms of theology. Both Deut 4:1–40 and 1 K 8:23–53 encourage repentance and stress the possibility of return. Levenson concludes, therefore, that 1 K 8:23–53 is a composition of Dtr 2. In the final stage of his article Levenson suggests that 8:56–61 is also the work of Dtr 2 because of v 60's reference to the universal recognition of Yahweh's unique divinity (cf. v 23; Deut 4:39). Also, these verses emphasize Yahweh's blessing through Moses, and this is a particularly appropriate focus for a document that introduces the core of Mosaic revelation into Deuteronomy. This final point relies heavily on Levenson's own view that Dtr 2 inserted the book of the Torah into Deuteronomy.

Levenson's arguments for the unity of 1 K 8:23–53 are strong. The phrase, *lihyôt 'ênêkā pĕtūḥôt*, used in vv 29 and 52 indicates unity not only because of its rarity but also because it forms an *inclusio* around the series of hypothetical situations followed by petitions in vv 31–50. Levenson's observation that 1 K 8:23–53 resembles Deut 28:15–68 in its treatment of several possible situations ending in exile is especially significant. A similar pattern recurs throughout the series of petitions in vv 31–50. In each case a hypothetical situation is proposed. Usually it is a disaster brought about as a result of the people's sin. In all cases the persons in question pray to Yahweh. In the case of disaster they repent and pray. Yahweh is requested to hear the prayer of the petitioner and to act on it. In the case of disaster because of sin Yahweh is usually requested to forgive. This outline of the pattern in the petitions may appear somewhat obvious, but it is important that the two petitions in vv 44–53 follow the same pattern as the earlier petitions./27/

Nelson's arguments for 1 K 8:44–51 being a separate unit, in contrast, are not compelling. The fact that "Israel" is not used in vv 44–51 does not necessarily signal a separate unit, especially since its presence is textually dubious in vv 38 and 41 where the OG lacks it. The use of the root *pš'* twice in v 50 along with the "sombre hope" expressed there may indicate some secondary revision within vv 44–51. But these things hardly furnish sufficient evidence for seeing all of vv 44–51 as separate, particularly in the light of the other evidence for the unity of vv 23–53. Finally, the fact that vv 46–51 take up the topic of vv 33–34 is not necessarily an indication that the passage is composite. In the first place, there is a different emphasis in the two passages. While both mention exile, the main concern in vv 33–34 is military defeat, and exile is not described in the same detail as in vv 44–51. Secondly, Deut 28 is again instructive. There, defeat and exile are mentioned repeatedly as curses (vv 25, 33, 36–37, 47–52, 64–65). Even if vv 36–37 and 64–65 stem from Dtr 2, which is not certain, the theme of defeat and exile is still prominent and repeated in the chapter. Thus, in 1 K 8, the repetition of this theme does not signal different hands. It merely reflects the fact that this theme was a common one in Ancient Near Eastern treaty curses because defeat and exile were common and dreaded fates in the Ancient Near East./28/ Hence, though there may be secondary elements here, particularly in v 50, there are good reasons for seeing vv 44–53 as a whole as part of the unit that begins in v 23.

I begin my own treatment of 1 K 8 by noting that 2 C 6:14–39 provide a close parallel to 1 K 8:23–49, and there is no literary or thematic reason for regarding any part of the C parallel as secondary to the original edition. Therefore, according to the theory that Chr used only Dtr 1's edition 1 K 8:23–49 should derive from Dtr 1. While I agree with Levenson that 1 K 8:23–53 is essentially a unit, I cannot agree with his attribution of all of this material to Dtr 2. As has been observed, the reference to exile does not automatically indicate the work of Dtr 2. Nelson recognizes this fact when he assigns vv 33–34 to Dtr 1. Levenson, however, refers to the "unambiguous hope of return" found only in exilic material in his treatment of vv 44–53. However, vv 44–53 nowhere mention restoration. The request is only that Yahweh forgive his people and grant that their captors treat them compassionately. Restoration is mentioned in vv 33–34, but it is hardly the "fervent hope" described by Levenson. There, the mention of restoration merely falls in line with the pattern found

in others of these petitions which often end with a request that
Yahweh deliver his people from distress. Even more significant is
the fact that the hypothetical situations posed in vv 23–53 presume
a pre-exilic setting, as Nelson argues. The frequent reference to
praying toward the Temple presumes that the Temple is standing,
as is clearly the case in v 31. Moreover, these verses reflect a
settled, agricultural *Sitz im Leben*./29/ Thus, vv 35–36 speak of
drought in the land, vv 37–40 of famine, plague, etc., again in the
land. Verse 40 explicitly requests that the people may fear Yahweh
so long as they live in the land. The setting for all of these verses is
clearly not exilic. Verses 41–43 imply that Israel is still in its
homeland in a pre-exilic setting. The hope that Israel would attract
foreigners because of its God existed in the pre-exilic period. There
are stories within DH itself that provide a precedent for such a
hope./30/ These verses apparently stem from a period before the
exile when Judah might still attract foreigners other than conquerors. Finally, even v 48 has the Temple still standing, thus
implying a pre-exilic setting.

Levenson's theological argument is an important part of his
article, because he sees 1 K 8 as a pivotal passage in the incipient
stages of the movement "from Temple to synagogue." However,
he builds a false contrast between the notions of the Temple as a
house of sacrifice in the empire and the Temple as a house of
prayer in the exile. It is clear from RS 24. 266 (n. 27) that Baal's
temple was considered a house of sacrifice and prayer. Certainly
from its construction, Yahweh's temple was also regarded as a
house of both sacrifice and prayer. More to the point, the
dedication ceremony in 1 K 8 clearly involves both sacrifice and
prayer, and Solomon's prayer seems no more important to the
narrator than his great sacrifice.

What is striking about this chapter is the tension that exists
within its understanding of the Temple's importance for Israel's
faith. Throughout the petitions in vv 31–53 the request is made
that Yahweh in heaven, *his dwelling place*, will hear the prayers of
his people *wherever* they may be. At the same time, Friedman is
correct in his observation that the passage consistently refers to the
Temple as a channel of blessing for Israel. Yahweh is to hear his
people's prayers when they pray toward the Temple. This is more
than an attempt to avoid anachronism. As Friedman argued, it is
difficult to imagine an exilic writer making the Temple, which he
knows has been destroyed, the chief channel for Israel to Yahweh.

The theological tension here presupposes a pre-exilic writer. The writer may have had the exiled Northern tribes in mind. In short, there are strong indications within 1 K 8:23–53 that it was written as a whole before the exile of 586 B.C.

Nevertheless, there are difficulties with seeing some of the material in 8:23–53 as pre-exilic. This is particularly true of most of vv 50–53. Here, as Nelson observed, the hope expressed is a sombre one. Contra Levenson, there is no "unambiguous hope of return" here at all. On the contrary, the writer pleads only for Yahweh to grant his people compassion before their captors (v 50b). This request is made on the basis of Israel's status as Yahweh's elect from the exodus (vv 51, 53). Furthermore, this request appears superfluous after the earlier request for Yahweh to maintain the cause of his people (*wĕ'āśîtā mišpāṭām*, v 49) and to forgive their sins (v 50a). In v 50a , the request for forgiveness is extended twice using the root *pš'*, as Nelson observes. Nelson is correct in attributing the double use of *pš'* and the sombre hope in v 50 to the exilic editor. The simple request for compassion in captivity is exactly the kind of prayer one expects from Dtr 2 who holds an uncertain hope for the future. Also, the request that Yahweh maintain the cause and forgive the sins of his people in vv 49b–50a is the apt conclusion to the hypothetical defeat and exile posed in v 46. This is essentially the way in which the previous hypothetical crisis ends (v 45), and it is also the way in which the parallel crisis in 2 C 6:39 ends. 2 C 6:40 provides a fitting conclusion to Solomon's prayer. It is parallel to 1 K 8:52, though the two verses are not as close as the rest of the parallel material in 1 K 8 and 2 C 6. As has been noted, the phrase *lihyôt 'ênêkā pĕtūhôt* in 1 K 8:52 forms an *inclusio* along with v 29 around the series of crises posed in this chapter. The *inclusio* and the similar verse in 2 C 6:40 indicate that 1 K 8:52 derives in some form from Dtr 1. However, it has probably been revised by Dtr 2. This is suggested by its difference from 2 C 6:40, particularly in the final phrase of the verse. In 2 C 6:40 Solomon asks Yahweh to be attentive to any prayer offered in "this place" (*litpillat hammāqôm hazzeh*), i.e., in the Temple. In 1 K 8:52, in contrast, the request is that Yahweh hear his people's prayer wherever they cry out to him (*bĕkōl qorām 'ēlêkā*). Thus, I regard 1 K8:23–50a (up to *lāk*) as the work of Dtr 1. Dtr 2 has added the rest of v 50, vv 51 and 53, and has revised v 52. Undoubtedly, Dtr 2 also interpreted Dtr 1's references to exile in the previous material as referring

very concretely to the Babylonian captivity. This understanding of
the redactional levels in 1 K 8 accords well with the theory that
Chr used only the Dtr 1 edition of the Deuteronomistic History.

It remains to comment briefly on Levenson's treatment of
Solomon's fourth speech in 1 K 8:56–61. Since these verses are
unparalleled in C, there is a possibility that they are Dtr 2
material. However, Levenson's arguments are not convincing. The
hope in v 60 for universal recognition of Yahweh's unique divinity
is similar to vv 41–43. Again, there are pre-exilic parallels for such
a hope. Levenson's view about these verses also depends partially
on his theory that Dtr 2 inserted the book of the Torah in
Deuteronomy. This theory is far from certain. More telling is the
strong optimism of these verses. It is difficult to believe that the
same Dtr 2 who finds himself in the exile and offers little real hope
in his addition to DH could have written that Yahweh had given
his people rest as promised (v 56).

B. *1 K 9:6–9*

Cross, Friedman, and Nelson all attribute these verses to Dtr 2.
There are basically two reasons for this position. First, there is
literary disunity in the shift from addressing Solomon (second
person plural) in vv 3–5 to addressing the entire people (second
person plural) in vv 6–9. Secondly, the reference to the destruction
of the Temple in vv 7–8 in their view requires an exilic hand.
Nelson adds a further argument to these two. He points out the
similarity of 1 K 9:6–9 to Jer 22:8–9 and Deut 29:24–25. Based on
Weinfeld's conclusion that Deut 29:23–25 is the primary text/31/
and on his (Nelson's) view that the addition of Deut 29 was
subsequent to the work of the Deuteronomistic historian, Nelson
argues that 1 K 9:6–9 must derive from Dtr 2./32/

This is an extremely difficult passage for the present study
because the evidence for isolating different redactional levels is
contradictory. There is obvious disruption within these verses
indicating that the passage has been reworked./33/ Thus, literary
considerations favor attributing the passage to Dtr 2. However, the
best parallels to the passage, both biblical and extra-biblical, are
pre-exilic, thus favoring a Dtr 1 origin./34/ 2 C 7:19–22 provides a
close parallel to 1 K 9:6–9, but the pessimistic view of the Temple
in this passage is troublesome in a work which served as a program
for the restoration of the Temple and its cult. This may indicate

that the C passage has been revised or inserted by a later editor./35/ Thus, I am forced to conclude as with 2 K 22:15–20 that both Dtr 1 and Dtr 2 material are likely in 1 K 9:6–9.

The preceeding study indicates that as it now stands C cannot be used as an objective criterion for isolating Dtr 2 material. It is probable that some of C's parallels to alleged Dtr 2 passages are secondary to Chr 1's edition. Still, it is important to point out that there is no evidence for systematic revision of C toward K by an editor or a copyist. Therefore, C can be of some help in separating reductional levels in DH. Its evidence has helped to refine the limits of Dtr 2's extension of DH (2 K 23:26–25:30), of his editorial work in omitting the story of Manasseh's repentance and blaming Manasseh for Judah's fall (2 K 21:10–16), and of his revision of the end of Solomon's speech at the dedication of the Temple (1 K 8:50–53). On the basis of C's evidence I have argued for the addition of the *bāmôt* passages to the list of Dtr 2 revisions (1 K 15:14; 22:44; 2 K 12:4; 14:4; 15:4, 35). C has not been particularly helpful in determining the origin of 1 K 2:4; 6:11–13; 2 K 17:7–40; or 20:17–18. However, on other grounds I have suggested that 1 K 6:11–14 is a secondary addition (not from Dtr 2) and 2 K 17:19–20 and 20:17–18 may contain light retouching by Dtr 2. Finally, in two C parallels to alleged Dtr 2 passages (1 K 9:6–9; 2 K 22:15–20), C includes statements that do not seem to accord well with the purpose of Chr 1's work as a program for the restoration of the Temple. Hence, one can only conclude that both Dtr 1 and Dtr 2 material are possible in the K passages. Thus, although C is not a completely reliable criterion for isolating Dtr 2 material, at least where C has a parallel to a K passage, one must be extremely cautious about attributing the latter to Dtr 2. There must be reason to suspect that the C passage as it stands is not from Chr 1's edition.

NOTES

/1/ No material in 2 S has been ascribed to Dtr 2 by any of the four scholars whose arguments are considered below.

/2/ These lists are not to be considered complete. Cross and Nelson, in particular, leave open the possibility that other passages may be found which should be attributed to Dtr 2. Levenson is included here because he ascribes much of 1 K 8 to Dtr 2. The fact that no other passage is given under his name does not mean that he believes the rest of 1–2 K to be Dtr 1 material. It simply reflects the fact that he does not attempt to list other Dtr 2 passages.

/3/   Cross, *CMHE*, 285–87.

/4/   These are my categories, not Cross's. He merely refers to these passages as brief glosses of Dtr 2.

/5/   Friedman, *The Exile*, 7–8.

/6/   Nelson, *Double Redaction*, 83–84. It is perplexing that Nelson also ascribes 23:4b–5, 19–20 to the exilic editor (Nelson does not use the nomenclature "Dtr 1" and "Dtr 2" but "historian" and "exilic editor"). In both cases an implicit contrast is drawn between Josiah and Jeroboam. In 23:4b Josiah defiles Jeroboam's cult site at Bethel. In vv 19–20, as Nelson correctly observes, a link is made with the story in 1 K 12:32–13:32. It was the contrasting theme of Jeroboam's apostasy and the blameless Davidide, Josiah, that first led Cross to perceive the Josianic edition of DH (cf. *CMHE*, 279–80). In addition, Friedman has noticed a series of correspondences between Manasseh's sins in 2 K 21:1–7 and Josiah's reforms in this context, including the reference to the *bāmôt* and the "host of heaven" in 23:5. This concern for Josiah's reform again signals the hand of Dtr 1. Finally, the fact that Josiah assumed control over the Assyrian provinces to the North has long been recognized. Both of these passages reflect that situation. Yet there is no indication that Dtr 2 was concerned with the North or the restoration of the Davidic empire. These passages, then, accord well with Dtr 1's themes.

/7/   Nelson, *Double Redaction*, 65–69.

/8/   Friedman, *The Exile*, 10–11.

/9/   Ibid., 12–13. Nelson, *Double Redaction*, 118.

/10/   Friedman, *The Exile*, 24.

/11/   Ibid.

/12/   Nelson, *Double Redaction*, 55–62.

/13/   On this aspect of Dtr 1's theology Cross has written as follows: "It speaks equally or more emphatically to Judah. Its restoration to ancient grandeur depends on the return of the nation to the covenant of Yahweh and on the wholehearted return of her king to the ways of David the servant of Yahweh." See *CMHE*, 284.

/14/   Friedman, *The Exile*, 24–25.

/15/ Nelson, *Double Redaction*, 63–65.

/16/ M. Cogan, "Israel in Exile—The View of a Josianic Historian," *JBL* 97 (1978): 40–44.

/17/ Nelson, *Double Redaction*, 129–32.

/18/ Cross, *CMHE*, 286, n. 46. Cf. Friedman, *The Exile*, 25.

/19/ Nelson, *Double Redaction*, 76–79.

/20/ See especially Weinfeld, *DDS*, 25–26.

/21/ See D. Hillers, *Treaty Curses*, esp. 33–34. Cf. Weinfeld, *DDS*, 116–46.

/22/ Friedman, *The Exile*, 21.

/23/ Ibid.

/24/ Nelson, *Double Redaction*, 69–73.

/25/ Levenson, "From Temple to Synagogue," 144–65.

/26/ Ibid.

/27/ There is an intriguing parallel to this pattern, indeed to 1 K 8 in general, in RS 24. 266. The text is composed of two parts. The first twenty-five lines are predominately a list of animal sacrifices to Baal of Ugarit at his temple. See KTU, 123–24. This part of the text apparently describes a special ritual in which the king is involved. The second part of the text reads as follows according to the transcription of A. Herdner ("Une priére a Baal des Ugaritain en danger," *CRAIBL* [1972]: 694):

kgr ʿz. t̮ǵ[r]km[.]	When a mighty (army) attacks your gates,
[q]rd ḥmytkm.	A strong (army) your walls,
ʿ[n]km. l[b]ʿl tšʾun	Raise your eyes to Baal.
yb[ʿ]lm. [ʾal. t]dy ʿz l[t]ǵrny	O Baal, drive the mighty (army) from our gates,
qrd[. lḥ]mytny	The strong (army) from our walls.
ʾibr ybʿl. n[š]qdš	A bull, O Baal, we will consecrate.
mdr bʿ[l]. nmlʾu[.]	(Our) vow to Baal we will fulfill.
[b]k̄r b[ʿ]l. nš[q]dš	A first-born to Baal we will consecrate.
ḥtp bʿ[l. n]mlʾu	The spoil to Baal we will devote.
ʿš[r]t [bʿl. nʿ]šr	A banquet for Baal we will prepare.
qdš bʿ[l.] nʿl	To the sanctuary of Baal we will ascend.
ntbt b[t. bʿl] ntlk	In the way of the temple of Baal we will go.
wš[mʿ b]ʿ[l.] lṣlt[km]	And Baal will hear your prayer
ydy. ʿz lt̮ǵrkm[.]	He will drive the mighty (army) from your gates,
[qrd] lḥmytkm	The strong (army) from your walls.

As in 1 K 8, so also in this text, a hypothetical situation of distress is posed. In RS 24. 266 that proposal begins with the particle *kī* just as in 1 K 8:37, 42, 44. The sufferers are instructed in each text to call upon their respective deities in prayer. In each case it is stated that the deity will hear the prayer and deliver the petitioners from their distress. There are, of course, some important differences between the two texts, but they do seem to follow the same basic pattern in instructing the people how to respond in times of crisis. This Ugaritic parallel may also prove instructive in the further treatment of 1 K 8.

/28/ Again, see Hillers, *Treaty Curses.*

/29/ Compare the arguments for this position given by Gray, *I & II Kings,* 197–213.

/30/ One could cite the stories of Naaman (2 K 5), Rahab (Josh 2), and the Gibeonites (Josh 9). Note especially the similarity of language in the phrase *mē'ereṣ rĕḥôqâ* in Josh 9:6 and 1 K 8:41.

/31/ Weinfeld, *DDS,* 100–116, esp. 115 (note). Nelson also argues for literary dependence of Jer 22:8–9 and 1 K 9:6–9 on Deut 29:24–25.

/32/ Nelson, *Double Redaction,* 74–76. Here he cites N. Lohfink's discussion of Deut 29 in "Der Bundesschluss im Land Moab," *BZ* 6 (1962): 36–42. Lohfink suggests that Deut 29:21–27 is an exilic expansion. Levenson adopts Lohfink's conclusion in his article on "Who Inserted the Book of the Torah?" Lohfink regards it as exilic because of v 27. This is also the only verse in the chapter ascribed to Dtr 2 by Cross. This entire passage is cast in terms of a future generation that has experienced the covenant curses. The fact that vv 24–27 are in the past tense does not necessarily signal an exilic hand, as Lohfink argues. The past tense is merely the result of casting the passage in a context in which people in the future discuss the judgment wrought against them. Even v 27, when understood in this setting, need not be ascribed to Dtr 2. Furthermore, Lohfink's view does not take into account the excellent parallels to this passage in Neo-Assyrian texts. See Weinfeld, *DDS,* 115.

/33/ Not only is there a change from singular to plural in v 6, but there is also a change in v 7 from second to third person. The protasis in v 6 is in the second person. One expects the apodosis in v 7 to be directed against "you," yet it is given against "Israel." The change is even more abrupt in C where the pronominal suffix alone is used (*ntštym*). Thus, the unit in vv 1–9 appears to be an artificial one. The threat in vv 6–9 against the people does not balance perfectly the promise to Solomon in vv 3–5.

/34/ The motif of the astonished passers-by occurs in Deut 29:24–25 and Jer 22:8–9. It has good parallels in Neo-Assyrian treaty curses (*DDS,*

100–116). Nelson argues for the literary dependance of both Jer 22:8–9 and 1 K 9:8–9 on Deut 29:24–25. He then argues that Deut 29:24–25 is exilic, hence 1 K 9:8–9 is exilic (*Double Redaction*, 74–76). The problem with this argument is that Jer 22:8–9 falls within a unit addressed to the king of Judah and hence is presumably pre-exilic. Thus, the closest parallels to 1 K 9:8–9 are treaty curses.

/35/ It is interesting that in Jer 22:8–9 the passers-by are appalled at what Yahweh has done to the city (Jerusalem). In 1 K 9:8–9//2 C 7:21–22 the Temple has received the brunt of Yahweh's judgment. The focus on the Temple's destruction would seem opposed not only to the goals of Chr 1 but also to the importance attached to the Temple by Dtr 1 as suggested by 1 K 8. Thus, it is dubious that 1 K 9:6–9 and 2 C 7:19–22 as they now stand derive from Dtr 1 and Chr 1 respectively.

Bibliography

Ackroyd, P. R. *I & II Chronicles, Ezra, Nehemiah.* Torch Bible Commentaries. London: SCM, 1973.

Albright, W. F. "The Date and Personality of the Chronicler," *JBL* 40 (1921) 104–24.

_____. "The Judicial Reform of Jehoshaphat," *Alexander Marx Jubilee Volume.* New York: Jewish Publication Society, 1950, 61–82.

_____. "New Light on Early Recensions of the Hebrew Bible," *BASOR* 140 (1955) 27–33.

Allen, L. C. "Further Thoughts on an Old Recension of Reigns in Paralipomena," *HTR* 61 (1968) 483–91.

_____. *The Greek Chronicles.* I: *The Translator's Craft.* VTSup 25. Leiden: E. J. Brill, 1974.

_____. *The Greek Chronicles.* II: *Textual Criticism.* VTSup 27. Leiden: E. J. Brill, 1974.

Baillet, M., Milik, J. T., and de Vaux, R. *Les 'Petites Grottes' de Qumran.* DJD 3. Oxford: Clarendon Press, 1962.

Barthélemy, D. *Les devanciers d'Aquila.* VTSup 10. Leiden: E. J. Brill, 1963.

_____. "La qualité du Texte Massorétique de Samuel," *The Hebrew and Greek Texts of Samuel.* 1980 Proceedings IOSCS–Vienna, ed. E. Tov. Jerusalem: Academon, 1980, 1–44.

_____. "Redécouverte d'un chainon manquant de l'histoire de la Septante," *RB* 60 (1953) 18–29.

Biblia Hebraica. Ed. R. Kittel et al. 16th ed. Stuttgart: 1973.

Bin-Nun, S. "Formulas from Royal Records of Israel and of Judah," *VT* 18 (1968) 414–32.

Botterweck, G. Joh. "Zur Eigenart der chronistischen Davidgeschichte," *TQ* 136 (1956) 402–35.

Braun, R. L. "Chronicles, Ezra, and Nehemiah: Theology and Literary History," *Studies in the Historical Books of the Old Testament.* VTSup 30. Ed. J. A. Emerton. Leiden: E. J. Brill, 1979, 52–64.

_____. "Solomon, the Chosen Temple Builder: The Significance of 1 Chronicles 22, 28, and 29 for the Theology of Chronicles," *JBL* 95 (1976) 581–90.

_____. "The Message of Chronicles: Rally 'Round the Temple," *CTM* 42 (1971) 502–14.

_____. "Solomonic Apologetic in Chronicles," *JBL* 92 (1973) 503–16.

Brown, F., Driver, S. R., and Briggs, C. A. *A Hebrew and English Lexicon of the Old Testament.* Oxford: Clarendon, 1974.

Brunet, A. M. "Le Chroniste et ses sources," *RB* 60 (1953) 481–508, 61 (1954) 349–86.

_____. "La théologie du Chroniste: Theocratie et messianisme," *Sacra Pagina.* Paris: Gamblous, 1959, 384–97.

Burney, C. F. *Notes on the Hebrew Text of the Books of Kings.* Oxford: Clarendon Press, 1903.

Childs, B. S. *Isaiah and the Assyrian Crisis.* SBT 2/3. London: SCM, 1967.

Cogan, M. *Imperialism and Religion: Assyria, Judah and Israel in the Eighth and Seventh Centuries B. C. E.* SBLMS 19. Missoula, MT: Scholars Press, 1974.

_____. "Israel in Exile—The View of a Josianic Historian," *JBL* 97 (1978) 40–44.

_____. "Tendentious Chronology in the Book of Chronicles," *Zion* 45 (1980) 165–72.

Coggins, R. J. *The First and Second Books of the Chronicles.* The Cambridge Bible Commentary. Cambridge: Cambridge University, 1976.

Coogan, M. D. "The Use of Second Person Singular Verbal Forms in Northwest Semitic Personal Names," *Or* 44 (1975) 194–97.

_____. *West Semitic Personal Names in the Murašu Documents.* HSM 7. Missoula, MT: Scholars Press, 1976.

Cross, F. M. *The Ancient Library of Qumran and Modern Biblical Studies.* Rev. ed. New York: Doubleday, 1961.

_____. *Canaanite Myth and Hebrew Epic.* Cambridge, MA: Harvard, 1973.

_____. "The Contribution of the Qumran Discoveries to the Study of the Biblical Text," *IEJ* 16 (1966) 81–95.

_____. "The Development of the Jewish Scripts," *BANE.* Ed. G. E. Wright. Winona Lake: Eisenbrauns, 1979.

_____. "The Evolution of a Theory of Local Texts," *Qumran and the History of the Biblical Text.* Ed. F. M. Cross and S. Talmon. Cambridge, MA: Harvard, 1975, 306–15.

_____. "The History of the Biblical Text in the Light of Discoveries in the Judean Desert," *HTR* 57 (1964) 281–89.

_____. "Papyri of the Fourth Century B. C. from Dâliyeh: A Preliminary Report on Their Discovery and Significance," *New Directions in Biblical Archaeology.* Ed. D. N. Freedman and J. C. Greenfield. New York: Doubleday, 1969, 41–62.

_____. "Problems of Method in the Textual Criticism of the Hebrew Bible," *The Critical Study of Sacred Texts.* Ed. W. D. O'Flaherty. Berkeley: Graduate Theological Union, 1979, 31–54.

_____. "A Reconstruction of the Judean Restoration," *Int* 29 (1975) 187–203.

_____. "Samaria and Jerusalem: The Early History of the Samaritans and Their Relations with the Jews (722–64 B. C. E.)." Unpublished paper, Harvard University, 1983.

_____. "The Structure of the Deuteronomic History," *Perspectives in Jewish Learning.* Annual of the College of Jewish Studies 3. Chicago, 1968, 9–24.

_____, and Freedman, D. N. "Josiah's Revolt Against Assyria," *JNES* 12 (1953) 56–58.

_____, and Wright, G. E. "The Boundary and Province Lists of the Kingdom of Judah," *JBL* 75 (1956) 202–26.

Curtis, E. L. and Madsen, A. A. *The Books of Chronicles.* ICC. Edinburgh: T & T Clark, 1910.

Dietrich, M., Loretz, O., and Sanmartin, J. *Transkription.* KTU I. Neukirchen: Neukirchener Verlag, 1976.

Dietrich, W. *Prophetie und Geschichte.* FRLANT 108. Göttingen: Vandenhoeck & Ruprecht, 1972.

Driver, S. R. *Notes on the Hebrew Text of the Books of Samuel.* Oxford: Clarendon, 1890.

Eissfeldt, O. *The Old Testament. An Introduction.* Trans. P. R. Ackroyd. New York: Harper & Row, 1965.

Freedman, D. N. "The Chronicler's Purpose," *CBQ* 23 (1961) 432–42.

Friedman, R. E. *The Exile and Biblical Narrative.* HSM 22. Chico, CA: Scholars Press, 1981.

_____. "From Egypt to Egypt: Dtr 1 and Dtr 2," *Traditions*

in Transformation. Ed. B. Halpern and J. Levenson. Winona Lake: Eisenbrauns, 1980, 167–92.

Gerleman, G. *Studies in the Septuagint*. II. *Chronicles*. Lunds Universitets Årsskrift N. F. 43/3. Lund: C. W. K. Gleerup, 1946.

Gooding, D. W. "Jeroboam's Rise to Power: A Rejoinder," *JBL* 91 (1972) 529–33.

—————. "The Septuagint's Rival Versions of Jeroboam's Rise to Power," *VT* 17 (1967) 173–89.

Graham, M. P. "The Composition of 2 Chronicles 24," *Christian Teaching*. Abilene, TX: Biblical Research Press, 1981.

Gray, J. *I and II Kings*. OTL. London: SCM, 1963.

Halpern, B. "Sacred History and Ideology: Chronicles' Thematic Structure—Indications of an Earlier Source," *The Creation of Sacred Literature, Composition and Redaction of the Biblical Text*. Near Eastern Studies 22. Ed. R. Friedman. Berkeley: University of California Press, 1981, 35–54.

Hanson, P. D. "The Song of Heshbon and David's *Nîr*," *HTR* 61 (1968) 297–320.

Herdner, A. "Une priére a Baal des Ugaritains en danger," *CRAIBL* (1972) 693–97.

Hillers, D. *Treaty Curses and the Old Testament Prophets*. Rome: Pontifical Biblical Institute, 1964.

Hoffmann, H.-D. *Reform und Reformen*. ATANT 66. Zurich: Theologischer Verlag, 1980.

Howard, G. "Frank Cross and Recensional Criticism," *VT* 21 (1971) 440–50.

Howorth, H. H. "The Real Character and the Importance of the Book of 1 Esdras," *The Academy* 43 (1893) 13–14, 60, 106, 174–75, 326–27, 524.

—————. "Some Unconventional Views on the Text of the Bible," *Proceedings of the Society of Biblical Archaeology* 23 (1901) 147–59, 305–25; 24 (1902) 147–72, 332–40; 26 (1904) 25–31, 63–69, 94–100; 27 (1905) 267–78; 29 (1907) 31–38, 61–69.

Janzen, J. G. *Studies in the Text of Jeremiah*. HSM 6. Cambridge, MA: Harvard, 1973.

Japhet, S. "Chronicles, Book of," *Encyclopaedia Judaica*. Jerusalem: Keter 1971. Vol. 5. Cols. 517–34.

—————. *The Ideology of the Book of Chronicles and its Place in Biblical Thought*. Jerusalem: Bialik Institute, 1977.

──────────. "The Supposed Common Authorship of Chronicles and Ezra-Nehemiah Investigated Anew," *VT* 18 (1968) 330–71.

Jepsen, A. *Die Quellen des Königsbuches.* Halle: Max Niemeyer, 1956.

──────────. "Die Reform des Josia," *Festschrift Friedrich Baumgartel.* Ed. W. Baumgartner et al. (Tübingen: J. C. B. Mohr, 1950) 97–108.

Josephus, F. *The Jewish Antiquities.* Vols. V and VI. LCL. Trans. H. St. J. Thackeray and R. Marcus. Cambridge, MA: Harvard, 1958.

Joüon, P. *Grammaire de l'hebreu biblique.* Rev. ed. Rome: Pontifical Biblical Institute, 1965.

Kittel, R. *Die Bücher der Chronik und Esra, Nehemia und Esther.* HAT 1/6. Göttingen: Vandenhoeck & Ruprecht, 1902.

Klein, R. W. "Jeroboam's Rise to Power," *JBL* 89 (1970) 217–18.

──────────. "New Evidence for an Old Recension of Reigns" *HTR* 60 (1967) 93–105.

──────────. "Once More: Jeroboam's Rise to Power," *JBL* 92 (1973) 582–84.

──────────. "Studies in the Greek Texts of the Chronicler." Unpublished Th.D. Thesis, Harvard University, 1966.

──────────. "Supplements in the Paralipomena: A Rejoinder," *HTR* 61 (1968) 492–95.

──────────. *Textual Criticism of the Old Testament.* Philadelphia: Fortress, 1974.

Kropat, A. *Die Syntax des Autors der Chronik verglichen mit der seiner Quellen: Ein Beitrag zur historischen Syntax des Hebraischen.* BZAW 16. Giessen: A. Töpelmann, 1909.

Lemke, W. E. "The Synoptic Problem in the Chronicler's History," *HTR* 58 (1965) 349–63.

──────────. "Synoptic Studies in the Chronicler's History." Unpublished Th.D. Thesis, Harvard University, 1963.

──────────. "The Way of Obedience: 1 Kings 13 and the Structure of the Deuteronomistic History," *Magnalia Dei.* Ed. F. M. Cross, W. E. Lemke, and P. D. Miller. Garden City, NY: Doubleday, 1976, 301–26.

Levenson, J. "From Temple to Synagogue: 1 Kings 8," *Traditions in Transformation.* Ed. B. Halpern and J. Levenson. Winona Lake, IN: Eisenbrauns, 1980, 143–66.

_____. "Who Inserted the Book of the Torah?" *HTR* 68 (1975), 203–33.

Lohfink, N. "Der Bundesschluss im Land Moab," *BZ* 6 (1962) 32–56.

McCarter, P. *1 Samuel*. AB. New York: Doubleday, 1980.

McCarthy, D. J. "II Samuel 7 and the Structure of the Deuteronomistic History," *JBL* 84 (1965), 131–38.

_____. "The Wrath of Yahweh and the Structural Unity of the Deuteronomistic History," *Essays in Old Testament Ethics*. Ed. J. L. Crenshaw and J. T. Willis. New York: KTAV, 1974, 97–110.

McKay, J. W. *Religion in Judah under the Assyrians 732–609 B.C.* SBT 2/26. Naperville, IL: Alec R. Allenson, 1973.

Macy, H. R. "The Sources of the Books of Chronicles: A Reassessment." Unpublished Ph.D. Thesis, Harvard University, 1975.

Mez, A. *Die Bibel des Josephus untersucht für Buch V-VII der Archäologie*. Basel: Jaeger Kober, 1895.

Montgomery, J. A. *The Books of Kings*. ICC. Edinburgh: T & T Clark, 1951.

_____. "A Study in Comparison of the Texts of Kings and Chronicles," *JBL* 50 (1931), 115–16.

Moriarty, Frederick L. "The Chronicler's Account of Hezekiah's Reform," *CBQ* 17 (1965) 399–406.

Mosis, R. *Untersuchungen zur Theologie des chronistischen Geschichtswerkes*. Freiburg: Herder, 1973.

Mowinckel, S. *Studien zu dem Buche Ezra-Nehemia. I: Die Nachchronische Redaktion des Buches. Die Listen*. Oslo: Universitetsforloget, 1964.

Myers, J. M. *I Chronicles*. AB. New York: Doubleday, 1965.

_____. *II Chronicles*. AB. New York: Doubleday, 1965.

_____. "The Kerygma of the Chronicler," *Int* 20 (1966) 259–73.

Nelson, R. D. *The Double Redaction of the Deuteronomistic History*. JSOT Supplement 18. Sheffield: JSOT, 1981.

Newsome, J.D. "Toward an Understanding of the Chronicler and his Purposes," *JBL* 94 (1975) 201–17.

Nicholson, E. W. *Deuteronomy and Tradition*. Philadelphia: Fortress, 1967.

Noordtzij, A. "Les intentions du Chroniste," *RB* 49 (1940), 161–68.

North, R. "Theology of the Chronicler," *JBL* 82 (1963) 369–81.

Noth, M. *Die israelitischen Personennamen im Rahmen der gemeinsemitischen Namengebung.* Stuttgart: W. Kohlhammer, 1928.

_____. *Überlieferungsgeschichtliche Studien: die sammelnden und bearbeitenden Geschichtswerke im Alten Testament.* Tübingen: Max Niemeyer, 1943.

Oded, B. "Judah and the Exile," *Israelite and Judean History.* Ed. J. H. Hayes and J. M. Miller; OTL; Philadelphia: Westminster, 1977, 435–88.

The Old Testament in Greek. II. *The Later Historical Books.* Ed. A. E. Brooke, N. McClean, and H. St. J. Thackeray. Cambridge: Cambridge University, 1927.

Olmstead, A. T. "Source Study and the Biblical Text," *AJSL* 30 (1913) 20.

Peckham, B. "The Composition of Deuteronomy 5–11." *The Word of the Lord Shall Go Forth.* Ed. C. L. Meyers and M. O'Connor. Winona Lake, IN: Eisenbrauns, 1983, 217–40.

Petersen, D. L. *Late Israelite Prophecy: Studies in Deutero-Prophetic Literature and in Chronicles.* SBLMS 23; Missoula, MT: Scholars Press, 1977.

Pfeiffer, R. H. *Introduction to the Old Testament.* New York: Harper & Brothers, 1941.

Plöger, O. "Reden und Gebete im deuteronomischen und chronistischen Geschichtswerk," *Festschrift für Günther Dehn.* Neukirchen, 1957, 35–49.

Polzin, R. *Late Biblical Hebrew: Toward an Historical Typology of Biblical Hebrew Prose.* HSM 12. Missoula, MT: Scholars Press, 1976.

Pratt, R. "The Incomparability of Hezekiah in the Deuteronomistic History," Unpublished paper. OT 200, Harvard University, Fall, 1982.

von Rad, G. "The Deuteronomic Theology of History in I and II Kings," *The Problem of the Hexateuch and Other Essays.* Trans. E. W. T. Dicken. New York: McGraw-Hill, 1966, 205–21.

_____. *Das Geschichtsbild des chronistischen Werkes.* Stuttgart: W. Kohlhammer, 1930.

_____. "The Levitical Sermon in I and II Chronicles," *The Problem of the Hexateuch and Other Essays,* 267–80.

_____. *Studies in Deuteronomy.* SBT 9. Trans. D. Stalker Chicago: Henry Regnery, 1953.

Rehm, M. *Textkritische Untersuchungen zu den Parallelstellen der Samuel-Königsbücher und der Chronik.* Alttestamentlich Abhandlungen 13/3. Münster, 1937.

Richardson, H. N. "The Historical Reliability of Chronicles," *JBR* 26 (1958) 9–12.

Rosenbaum, J. "Hezekiah's Reform and the Deuteronomistic Tradition," *HTR* 72 (1979) 24–43.

Rothstein, J. W. and Hänel, D. J. *Das erste Buch der Chronik.* KAT 18/2. Leipzig: D. Werner Scholl, 1927.

Rudolph, W. *Chronikbücher.* HAT 21. Tübingen: J. C. B. Mohr, 1955.

————. "Problems of the Books of Chronicles," *VT* 4 (1954) 401–9.

Shenkel, J. D. *Chronology and Recensional Development in the Greek Text of Kings.* HSM 1. Cambridge, MA: Harvard University Press, 1968.

Smend, R. "Das Gesetz und die Völker. Ein Beitrag zur deuteronomischen Redaktionsgeschichte," *Probleme biblischer Theologie.* Ed. H. W. Wolff. Munich: Chr. Kaiser, 1971.

Smit, E. J. "Death and Burial Formulas in Kings and Chronicles Relating to the Kings of Judah," *Biblical Essays.* Proceedings of the Ninth Meeting of Die Ou-Testamentiese Werkgemeenskap in Suid-Afrika. Potchefstroom, 1966.

Talmon, S. "Double Readings in the Masoretic Text," *Textus* 1 (1960) 144–84.

————. "The Old Testament Text," *The Cambridge History of the Bible. I. From the Beginnings to Jerome.* (Ed. P. R. Ackroyd and C. F. Evans; Cambridge: Cambridge University, 1970) 159–99.

————. "The Textual Study of the Bible—A New Outlook," *Qumran and the History of the Biblical Text.* Cambridge, MA: Harvard, 1975. 321–400.

Thackeray, H. St. J. "The Greek Translators of the Four Books of Kings," *JTS* 8 (1907)262–78.

————. *Josephus The Man and the Historian.* New York: Jewish Institute of Religion, 1929.

Trontveit, M.A. "Linguistic Analysis and the Question of Authorship in Chronicles, Ezra, and Nehemiah," *VT* 32 (1982) 201–16.

Torrey, C. C. "The Chronicler as Editor and as Independent Narrator," *AJSL* 25 (1909) 157–73, 188–217.

_____. *The Chronicler's History of Israel*. New Haven: Yale, 1954.

_____. *Ezra Studies*. Chicago: University of Chicago, 1910.

_____. "A Revised View of First Esdras," *Louis Ginzberg Jubilee Volume*. New York: The American Academy for Jewish Research, 1945, 395–410.

Tov, E. "Determining the Relationship between the Qumran Scrolls and the LXX: Some Methodological Issues," *The Hebrew and Greek Texts of Samuel*. 1980 Proceedings IOSCS-Vienna. (ed. E. Tov. Jerusalem: Academon, 1980) 45–68.

_____. "The Textual Affiliations of 4QSam^a," *The Hebrew and Greek Texts of Samuel*.

Ulrich, E. C. "The Old Latin Translation of the LXX and the Hebrew Scrolls from Qumran," *The Hebrew and Greek Texts of Samuel*.

_____. *The Qumran Text of Samuel and Josephus*. HSM 19. Missoula, MT: Scholars Press, 1978.

Vannutelli, P. *Libri Synoptici Veteris Testamenti*. Rome: Pontifical Biblical Institute, 1931.

Wallace, H. "The Oracle Against the Israelite Dynasties." Unpublished paper, OT 200, Harvard University, Fall, 1979.

Welch, A. C. *The Work of the Chronicler: Its Purpose and its Date*. London: Oxford University, 1939.

Weinfeld, M. *Deuteronomy and the Deuteronomic School*. Oxford: Clarendon Press, 1972.

Wellhausen, J. *Prolegomena to the History of Ancient Israel*. Gloucester: Peter Smith, 1973.

_____. *Der Text der Bücher Samuelis*. Göttingen: Vandenhoeck & Ruprecht, 1871.

Willi, T. *Die Chronik als Auslegung*. FRLANT 106. Göttingen: Vandenhoeck & Ruprecht, 1972

Williamson, H. G. M. "The Accession of Solomon in the Books of Chronicles," *VT* 26 (1976) 351–61,

_____. "The Death of Josiah and the Continuing Development of Deuteronomic History," *VT* 32 (1982) 242–47.

_____. *Israel in the Books of Chronicles*. Cambridge: Cambridge University, 1977.

Wolff, H. W. "Das Kerygma des deuteronomischen Geschichtswerk," *ZAW* 73 (1961) 171–86.